MODERN TEACHING AND CURRICULUM MANAGEMENT

MODERN TEACHING AND CURRICULUM MANAGEMENT

[For B.Ed. Course]

By

UDAI VEER

ANMOL PUBLICATIONS PVT. LTD.

NEW DELHI - 110 002 (INDIA)

ANMOL PUBLICATIONS PVT. LTD.
4374/4B, Ansari Road, Daryaganj
New Delhi - 110 002
Ph.: 23261597, 23278000
Visit us at: www.anmolpublications.com

Modern Teaching and Curriculum Management

First Published, 2004

ISBN 81-261-1944-6

PRINTED IN INDIA

Published by J.L. Kumar for Anmol Publications Pvt. Ltd., New Delhi - 110 002 and Printed at Mehra Offset Press, Delhi.

Contents

Preface

Education is a vast discipline and Teachers' Training is a vital part of it. The responsibilities of the educationists and educators are focused on the task of providing better training to the future teachers for their better learning and proper development. Needless to say that this responsibility can only be exercised, if the trainers are equipped with the required knowledge of the subject concerned. That's why it becomes essential for making adequate provisions for each course to the student-teachers or teacher trainees. The present series is designed for providing a solid workable base for all course-papers. It has been prepared strictly according to the syllabus of the B.Ed class, prescribed by the UGC for different universities.

No doubt, there are so many other books on the subject, available in the market, written by worthy authors. However, every writer has his or her own style and way of presentation. The present work also has its own features and characteristics.

In preparation of this series of texts, the editor had to refer to the works of other authors and information sources. The editor feels a deep sense of gratitude for incorporating their ideas in the text. Hopefully, this series would serve as a 'ready to refer' tool for all teachers, teacher-students and others.

—**Editor**

1

Introduction

Education is a process of development. It is designed for the all-round development of a child. The term education is closely related to curriculum development. It is the most important component of educational programme. The answers of three fundamental questions, why are education and curriculum needed? what should be taught in education? and how should we teach? provide the awareness and basis of education.

Why do we need curriculum? This question can only be answered by philosophy and sociology.

What should be the curriculum? The answer of this question can be given by sociology and national needs.

How the curriculum should be used in our schools? This question can be answered by psychology and educational technology.

These fundamental questions are answered by the experts of different disciplines. Thus, the curriculum development and education have the following bases:

1. Philosophical Basis of Curriculum.
2. Sociological Basis of Curriculum.
3. Psychological Basis of Curriculum.
4. Tendencies and Curriculum.

The contributions of the bases have been discussed in the present chapter and provided in the following paragraphs.

Philosophy and Education

Philosophy has been defined in several ways but the essence of all definitions is that it is a branch of knowledge concerned with the quest for Truth. The human mind has always been puzzled by the questions regarding the nature of Truth. Two strong philosophical thoughts have held ground in that connection. According to one, the final reality is in nature of mind, and according to the other it is matter. The first school of thought is that of the idealists and the second of the materialists. The idealists hold that the universe is a manifestation of intelligence and will, that behind the fugitive phenomena that we behold is a reality which is unchangeable and imperishable, and that the external phenomena are manifestations of that. This philosophy is psycho-centric and it places emphasis on the soul rather than the body. Materialists regard matter as the final reality. Everything originates from matter and it is reduced to matter in the end. The final truth is the truth established by science ; truth that our senses can comprehend. Both these philosophies have influenced education. All philosophies of life have a general rather than a specific influence on education and idealism and materialism have both influenced education in its various aspects.

Modern education has also been influenced a great deal by pragmatism, which attaches importance to human experience. It is not a philosophy in the sense in which idealism or materialism is. Pragmatism is the empiricist's attitude and it recognises the existence and significance of only those values and truths that are related to human purposes. Nothing is absolutely fixed and nothing is determined for ever. The ultimate reality does not exist. Human beings, in the course of their experience, make realities, truths and values. Whatever is found real, useful, or true, is retained and whatever is not, ceases to exist. Pragmatism comes midway between idealism and materialism and in education its influence is significant. By its relationship with idealism it has often been called dynamic idealism.

Philosophy has close relationship with life. Divorced from the context of life philosophy might just be an intellectual exercise but that would not have any bearing upon human life. Philosophies of life are systematic thoughts about human existence and how it can be made gracious and harmonious. Wherever philosophy has been taken seriously, it has always been a source of inspiration for the conduct of life. That is the significance of philosophy for life. It is closely tied with human life. An individual's philosophy of life determines his behaviour, and his philosophy may be inferred from his reactions to different situations.

Each individual or group of individuals with similar thinking has a tendency to spread ideas, and the process of doing that is called education. Education may be called the dynamic side of philosophy.

These philosophical thoughts - idealism, naturalism, and pragmatism have influenced education. Idealism is psycho-centric, naturalism is nature-centric and pragmatism is anthropocentric. Detailed study will be taken up in the chapters that follow.

There might be many philosophies of education, a theory of education would mean a composite view of educational ideals, aims and objectives, programmes and organisation, etc., determined on the one hand by the philosophy of life and on the other, by the exigencies of the situations. Educational theory cannot be divorced from educational practice. It does not have any meaning if it is not practicable. Similarly, educational practices do not have a solid foundation if they are not supported by a sound educational theory. Theory provides the necessary support to practise and practice gives theory a real and practical meaning. Their relationship is thus vital. It may be said that theory is made explicit through practice, and practice gains strength when a sound theory is implicit. Whatever may be the realm of pure philosophy, educational philosophy has come to mean theory of education which can be transferred into action.

Philosophical Basis

The philosophical basis of education emphasizes that philosophy is the education is the means to achieve that end. In other words, philosophy determines the goal of life and education tries to achieve that goal through its aims and curriculum. As goals of life and aims of education change from time to time, from place to place and according to philosophical ideologies, the curriculum of education can not escape from these transformations. It also changes according to change in times, places, circumstances and prevalent ideologies. In other words, there is a very close relation between the philosophy and the curriculum. The shape and form as well as the contents of curriculum change to suit the prevalent ideologies and social ways of thinking. !ts contents fulfil the needs and aspirations of the society for which it is organized and formulated. To quote an example let us understand that present day curriculum for Indian society is not the same as it was when it tried to fulfil the needs of the society in ancient times. This is because the present day ideology, goals of life and aims of education of modern society are quite different from those of ancient times. Hence, we conclude that curriculum is positively correlated with the needs and requirements of the society for which it is formulated, organised and developed. In the following lines we are throwing light on curriculum construction according to Idealism, Realism Naturalism and Pragmatism.

Idealism and Aims of Education

In discussing the aim of education, we shall proceed with a few statements made in respect therefore by some educational philosophers—

(1) "Education should be thought of as the process of man's reciprocal adjustment to his nature, to his fellows, and to the ultimate nature of the cosmos."

(2) "Education should lead to self-emancipation and self-realisation."

(3) "Knowledge is virtue." (Socrates) "It is the recognition of the harmony between phenomenon and form."

(4) "In all things there reigns an eternal law .... This all-pervading law is necessarily based on an all-pervading, energetic, self conscious, and hence eternal unity .... This unity is God .... The divine effluence that lives in each thing is the essence of each thing .... The object of education is the realisation of a faithful, pure, inviolable, and hence holy life .... education should lead and guide man to clearness concerning himself and in himself, to face with nature, and to unity with God."

(5) "Education consists in giving to the body and the soul all the perfection of which they are susceptible."

(6) "The purpose of education is to enable the child to reconcile himself to reality in all its manifestations, not merely to adapt himself to a natural environment. Such a reconciliation is not impossible, because the cultural environment is the product of man's creative activity, and the physical environment has been likewise fashioned by his inventive powers. The conflict is not something quite alien to man, it is with those of his household: it is a fight that has begun within himself. When

we recognise the priority of man's cultural environment, when we realise that in the transmission and increase of this cultural inheritance though its constant recreation lies the supreme task of education that man possesses spiritual powers adequate to the task, then our philosophy of education is idealistic and doubtless, only then adequate."

(7) "To live in the trade I wish to teach him .... In the natural order of things, all men being equal their common vocation is manhood."

(8) "Education is not simply growing, it is growing towards a goal. It is not simply an ongoing process, it is a process going on toward an objective. The immediate objective is the realisation of the values. The remote objective, the absolute goal, is likeness to the spiritual order to the universe. Education, in the final analysis is the up building of humanity, is the image of divinity."

Idealism and Curriculum

Idealism employs the logical point of view in the construction of curriculum. This doctrine attaches greater importance to the experiences of the whole human society in preference to the present and future experiences of a child. In other words, an idealistic curriculum reflects the cultural heritage and civilization of the whole human race. As these experiences can be gained through physical environment and also from the contacts with fellow human beings, an idealistic curriculum contains humanities and scientific subjects in proper balance and proportion.

As to the form the curriculum, there is a difference of opinion among idealists. According to Plato, curriculum should be constructed according to human thoughts, feelings, ideals and values. On the other hand Ross holds that construction of curriculum should be based on psychological facts and needs. According to him, experience has three activities - (1) Cognition, (2) Affection and (3) Conation. In other words, what does a man think, feel and act? According to the first criteria, the curriculum should have Language, Literature, Arithmetic, Science, Geography and History whereas according to the second criteria, it should have Music, Art, Poetry and as to the third, it should include those activities, which satisfy the basic needs of food, clothes and shelter which may be called practice of arts and capacities to work. T. P

Nurn, in view of his insistence on human civilization, advocates the inclusion, in any curriculum, of those subjects and activities which express the grand expressions of human spirit. Such activities may be divided into two categories- (1) those which protect and preserve individual life and the life of society and (2) those which create human civilizations, moral laws, religious sentiments, physical resources, physical hygiene and health education, good conduct, love and so on. These can be guided by study and teaching only. The other category includes subjects as Literature, Arts, Handicrafts, Science, Geography and History etc.

Realism and Aims of Education

"The ultimate end of man is eternal happiness with God," Comenius stated in his, Great Didactic'. This aim could be realised not by suppression of appetites, instincts or emotions but by a man's moral control over himself, which was to be acquired through knowledge of oneself and the knowledge of all things. Knowledge, virtue and piety are the aims of education. The purpose of the school of universal wisdom was, therefore, the aim of education—

"They will learn, not for the school, but for life, so that the youth shall go forth energetic, ready for everything, apt, industrious and worthy of being entrusted with any of the duties of life, and this all the more if they have added to virtue a sweet conversation, and have crowned all with the fear and love of God. They will go forth capable of expression and eloquence."

Aims of Education and the Nature of Subject-matter : Bacon advocated exactly what his contemporaries, William Gillbert, and many others did. "Turn to Nature," he advised, "contrive experiments by means of which She will be compelled to furnish the data you require; observe weigh and relate your observations with the utmost care, and elaborate your generalisations with regard to the principles of inductive logic. It was dishonourable that the boundaries of the intellectual world should be confined to discoveries and straits of the ancient." Bacon laid emphasis on the study of the phenomena of Nature. The natural sciences as well as the physical sciences alone would relieve the suffering of men, raise and refine their standard of living, enrich their mind, and enable them to live happily together. In the new Atlantis, Bacon elaborated a utopian scheme for scientific research.

Bacon's contribution is not of the scientist, but of the publicist. His high position, his learning, his writings-all won for him a wide audience. He stimulated men to discover the truth and turned their energies in so doing from assumption and disputation to patient experimentation. His writings gave impetus to the formulation of the Royal Society of London and to a movement in the theory of education in connection. He gave considerable impetus to empiricism also of which Locke was the most important protagonist.

Realism and Curriculum

Realism is based on materialism which believes that matter is everything and this material world is all in all. Hence realists attach great importance to physical sciences in preference to academic and bookish knowledge in the curriculum. They believe that only such useful knowledge in the curriculum can be include. They believe which is closely related to their actual life and which is capable to solve the problems of their future life.

Realism and Modern Education

Like idealism and naturalism, realism today has a broad meaning and it has also exercised a potent influence on education by emphasising the following principles :

(1) Since we live in a world which is rapidly changing, it is necessary that we remain prepared to adjust ourselves to any psychological, intellectual and social change that occur at any time.

(2) A philosophy of education should be based on the realities of life and it can prove is worth by being practical.

(3) No 'ism' can solve problems of education. To be useful, Education must be organised by harmonising values, past and present.

(4) Things and objects exist independently. Human experience is limited. Truths of science are more reliable.

(5) The surest way of acquiring knowledge is the scientific way but this does not mean that science has discovered all truth. There might be many truths which have not yet been discovered.

(6) Curriculum should be many-sided and it should present to the children a rounded view of the universe.

(7) Like naturalism, realism also lays emphasis on sense-training, study of science, diversified curricula, catering education to varied interests, making methods of teaching interesting and basing them on psychological principles.

(8) Realism places more emphasis on curriculum and content of studies rather than on behaviour training like the pragmatists. "Education may be defined as behaviour training, but there are no possibilities of behaviour training without regard to the content of experiences."

(9) By emphasising the independence of objects, the realists' outlook is more balanced than the pragmatic view which over estimates the worth of human experience.

Naturalism and Aims of Education

Of the forms of naturalism, it is the biological naturalism which has exercised the greatest influence of education. The influence of physical and mechanical is practically nil in education, specially that of the former which seeks to interpret the entire universe in terms of physical science. As regards educational aims the interpretation centres round the following points—

(1) According to mechanical naturalism, the individual is also like a machine and consequently, the aim of education should be to make the machine work with as much perfection and efficiency as possible. According to this view, all activities of human beings originate on receiving some stimuli from the environment, and hence they are functioning in the form of conditioned reflex actions. The process of education should be to improvise the stimuli in such a way that desired activities proceed from them. As has been mentioned above, the form of naturalism has given birth to behaviour psychology which has also influenced education.

(2) Biological naturalism interprets educational aims in several ways:

(a) McDoughll's psychological discoveries tell us that the aim of education is the sublimation of the native instincts and energies of the individual-the redirection, co-ordination and harmonious working of the native impulse.

(b) According to Neo-Darwinism, the struggle for existence is very important and therefore, the aim of education is to equip the individual for struggle to ensure survival.

(c) Neo-Lamarckianism emphasises adjustment to environment and states that the aim of education is to enable the individual to adjust himself to the environment. It will be through the process of adjustment that an individual will grow physically and mentally.

(d) Herbert Spenser states that to prepare for complete living is the aim of education.

(e) Some naturalists, like George Bernard Shaw, say that the purpose of education is not only to enable the individuals to grow and develop naturally but it is also to enable them to accelerate the process of evolution. By preserving, increasing and handling on the successive generations, the racial heritage, individuals can increase the speed of evolution.

(f) T.P. Nunn is a naturalist in a very broad sense and he maintains that the purpose of education is to enable the individual to develop his individuality and also be able to contribute to the development of the society. He seeks to establish a harmony between individual and social claims in education and does not believe that there is any dichotomy existing between the two.

Naturalism and Curriculum

Naturalism does not believe in the aims of education as knowledge for the sake of knowledge. Breaking all restrictions of religion and morality this doctrine advocates the development to the full of the inherent instincts and impulse of a child. Hence the construction of curriculum, according to naturalism, should be according to the individual differences of children with regard to and according to the individual differences of children with regard to their natural interests, abilities, capacities, basic impulses and tendencies of action. It may be noted that different naturalists, for example Rouseseau, advocate the curriculum which satisfies and meets all the varying needs of varying stages of a child's developmental process and growth. With this view, the curriculum should contain games and sports, nature-study, physical care, psychology, material sciences, language, geography and history. According to Herbert Spenser, a man is by nature an individualist. Hence the aim of education becomes self preservation and only those subjects should be included in the curriculum which promote this capacity of self protection, viz psychology, health hygiene, chemistry, arithmetical, biology, home science, physiology and other scientific subjects as main items of curriculum, keeping cultural and academic subjects at the secondary place.

Pragmatism and Aims of Education

According to the pragmatic view, the function of education is to bring about certain changes in the behaviour of the individual. These changes relate to the physical, intellectual, and moral development of the human being. They reflect the growth of the individual, as the process of education goes on and the individual continues growing physically, mentally, and morally. Since this process starts from birth and continues throughout life-sometimes some type of growth occurring and sometimes of another type-education is broadly conceived as a life-long process. The process of growth is not without any restrictions or guidance. It is important to realise that the growth of the individual does not take place through anti-social channels. When we see a person doing some crime of indulging in anti-social behaviour we may say that in his case also some growth in the behaviour has taken place. But that growth is undesirable and detrimental to the interests of the individual as well as to those of the society. All growths must be conducive to the welfare of the individual and the group; life that is parasitic is the frustration of other life. Growth must signify growth in general, a continuum of growth. Society establishes educational institutions for enabling individuals to grow physically, mentally, and morally so that they can develop their capacities and help themselves in life. But it also expects them to acquire those traits of character, outlooks and dispositions, and learn those trades by which they also strengthen the social framework and do not in any way prove injurious to the interests of other members of the society. That is why there is need of a properly controlled and organised education.

Pragmatism and Curriculum

Pragmatism covers and completes the drawbacks of naturalism. According to this ideology, curriculum construction should confirm to the principles of utility, creativity inherent interests of children. In other words, curriculum should be child-centred. According to Pragmatism, the principle of utility is concerned only with those subjects which are not only relevant and useful to the present life of a child but also prove worthy for the needs of his future life as an adult. According to this principle, the minimum curriculum should include language, health hygiene, physical, science, geography, history, agricultural science and home science for girls. Study of these subjects will enable the child to solve the day to day problems of life easily and intelligently. This principle of utility later on emphasizes the need for vocational education. It may be noted that insistence of pragmatism on the principle of utility should not be interpreted in a narrow sense to march away progress. As a matter of fact in its wider and true interpretation, the principle of utility advocates more and more human progress and welfare.

The second principle of curriculum construction according to pragmatism is the principle of creativity. According to this ideology, a child is active by nature. Hence his activity should be exploited for education. In other words, the curriculum should be activity-centred. Hence more and more opportunities should be provided to children to indulge in conductive and useful activities to develop themselves physically, mentally, socially and culturally in a free environment. Through these activities, a child will acquire various experiences. John Dewey asserts thus - “If these activities take the character of the activities of the community, of which the school is an organ, they will develop more virtues, result is attitudes of initiative and independence and will give training in citizenship and promote self-discipline.”

The third principle of curriculum construction according to pragmatism is the principle of natural interests. According to John Dewey there interest are of four varieties - (1) Interest in conversation, (2) Interest in investigation, (3) Interest in creation and (4) Interest in artistic creation. Hence curriculum for primary classes should be constructed with full consideration of these interests. All children should be free to express their basic interests through music, art, calculation, spinning, weaving, knitting, tailoring, drawing, painting and creating models. Only after these free experiences and expressions, children should learn, reading, writing and calculation. These mini activities will later develop into fullfedged actions and practical achievements. The result will be that in senior classes, a child will easily learn about biology, agricultural science, botany, arithmetic, algebra, engineering and other technical arts of like nature. In short, the curriculum should confirm to the real needs and realities of actual life of all children. This is the point of departure from pure nationalism.

Psychological Basis

Psychological basis of education emphasizes that education is for the child and not that child is for education. In other words, child is the centre of educational process. Psychology has also established the fact that a child develops through various stages. Not only this, there are individual differences to interests, impulses, urges needs capacities and abilities among children. Hence curriculum should be so flexible that it is able to meet the individual difference needs effectively and allow each child to, develop along his natural part and progress at his own speed according to his natural directions of development. For this, the curriculum should contain various, games, sports, creative activities and useful developing experiences.

Herbart's Aims of Education : It has been very early impressed upon Herbart's mind that "the aims of all instruction is to cultivate cleaners, definiteness and continuity of thought." This view was maintained by him throughout his life. Herbart recognised that education is an art and that it must aim at enabling the man to achieve a definite end. That end, according to him, is "morality." The one and the whole work of education may be summed up in the concept-Morality. Morality means good character, disposition and adaptability to the society. Education will produce a cultured man, who will conform to morality and thus attain the highest good. An uneducated man cannot do so. He will be good but he will be only mechanically good-good by habit or by imitation. He cannot be "intelligently good, so freely good," or good in so many minute ways as the educated man. At one place Herbart says, "The moral man commands himself." and so the youth should be so trained that his training results in making him a moral man.

Herbart's Doctrine of Interest : For the sake of making a man moral, it is essential that his outlook should be broadened and his experiences and interests be widened. The breadth of training is called "many-sidedness of interest" by Herbart. Interests are of various kinds and they proceed from various sources; but mainly they are two: (1) knowledge (2) participation. They are further divisible.

Interest

Knowledge	**Sources**	**Participation**
Empirical (appealing directly to senses depending upon causes and sense observation of object's nature)	Speculative (depending upon the relation of effect)	Aesthetic (concerned with enjoyment of beauty)
Sympathetic (relations between man and man as a whole)	Social (dealing with relations with community)	Religious (dealing with relations of oneself with God)

These interests are to be developed in each youth for making him a moral man. Only when they have cultivated a many-sidedness of interest, they will do good to themselves and fit in the society and achieve its welfare. This many-sidedness of interest will create a circle of thought in the mind and that circle will enable individuals to act successfully under all circumstances.

Need of Instructions

As has already been pointed out, instruction alone can help in the realisation of the true aims of education. Instruction will systematise the ideas. It will alone modify them and determine the volutions; it will fill in the blanks, reject and brush aside the erroneous and the faulty ones; it will determine the relation of idea to idea; it will foster many-sidedness of interest and lastly, it will alone create a good circle of thought. But instruction should be really meaningful. Instruction in the sense of mere information contains on guarantee whatsoever, as to whether it will materially counteract faults, and influence existing groups of ideas that are independent of the imparted information.

Curriculum and Correlation

If a many-sidedness of interest is to be developed, a wide range of studies must be include in the curriculum. Herbart divided all studies into two groups: (a) historical and (b) scientific. Herbart says that the former are of utmost importance. They furnish concrete and personal situations which call into action the moral judgments of man. History and literature are the dominant subjects, while scientific studies are subordinate.

Since mind acts as a unit and is a unity, so all studies must ultimately lead to produce the unified mind functioning as a unity. This position leads to a further conclusion, i.e. studies must bear relation to each other or, in other words, they must be correlated. Correlation means that all studies should be centred round one subject which would be core subject and should be taught with their relation to the core subject. Herbart chose History around which other subjects of the curriculum could be correlated.

Method of Instruction

Herbart was the first to lay emphasis on proper instruction and to exalt the teaching procedure. He believed that it is only through instruction that a compact body of knowledge can be systematically presented to the child. If proper instruction is not given, knowledge would only be retained in the memory and would not have any significance in life. With a view to rate permanent interest it is necessary that knowledge must be assimilated. This can be done only through instruction.

Scientific Basis

Scientific tendency in education or scientific basis of education emphasizes that in the curriculum the main and important place should be given to scientific subjects and secondary place to the academic disciplines. The credit of introducing and developing the scientific tendency in education goes to Herbert Spenser. According to him the development of a human being should not be one-side but complete in all aspects. Hence education should so achieve this complete development that an individual is able to solve all the problems and thus lead a happy life. In other words, the main aims or education should be to prepare the individual for complete living. For this, Herbert Spencer divided human activities into five categories and in order of their priority prescribed definite subjects for each category.

Sociological Basis

Sociological basis of education emphasizes the need that through education, the individual needs, propensities, interests, capacities and tendencies should be moulded to achieve social welfare and social development. Hence only those subjects and activities should be included in the curriculum which are useful from the point of view of society. In other words, curriculum should be constructed in accordance with the needs, requirements, conditions and aspirations of society so that qualities of sociability and citizenship and inculcated in each child. With this view point, the curriculum should contain Language, Arithmetic, Health education, Physical education, Social studies, General science, subjects to enable children to earn livelihood. Experimental arts, Music and such other socially useful subjects which develop the individual side by side with the society.

Sociological Tendency

In modern education, the sociological point of view is reflected in widening the scope of curriculum, attaching importance to co-curriculum activities, regarding school as a miniature society where all the activities are rehearsed. The sociologists hold that the programme of education should be life-centred, and that the aim of education is to foster efficient citizenship among the pupils. Modern education holds a balance between the individual and social claims in education and regards their interests as closely bound with each other.

The sociological movement is not concerned with the reform of education; it keeps rather of the whole society within its purview. In the beginning, the movement for reform in education from the stand point of public welfare was started in Germany, but the problems of social welfare gradually cropped up in many European countries where industrial revolution made progress. Consequently, the movement for reform of education with a view to eradicate social evils became popular as a part of bigger movement of social reform. Education, according to the sociological view point, aims at strengthening the social structure and through that improving conditions of living and growth of all individuals. This view is dominating our outlook today as well.

Eclectic Tendency

'Adjustment' is the key to success in the present-day life which is very much complicated. The conditions of living today are very different from those we had only two decades ago. Science has made tremendous progress and men and women all over the world are coming closer and closer. Science has also brought about changes in our attitudes and outlook on life. In addition to the rapid advances made by science, we have also to face complexities of different cultures, and their diversities as we come in contact with people of different parts of the world. We cannot live in isolation and we must learn to live with others. This makes its necessary for as to learn the value of adjustment. Conflicts are to be avoided and life is to be lived graciously and harmoniously.

Eclecticism is a term used to denote an outlook which does not conform to one single philosophy or principle but which believes in a fusion of a worthwhile ideas, concepts and practices, whether they relate to individual ways of living and thinking or to a group life. The diverse elements have utility of their own if they cater effectively to new situations which do not run contrary to the spirit of other ideas already accepted. Eclecticism is characteristic of the present-day modes of living, thinking, and behaving. We do not stick to one rigid or fixed dogma, creed, or belief. But on the other hand, we express through our behaviour and thinking, in our dresses, manners and concepts, in our relationship with others, our adherence to a comprehensive philosophy which is a harmonious blending of several philosophies and cultures. In education, we do not follow and dogmatic approach, nor do we exhibit boundless regard for one single doctrine; rather, we believe in borrowing from, and accepting useful features of the diverse educational philosophies and tendencies and harmonising them for our purpose so as to help ourselves in preparing policies and programmes for meeting the needs of our society. If we analyse the trends in present-day education we find that their origin is traceable not to one school of philosophical thought or to one movement in education but to different educational philosophies and movements. Idealism, naturalism, pragmatism, psychological, scientific, and sociological tendencies-all these have been harmonised to give education today its present shape.

The eclectic tendency in education reflects itself in the aims of education, contents and method of teaching. Present-day tendencies in this respect are not specially attributable to a single or particular school of thought or educational philosopher, but to the cumulative experience of the human race. They have taken the best and the acceptable out of many sources, presenting them in a unified and coherent educational philosophy as regards its aims procedures of instruction.

The Principles

In the above lines various bases in connection with the construction of curriculum have been discussed. From this, we can deduce some salient principles of curriculum construction which are as under—

Principle of Child-centred Education - Curriculum should be child-centred. In other words, while constructing a suitable curriculum, the interests, needs, capacities, abilities, age and the level of intelligence of children should be kept in full view and close attention

Principle of Relation with Life - In the curriculum, only those subjects should be included which are relevant to actual living directly. The old and prevalent curriculum is under heavy fire only because to its irrelevancy to the actual living conditions of children.

Principle of Utilizing Creative and Constructive Powers - Those subjects should be assigned prominent place in the curriculum which develop the creative and constructive capacities and abilities of children. Rayment rightly says - "fit a curriculum that is suited to the needs of today and of the future, there must be a definite bias towards definite creative subjects."

Principle of Interrelation of Play and Work Activities - While constructing a curriculum, the learning activities and experiences should be made so much interesting that a child gains experiences should be made so much interesting that a child gains knowledge and learning form them in the play-way spirit, thinking them as very interesting and captivating. According to Crow and Crow- "The aim of those, who guide the learning process, should be so as to plan learning activities that the play attitude is introduced."

Principle of the Knowledge of Culture and Civilization - In the curriculum should be included those subjects, activities and experiences which convey to the children the knowledge and understanding of their cultural values and civilization. In other words, curriculum should preserve and develop culture and civilization.

Principle of Totality of Experience - In the curriculum should be include the integrated whole of human experiences as one unit. In other words, curriculum should include both the literary and academic subjects as well as the sum total of varied human experiences which a child receives in the school campus, in the classrooms, on the playing fields, in the libraries and laboratories and through the various informal contacts with the teachers and other educationists. The Secondary Education Commission Report also emphasizes this as - "Curriculum does not mean only the academic subjects, but it includes the totality of experiences."

Principle of Achievement of Wholesome Behaviour Pattern - Curriculum subjects, activities and experiences should inculcate in the children social and moral qualities which shape curious behaviour towards others. Crow and Crow aptly remarks - "The curriculum should be so framed that it may help the children in the achievement of wholesome behaviour patterns."

Principle of Utility - Curriculum should include those subjects, activities and experiences which are useful to the present life as well as the future life to children. Irrelevant and useless material should find no place in the curriculum. There is enough dead wood in the curriculum of modern times, which needs to be removed and replaced by needful and relevant materials.

Principle of Future Orientation - Curriculum subjects and materials should be forward looking so that the child is able to solve the various problems that are to come before him in the immediate as, well as remote future, and also the find out suitable solutions and achieve harmonious adjustment with the changing conditions and situations of life in a progressive way. This capacity for adjustment should also enable the child to modify the environment according to his needs.

Principle of Variety and Flexibility - Different children have different inherent interests, aptitudes, urges, tendencies, capacities and abilities. In view of these variations and differences, there should be enough flexibility and elasticity in the curriculum to suit the varieties. The Secondary Education commission Report (1952-53) expresses the view as- "There should he enough variety and elasticity in the curriculum to allow for individual differences and adaptation to individual needs and interest."

Principle of Education for Leisure - The problem of utilizing leisure time gainfully is of considerable magnitude in modern times. It is generally noticed that people have no plan to spend this time effectively. They often waste it or rather kill it. A good curriculum should develop capacities in the children to spend their leisure time in a useful manner as they spend the busy time in various developmental activities.

Principle of Inclusion of All Life Activities - According to Herbert Spencer, the prime aim of education is to achieve complete development of individuality. Hence in the curriculum all those activities and subjects should be included which promote physical, mental, moral, social and political development of a child in a harmonious manner.

Principle of Relationship with Community Life - While constructing curriculum, full consideration of local needs and situations should be kept in mind. Not only this, all those social beliefs, attitudes, traditions and problems of community life should be given due place to make children understand them well and realize their responsibility towards them. The Secondary Education Commission Report also lays down - "The curriculum should be vitally and organically related to community life."

Principle of Development of Democratic Spirit - India has accepted the ideal of a democratic republic. Hence curriculum should contain and emphasize those activities and experiences which promote in the children democratic spirit, feelings and attitudes together with democratic behaviour patterns based on democratic ideals and values.

Principle of Correlation - The impact and importance of a curriculum is destroyed when it is broken into unrelated fragments and unconnected units. On the other hand if the integrated approach is employed in teaching various subjects, then this correlation leads to wider and deeper understanding and wholesome knowledge. Hence the curriculum should keep various units interrelated and lay stress upon correlation, so essential and so vital to effective and successful teaching.

QUESTIONS

1. Try to answer the basic questions -
   (a) Why is the curriculum needed?
   (b) What Should be the curriculum?
   (c) How Should the curriculum be prepared?
2. Enumerate the basis of curriculum construction. Establish the relationship between philosophy and curriculum.
3. Describe the contributions of idealism, naturalism, realism and pragmatism for curriculum construction.
4. Indicate the contributions of tendencies of education in curriculum construction. Describe contribution of Eclectic tendency in curriculum construction.

2

Methods of Teaching

Curriculum development is a cyclic process. Method of teaching is the most important component of the process. An instructional procedure is followed by employing appropriate instructional method. Instructional method is used for generating conducive learning conditions and situations for implementing curriculum. Education is continuous process from pre-primary to college and university level. Curriculum is designed for different stages of education. Thus, various types of instructional methods are used in educational process. The instructional methods are classified on different bases.

Various Types

Instructional objectives	*Type of methods*
Cognitive objectives	Knowing Instructional methods
Affective objective	Feeling Instruction methods
Psychomotor objectives	Doing Instructional methods

Teaching is a group activity. Teacher, learner and content are three major components of teaching or variables of teaching. Teacher is considered as an independent variable and student is dependent variable when content and instructional method is known as interfering variable. The role of these components changes in different instructional methods.

Types of Instructional methods on the basis of roles of teaching variables:

1. Teacher-Controlled Instruction (TCI),
2. Learner-Controlled Instruction (LCI), and
3. Group-Controlled Instruction (GCI)

An instructional method determines the role of teacher and learners in teaching-learning situations. An instructional method is selected in view of subject-content to be taught. In the following table instructional methods and nature of teaching learning situations have been provided.

Nature of Methods

Method of Teaching	*Nature of Teaching-Learning*
Lecture Method	Teacher Controlled Instruction
Demonstration Method	(TCI)
Team Teaching Method	(Monologue Instruction)
Chalk and Talk method	
Questions Answer method	Interactive Procedure of
Interactive Procedure	Instruction
Group Discussion Method	(T LCI)
Tutorial Method	(Dialogue Instruction)
Programmed Instruction	Learner-Controlled Instruction
Library Method	(LCI)
Computer Assisted Instruction	(Self-Study)
Laboratory method	
Field work	
Project Method	Group-Controlled Instruction
Simulated Instruction	(GCI)
Field Trips and	(Action Orientation Instruction)
Field work	

There are various ways to classify instructional methods. Teacher controlled Instructions are also known as autocratic style or authoritarian method. Learner-controlled Instructions are termed as permissive style or democratic methods.

Aspects of Development

An Instructional method is used for developing certain aspects of learners. The method involves some components of content which is the part of school curriculum. The content components are the means for developing the cognitive, affective and psychomotor aspects of the learner. In the following table aspects of development and components of content have been classified.

Aspect of Development and Components of Content

Aspect of Development	*Components of Content*
Cognitive aspect-knowing	Terms and words
(Cognitive objectives)	Concepts
	Facts and Events
	Rules and Principle
	Theories
	Problem solving
.	Creativity
Affective Aspect-Feeling	Interests and feelings
(Affective objectives)	Attitudes and beliefs
	Values and character
Psychomotor Aspects-Doing	Skill Training
(Psychomotor objectives)	Verbal - concepts
	Linguistic training
	Habit formation

Teaching-Learning Competency

The knowledge and skill of these instructional methods is essential for classroom teacher because he is the manager of classroom activities whether these are teacher-controlled of learner-controlled or group controlled instruction. The effective teaching can be classified into four type competencies.

1. Competency of Subject-matter,
2. Competency of Teaching skills,
3. Competency of Teaching behaviour, and
4. Competency of Problem-solving.

These competencies develop the quality of teaching which are related to content and instructional methods. The following are the good qualities of teaching-learning.

(1) Managing classroom activities - organized dominer.
(2) Dynamism in teaching style.
(3) Warmth and acceptance in teaching.
(4) Flexibility in teaching, and
(5) Creative teaching style.

The competencies and quality of teaching enables the teachers to understand four stages of learning—

(a) Learning to know
(b) Learning to learn
(c) Learning to do and
(d) Learning to live cooperatively

The awareness of these aspects of teaching is essential for selecting appropriate instruction method. It is not that easy because teaching learning is very complex activity which involves several components in various subjects method. In the following paragraphs teacher-controlled instruction methods have been discussed.

Teacher-Controlled Instructions

A teacher plays significant and main role in classroom teaching learning situations. All the activities of teaching are controlled by the teacher. He dominates the classroom climate. It is assumed that teacher has the mastery of subject and possesses mature personality while students have less nature personality. It further assumes that the learners have the capacity to carry out the order and obey the teacher. Then, they are the passive listeners in the classroom. They can not argue or ask question in the classroom. This type of instruction has authoritarian type climate. The curriculum is content centred. The concept of teaching is explained in the following manner by H.C. Morrison:

"Teaching is an intimate contact between a more mature personality and a less mature which is designed to further the education of the later (student)."

This type of teaching and instruction confines to memory level, there is no place for developing feelings attitude and values. This type of instruction methods have their advantages and limitations which have been discussed along each instructional method. Even a teacher can teach wrong thing to the students. The following are the instruction methods which are known as Teacher Controlled Instruction. These are task-centred methods.

(1) Lecture Method,

(2) Demonstration method and

(3) Tutorial method.

The details of these methods have been provided in the following groups.

Lecture Method

It is one of the oldest teaching method given by idealism philosophy. It is still most important teaching method in our schools. It is one of the autocratic teaching strategies.

Focus: It may be used to achieve the cognitive and affective objectives. Lecture can be used to realize the highest order of cognitive objectives.

Structure: Lecture lays emphasis on the presentation of the content. Teacher is more active and students are passive participants but he uses question-answer technique to keep them attentive in the class. Teacher controls and plans for all students act.

Principles : It employs the following principles-

(a) The content is presented as whole.

(b) The main stress is on presentation.

(c) The students learn better through listening.

(d) The subject-content is correlated with other subject.

(c) The new knowledge is linked with student's previous knowledge.

Applications: The presentation can be made effective but it should be used with great precaution. Teacher should make use of the teaching aids in the description and explaining concepts. Developing questions should be asked to make the presentation purposeful and interesting.

Advantages: The following are the major advantages of lecture strategy-

1. The habit of concentration may be developed among the students.
2. It is an economical teaching strategy. A large subject content may be taught relatively in small duration.
3. Very high order of cognitive objectives may be achieved.
4. The personality of teacher influences the learner's personality.
5. The new content can be easily introduced.

6. It provides the opportunity to the teacher to use different types of teaching aids.
7. Teacher can employ his full verbal communication.

Limitations: It has the following limitations.

1. It has more emphasis on teacher presentation and has no place for the participation of the students.
2. This strategy can be used in higher classes but it can not easily used in elementary classes.
3. Teaching activities are dominated by the teacher and there is no place for student's abilities, interests and their learning.
4. It is not based upon the principle of psychology. The individual differences are not considered in implementing teaching strategy.
5. It can not be used for achieving the psychomotor objectives and the highest order of affective objectives.
6. Usually teacher deviates from, the subject-content and teaching points. Therefore, student can not perform well in examination.
7. An effective teacher can use this strategy effectively, because teacher should have mastery over the content.

Suggestions: The following precautions should be observed to use this strategy effectively-

1. The language of the lecture should be simple, easy and comprehensive.
2. The developing question should be asked to make the students attentive in the class.
3. The students remain inactive and passive participants hence the teacher uses humour to release their tension and monotony of the class.
4. The strategy should be used from secondary level to upward classes.
5. The teacher should explore their previous knowledge and make efforts to link with new one.
6. The strategy should be supported by question answer, technique and appropriate teaching aids, maps, charts, diagrams, pictures, etc.

Demonstration Method

The lesson demonstration strategy, is a traditional classroom method which is used in technical schools and training colleges. It is widely used by teacher-educators during teaching practice. As a permissive than a discussion.

Focus: It is used for achieving the psychomotor and cognitive objectives.

Structure: It consists of three successive steps:- (a) Introduction, (b) Development, and (c) Integration.

In the first step of introduction, the aims are stated. The second phase involves a good deal of question answers and other class activities. The last step, in which the lesson material is rehearsed, revised and evaluated.

Principles: It is mainly used as a leaching strategy for average and below average students or untrained and inexperienced teacher. The cognitive and psychomotor objective can be realized. It is more useful for pupil-teachers to develop his own lesson in classroom teaching.

Limitations: It suffers from the following limitations-

(1) It does not provide an opportunity to develop originality of pupil teachers. They try to imitate the model lesson in their teaching.

(2) Teacher-educators can not demonstrate the lesson correctly and effectively.

Suggestions: The following precautions should be taken in demonstrating the lesson.

(1) An effective or skilled teacher should demonstrate the lesson.

(2) The pupil-teacher should be given an opportunity to seek the clarification of their problems.

(3) The lesson-demonstration should be followed by discussion.

(4) The lesson -demonstration should be used as a supplementary techniques in simulated social skill training.

Tutorials Method

Tutorials strategy is considered both autocratic and permissive type of teaching. It is generally considered to be one of the most valuable educational experiences. Lecture strategy is followed by tutorials because individual difficulties can both solved in lecture. Tutorials are highly individualized type of teaching.

Focus: Tutorials aim at providing remedial help to the learner or to help individual difficulties of the learner. The cognitive and affective objectives may be achieved by the tutorials.

Structure: Tutorial classes are formed by considering the homogeneous type of difficulties of the learner. The small homogeneous group is assigned by one teacher. He has to give remedial help to the learner. Tutorial is a follow up programme.

Principles: It is based upon the following teaching principles.

(1) It considers the individual difference.

(2) It establishes the rapport with learners.

(3) It provides educational guidance.

(4) It organizes as remedial help to the weak learner.

Types: Tutorial covers a wide range of teaching activities. These may be classified under three heads:-

Supervision Tutorials: In this type of tutorial students and teacher meeting are arranged regularly. A student reads an essay and defends it with arguments. This strategy can provide an opportunely to dependant his understanding of subject can provide an opportunity to deepen his understanding of subject for able student. It stresses on the mastery over the basic skills of scholarship.

Group Tutorials: These tutorials are useful for an average student. These can satisfy the needs of less exceptional students. The teacher should have the background of social psychology and group dynamics so that he can deal with group tutorials effectively in solving their problems.

Practical Tutorials: These tutorials are commonly used for both, group and individual bases to achieve psychomotor skills in laboratory, workshop and rehearsal. These tutorials are basically employed to achieve the psychomotor objectives.

Group tutorials are more useful in adult teaching. A tutorial strategy is more useful for achieving higher-order cognitive, affective and psychomotor objectives.

Advantages: The following are major advantages of tutorials:

(1) It is a valuable teaching strategy from individual differences point of view.

(2) It provides an opportunity to organize remedial teaching.

(3) It can fulfil the need of entering behaviour of the learner.

(4) It provides full freedom to the learner to seek the clarification of their problems and can raise their level of performance.

Limitations: It has the following disadvantages-

(1) One teacher cannot solve the difficulties related to different subjects and different students.

(2) The teacher becomes biased and does not take interest in the problem of each and every student.

(3) Usually some students dominate the tutorials group and all students can not get equal opportunity to participate.

(4) Tutorial-groups develop the feeling of jealousy.

Suggestions: Tutorials may be improved by observing the following suggestions:

(1) Tutorial groups should be formed of some background, abilities and entering behaviours.

(2) Teacher should have very objective dealing with the students.

(3) Teacher should provide the remedial help in the subject of his won interest.

(4) The tutorial groups should be formed on the basis of students difficulties in different subjects.

(5) Teacher should encourage every student to place his difficulty.

Interactive Method

The participation of teacher and students is equally important in this method. This type of instruction method is used in democratic form of government. The transaction curriculum is objective-centred and teaching is an interactive process. B.C. Smith has rightly defined as follows:

"Teaching is a system of actions and activities which intends learning through interpersonal relationship."

This type of teaching helps in developing students as well as teacher. Interaction means development of both teacher and students.

Similarly Edmuned Anidon (1967) has defined teaching in view of the democratic model of behaviour.

"Teaching is defined as an interactive process primarily involving classroom talk which takes place between teacher and pupils and occurs during definable activities.

This type of teaching is relationship-centred rather than task-centred. Due weightage is given to the feeling and beliefs of the students in classroom teaching. The students are encouraged to ask questions and initiate the classroom talk. A student can argue with teacher, even he can criticise the teacher. Teacher role is take a guide and friend.

The teaching activities and action in this type of instruction-method are planning, organizing leading or motivating, counselling and evaluation (feedback to both), in the conductive classroom climate. The following are the methods which are used as dialogue in classroom-.

(1) Question-answer, Instruction method;
(2) Heuristics Instruction Method;
(3) Group-discussion- method.

The defects of these methods have been given in the following paragraphs.

Question-Answer Method

The Socratic method is known as question-answer method. It is developed by the famous philosopher Socrates. He assumes that all knowledge within the learner and teacher has to unfold it. He further assumes that teacher should present the subject-matter in such a way that learner recognizes, the truth and he can identify himself with it.

Focus: The strategy aims at achieving the cognitive objective and bringing knowledge at the conscious level.

Structure: Socrates has suggested three steps:

(1) To prepare questions and arrange them in a sequence..
(2) To present the questions in appropriate way so that curiosity may be created among the learners.
(3) To ask new questions by linking with the learner's responses. Teacher is able to recognize the intention of learner and provides motivation accordingly.

He has to identify the three phases of learning process: observation, experience and testing.

Principles: The question-answer strategy is based upon the following principles:

(1) Theory of unfoldment: All knowledge is within the learner, teacher can not impart any new knowledge to students.
(2) The knowledge can be emitted by linking the questions with his answers.

Example: Lesson does most of Indian population live in?

Teacher - Where does most of Indian population live in?

Pupil - Villages.

Teacher - What is their main occupation?

Pupil - Farming or Agriculture.

Teacher - What are the main agriculture crops in our country?

Pupil - Rice, Wheat and Sugarcane.

Thus, the teacher develops his lesson with the help of appropriate questions.

Advantages: The following are major advantages of question-answer strategy.

(1) The classroom verbal interaction can only be encouraged.
(2) The learner remains active and participates in teaching acts.
(3) The new knowledge is imparted by linking with earlier acquired knowledge.
(4) It involves psychological principles of learning.
(5) It is more useful at primary and secondary level.
(6) It reduces the chances of indiscipline in classroom teaching.
(7) While asking the questions teacher should keep in mind the abilities, needs and interests of the learners.

Limitations: It has the following disadvantages:

(1) It is very difficult to prepare good questions and arrange them in psychological sequence.
(2) It is a mechanical strategy and creates memory in the classroom climate.
(3) It can be used in the teaching of higher classes.
(4) All knowledge can not be imparted by questions-answer strategy.

Suggestions: The following precautions should be taken.

(1) It should be supplemented by lecture and narration devices.
(2) The questions should be evenly distributed among the whole class.
(3) The strategy should be used only those teachers who can prepare question immediately even at the time of teaching.
(4) The teacher should try to reduce the tension of the class by humour.

Heuristics Method

The term 'Heuristics' has been borrowed from the word 'Heurises'; it means, "discover or investigate". The purpose of communication is to develop the tendency of investigation. Arm Strong is the exponent of this strategy. It is based upon the assumption of Herbert Spencer that the learner should be told as little as possible and he should be encouraged to learn by himself as much as possible.

Pollio and Dankar (1945) have mentioned this method in their article entitled-Problem 'Solving.' The strategy involves 'trial and error' and invention techniques. This strategy is very economical and speedy. It requires more logical and imaginative thinking in formulating the number of tentative solutions for the problems.

Objectives: The following are the main objectives of 'Heuristics Strategy of Teaching:

(1) To develop problem-solving tendency.

(2) To develop logical and imaginative thinking ability.

(3) To develop scientific attitude towards the problem.

(4) To encourage free thinking for performing the task.

Structure: A problem is placed before the learners and they attempt to seek the solutions of the problem. The learners get full freedom of working and thinking. The number of devices are used for solving the problem. The problem is analysed in possible elements. The learner discuss themselves about the problem. The teacher encourages the students to work in laboratory and to study in the library. The teacher attempts to acquaint the leaner with relevance of the problems.

Advantages: The following are the main advantages of Heuristic strategy of teaching:

(1) It develops the scientific attitude of the leaner and tendency of observation.

(2) It evolves the feeling of self confidence and self reliance.

(3) The teacher provides the individual guidance to the learner.

(4) The teacher remains active.

(5) It develops logical and imaginative thinking among the learners.

(6) It is based upon psychological principles of learning.

(7) It creates the situation for divergent thinking.

Limitations: It suffers from the following limitations:

(1) It can not be used for lower classes.

(2) It is very time consuming strategy.

(3) It can not be used for the dull or poor students even for higher classes.

(4) It can be employed for a large number of students.

Precautions: The following precautions should be observed:-

(1) It has a number of possible solutions to a problem, hence most relevant solutions should be tried out.

(2) It has an unstructured curriculum, therefore, problem should be oriented towards the objective.

(3) It is full of risk, because most of the trials go waste, therefore, wrong solutions should not be accepted.

(4) There are more chance of indiscipline hence teacher should provide proper guidance to each and every learner.

Group Discussion Method

There is no comprehensive definition of 'group discussion' but it is considered as a democratic teaching strategy. The pupils are more active in it. Teacher's job is to supervise and to provide guidance to pupils activities. It is child-centred teaching strategy. It may be of two types: (1) By the teacher and (2) By the students.

(1) By the teacher: This type of discussion is more autocratic in style.

(2) By the student: In this situation, discussion is more permissive or democratic in style.

Objectives: The affective objectives and higher order cognitive objectives may be achieved.

Structure: The group discussion is organized in two forms: Formally and informally. In formal group discussion, proper schedule is prepared and certain rules are absence of a teacher, pupils have to select a student to act as a leader of the group. The leader of the group prepares a plan for discussion. In the group discussion, due weightage is given to the answers and questions of the pupils.

Principles: This strategy is based upon the following principles of teaching:

(1) Principle of active participation.

(2) Principle of freedom for work.

(3) Principle of group work and equal opportunities to ask questions and to answer them.

Advantages: The following are the main advantages of this strategy.

(1) It has the greater scope of criticism for incorrect approaches, ideas and concepts.

(2) It develops the feeling of group work and group participation.

(3) It helps in developing the creative ability and thinking among pupils.

(4) It develops the problem solving attitude and the tolerance to hear one's own criticism.

(5) It helps in developing the feeling of cooperation.

(6) The higher order of cognitive and affective objectives of teaching are achieved.

Limitations: It has the following limitations:

(1) It has chances for deviation from the main topic.

(2) In the discussion, only few students dominate and to discuss more and large number of students do not participate in the discussion.

(3) Generally groups are formed in this strategy and they are critical to one another.

(4) It involves more criticism rather than relevant discussion.

Suggestions: It may be improved and can be effectively employed by observing the following precautions:

(1) Every student should be provided an opportunity to participate in the discussion.

(2) Students should be encouraged and motivated to participate in the discussions.

(3) Irrelevant criticism should not be encouraged.

QUESTIONS

1. Indicate the need of instructional method in curriculum development. Enumerate methods in view of the objectives.
2. Explain the term teacher-controlled instruction. Enumerate methods which are as TCI.
3. Enumerate the teaching learning competency. Indicate the components of content which are taught by TCI.
4. Indicate the methods of teacher-controlled instruction. Describe the lecture method.
5. Enumerate the Instruction method used in interactive process of teaching. Describe question-answer method.

3

Modes of Teaching

A question of philosophy tends always to be framed in terms of concepts to be analysed and pattern of thinking to be clarified. The problems of philosophy are conceptual problems; therefore, when the philosophers of education wish to investigate the nature of teaching, they tend to ask not about teaching itself but about the concept of teaching how it is used, to what sorts of things we do not. Their course tends to be focused in a peculiar way upon the term 'teaching and learning and their relationship to other terms.

A concept is the focus of inferences, permitted by the various uses of term:

One way to study a concept is to extreme how it is related to others, which concepts are connected with it and which ones are not.

"Teaching is the task of a teacher which is performed for the development of a child."

"A close relationship exists between linguistic or conceptual analysis and the formulation of definition. A concept is analysed by studying the meaning of its related terms, and definition, like an analysis, is always a formulation of meaning."

The concept of teaching is immensely important to the philosophy of education, because it emphasises more fundamental:

"Teaching that ....and teaching to ...."

Teaching someone that to and so ....communication of knowledge and beliefs.

Teaching someone to do so and so ....shaping behaviour.

Thus, teaching is for some development. The term development implies shaping behaviour and conduct; communication of knowledge and beliefs. The relationship between these two emphasis in teaching is immensely important for the philosophy of education.

Teaching process involves certain modes of behaviour. These modes of behaviour are in a continuum. It means that teaching is a continuum for developing behaviour to the formation of beliefs. Thus, teaching is a continuum from conditioning to indoctrination. These terms (conditioning, training, instruction and indoctrination) can be understood with the help of the following diagram—

Teaching as Continuum

Behaviour	Conduct	Knowledge	Beliefs
Training			Instruction
Conditioning	Training	Instruction	Indoctrination

The Region of Intelligence

The diagram indicates that teaching has four modes of operations in a continuum. Teaching starts from conditioning and reaches upto indoctrination.

Conditioning as Mode of Teaching: The conditioning is a kind of teaching which refers to teaching someone to do .... (shaping behaviour). It is more concerned with shaping behaviour and habits. It seems to be related with the concept of training and enters the teaching concept.

Training as a Mode of Teaching: Teaching is a kind of training. Training refers to teach some to do .... (shaping conduct and skills). Training implies the manifestation of intelligence. They are trainable but not educable. Teaching implies the higher degree of intelligence. Training is related to conditioning.

Instruction as a Mode of Teaching: The instruction is a kind of teaching which refers to teach someone that .... (communication of knowledge). It is more concerned with imparting knowledge an information. Training may be the pre-requisite for instructing. Instructing is a good example of teaching. It requires thinking, reasoning and generalization. It is a higher level of teaching.

Indoctrination as a Mode of Teaching: The indoctrination is a kind of teaching which refer to the concept "teaching someone that ...... (formation of beliefs). It mainly concerns with shaping beliefs. It requires higher order in intelligence, *i.e.* reasoning with feeling. Indoctrination concerns with doctrine in way or transmission of doctrine.

The analysis indicates that the different modes of teaching are distinguishable, but they are related to one another. These modes of teaching help in development of a child. They all seem to be distributable along a continuum which represent the manifestation of intelligence. The continuum of teaching has been illustrated with help of the following chart.

Modes of Teaching

Teaching someone to do		Teaching someone that	
Shaping behaviour and conduct		Shaping knowledge and beliefs	
Conditioning	Training	Instruction	Indoctrinating
Behaviour	Conduct	Knowledge	Beliefs
	Trainable	Educable	

"The is an activity primarily concerned with manifestation of intelligence then it will follow that instructing is an activity which more perfectly displays the properties of teaching than does indoctrinating."

Activities of Teaching

The teaching activities are those which a teacher performs in his classroom teaching. These are many ways to group the teacher activities or teaching tasks. B.O. Smith has classified teaching activities in cognitive and affective activities of teaching. Thomas F. Green has classified teaching activities into three categories

1. The logical activities of teaching,
2. The strategic activities of teaching, and
3. The instructional activities of teaching.

Logical Acts: The logical acts are those activities relating primarily to the elements of thinking or reasoning in the conduct of teaching.

Green has identified eight logical acts of teaching. These are as follows:

1. Explaining, 2. Concluding, 3. Inferring, 4. Giving reason, 5. Amassing evidence, 6. Demonstrating, 7. Defining, and 8. Comparing.

Strategic Acts: The strategic acts are those items that have to do primarily with the teacher's plan or strategy in teaching the material is organized or students are directed in the course of teaching. The performance of strategic acts of teaching is appraised by their consequences for learning outcome.

Thomas F. Green has identified the following seven strategic activities of teaching—

1. Motivating, 2. Counselling, 3. Evaluating, 4. Planning, 5. Encouraging, 6. Disciplining and 7. Questioning.

Teaching can not occur independently without the logical and strategic acts. Activities associated with the logic and strategy of teaching are indispensable to the conduct of teaching wherever and whenever it is found.

The logical and strategic acts of teaching differ not only from the instructional acts but also from each other. They are distinguished primarily by the fact the performance of the strategic acts of teaching will be evaluated chiefly by their consequences, but performance of the logical acts of teaching will be evaluated independently of their consequences. This important difference between the logic of teaching and the strategy of teaching is usually obscured because, in practice, the logical acts of teaching never occur, or at least very seldom occur, except in the context of some teaching strategy. The performance of the logical acts is evaluated on logical grounds.

The Instructional Acts of training: The instructional acts of teaching are those activities that arise primarily because of the way the teacher's work is organised the institution or the school.

It is easy, of course to add the test under each of these categories, but it is not easy to decide under which heading each item should be placed.

Green has identified the following seven activities of teaching under this category:

1. Collecting money, 2. Patrolling hall, 3. Attending meeting, 4. Taking attendance, 5. Consulting parents, 6. Keeping reports. and 7. Chaperoning.

The activities of teaching can go without institutional activities of teaching. The institutional acts of teaching are distinguished because they are not necessary for the activities of teaching. The institutional acts of teaching might better be known as the 'institutional activities of teachers.'

The activity of teaching involves giving reasons, evidence, explanations and conclusions ; it can be evaluated quite independently of its results in getting some one to learn.

Teaching Variables

Teaching process involves three variables:

1. Independent variable is the teacher.
2. Dependent variable is the student.
3. Intervening variables are the content and strategies of presentation.

In the process of teaching, it plays the role of independent variable. The planning, organizing, leading and controlling of the teaching is done by him. The teacher has the freedom to perform the activities for providing the learning experiences to the pupils.

The student is the dependent variable in the process of teaching because student has to act according to the planning and organization of the teacher. The student's learning or performance is influenced by teaching activities.

The content of teaching, strategies, tactics of teaching and techniques of motivation are known as intervening variables. The interaction between teacher and student is performed through the intervening variables. The content determines the mode of presentation-telling, showing and doing.

These variables operate in the process of teaching and creating learning conditions or situations.

The Functions

The teaching variables have important place in the process of teaching. The independent and dependent variables perform three major function: (1) Diagnosis, (2) Prescription and (3) Evaluation.

Diagnostic Functions: The teacher as an independent variable is more active in this function. He has to diagnose the entering behaviour of the learners and structure of the content for writing teacher objectives in behavioural terms. This function helps the teacher to take the decision about the following aspects of teaching-

(a) Entering behaviour of pupils,
(b) Analysing teaching problems,
(c) Individual variations, and
(d) Content analysis in view of learning conditions.

The teacher uses two approaches in the diagnostic function (1) A diagnostic test is administered for the entering behaviour of the pupils. (2) The content is analysed into elements and they are arranged logically in a sequence.

The student as a dependent variable diagnoses on the basis of his perception for his activities and responses. The language comprehensions, abilities, skills and expressions are the main components of dependent variables. In the process of interaction teacher and student, both use intuition and response.

Prescriptive Functions: The teaching learning objective can be achieved by the appropriate interpersonal relationship between the teacher and student. The teacher takes decision about teaching strategies and tactics to be used.

The main objective of this function is to bring desirable change in learner's behaviour. Therefore, techniques of reinforcement are used for this purpose.

In selection teaching techniques and feedback devices, teacher has to keep in mind the individual differences among the students. The teacher attempts to organize the intervening variables in such a way so that learning objectives may be achieved. It has two main element:

(a) Teaching Skills are taken into practice.
(b) The feedback devices are used appropriately.

The teacher performs more prescriptive function in the presentation of the content whereas student is less active. The student helps the teacher in demonstration.

Evaluation Function: The evaluation function is the most important aspect of teaching and its main objective is to examine the effectiveness of prescriptive functions. The criterion of evaluation is the realization of objectives. If objectives could not be realized, it shows that prescriptive functions are not appropriate. Therefore, the weakness of the second function should be diagnosed students should not be blamed for this weakness but prescriptive functions should be modified and improved. The evaluation function has two main activities:

(a) Construction of criterion test, and
(b) Evaluation of change of behaviour.

In the evaluation function the student is more active. He has to diagnose the items of criterion test and then he has to respond. The student diagnoses the items to check the correctness of his responses. The teaching functions are similar to a medical doctor. The main job of a doctor is to diagnose and to give prescription. Thus, the source of teaching function is like medicine.

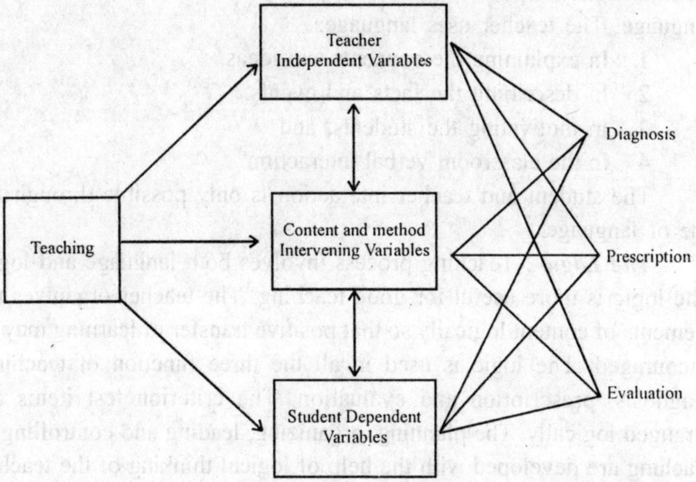

Structure of Teaching

B.O. Smith has pointed out that knowledge and understanding of teaching function is basic information theory of teaching. Theory of teaching explains the relationship of variables and their structure.

Structure of Teaching

Teaching has three dimensional process and a system development can be done by teaching process. It involves three types of activities.

(a) Signs and Symbols in Teaching,
(b) Teaching as a Linguistic process, and
(c) The Logic of Teaching.

Signs and Symbols : When we analyse teaching components, the signed and symbols are obtained. The teacher uses the signs symbols at diagnostic stage and the student begins to understand and takes interest in them. The teacher also employs signs and symbols at prescriptive and evaluative stages of teaching. The students also use them in communication and explaining the teaching concepts. Thus, these are the elements of teaching structure. The use of signs and symbols in teaching makes it more economical and effective.

Linguistic Process: The teacher not only uses signs and symbols in the instruction but also uses language for communicating ideas to the pupils. Teaching is not possible without the use of language. The communication aspect of teaching is purely based on the use of certain language. The teacher uses language:

1. In explaining the concepts and ideas,
2. In describing the facts and events,
3. In motivating the students, and
4. In the classroom verbal interaction.

The student and teacher interaction is only possible through the use of language.

The Logic : Teaching process involves both language and logic. The logic is more useful for good teaching. The teacher organizes the elements of content logically so that positive transfer of learning may be encouraged. The logic is used in all the three function of teaching: diagnosis, prescription and evaluation. The criterion test items are arranged logically. The planning, organizing, leading and controlling of teaching are developed with the help of logical thinking of the teacher.

The nature of teaching can be well understood with the help of the three components of teaching.

Teaching Prescriptions

E. Stones and Morris have classified teaching prescriptions under the three components of teaching.

Level I- Involves the Following Activities

(1) To provide for communication among the pupil, teacher and students.

(2) To develop teacher-pupil interpersonal relationship conducive to student learning.

(3) Maintain a social order conducive to pupil learning.

(4) Ensure that pupils are motivated to learn.

(5) Ensure that pupils are active.

Level II- It has the main activities

(6) To employ strategies to produce minimum interference with other objectives and that are to appropriate (a) the characteristics of the learner (b) how pupils learn (c) the specific curricular objectives.

Level III-

(7) To appraise student's progress towards curricular objectives with a view of teaching, revising teaching strategies, revising curricular objectives or combination of these.

(8) To provide a minimum level of performance in each prescription.

Objectives of Teaching

Teaching is a purposeful activity. It has the following objectives:

1. The purpose of teaching is to facilitate the learners transformation of egocentric assimilation into true deduction.
2. The purpose of teaching is to help learner, adjust his perceptions to reality attaining harmony between internal organization and external experiences-Piaget.
3. The purpose of teaching is to help students to become better thinkers and workers.
4. The purpose of teaching is to help someone, someday, somehow, somewhere that he is able to see beyond and feel a new creativity think and do.

Characteristics of Good Teaching

A good teaching is the main criterion of an effective teacher. An effective teacher has three types of characteristics: Presage, process and product factors. Teaching effect is considered the process factor. The characteristics of good teaching can be enumerated with reference to social structure and form of the government.

Good teaching in a totalitarian state would be done by people whose personal interaction would influence learners toward valuing the goals of the state, which is good, for the state is good for the individual.

Good teaching in a democratic state would be done by people who arrange for a vigorous market place of freely announced ideas which force all learns Constantly to adjust and assimilate their own values, structures thought patterns, and total configuration of what they know.

The characteristics of good teaching of democratic model have been given in the following paragraphs:

1. Good teaching requires appropriate responsiveness to the date, the child and group placing in the situation. The child activities can be rewarded properly.
2. Good teaching requires a reduction in the controlling functions exercised continuously by the teacher. Teacher behaviour should be indirect.

   Flanders found in his study that the indirectness of teacher who goes along with greater achievement on the part of their pupils.
3. Good teaching requires that the classroom should be well managed so that the business of learning may receive full attention. Teachers perform the functions of controlling with clarity and with consistency.
4. Good teaching requires that the human environment should be accepted by each individual, that in some way it tells him that he is important. It suggests a personal rapport between teachers and students.
5. Good teaching keeps or maintains the interpersonal relationship supportive within the classroom. Out of this a shared problem solving attitude develops.
6. Good teaching requires that the teacher should be a well educated mature person who has the insight and energy for this demanding job. It requires the responsive human environment that fosters exploration and initiative on.

QUESTIONS

1. Explain the term teaching. Enumerate the modes of teaching and describe their meaning.
2. Explain the phrase 'teaching a logical activity.' Indicate the teaching variables.
3. Enumerate the functions of teaching variables, and indicate the relationship among these variables.

4

Objectives of Teaching

The planning is most important task of a teacher. He has to utilize his imagination, creativity and insight in analysis teaching content into its elements and in defining and formulating the learning objectives in behavioural terms. This step is very scientific in nature because the teacher has to analyse the content systematically and arrange in its elements in a logical sequence that may suit to students-learning and desired objectives can be achieved. Thus, a teacher has to perform three activities in this step:

1. Analysing the task or content Analysis.
2. Identification of teaching objectives, and
3. Writing objectives in behavioural terms.

The detailed description of these activities has been provided in the following paragraphs.

Task Analysis

Ryle has given this concept of *'Task Analysis.'* The focus of training psychology is to analyse the task to be performed. This concept is very useful for developing the understanding and skills for teaching and training. This has emerged against the theories of learning because theories of learning could not provide substantial solution for the problems of classroom teaching and learning.

The effective teaching can only, be organized by analysing the content. This task is educational as well as intellectual in nature because it involves both the process of analysis and synthesis. The task analysis has four characteristics:

(a) Description of learning activities,
(b) Identification of desired behaviour,
(c) Identification of appropriate situation and techniques of motivation, and
(d) Developing Criterion test for measuring the desired behavioural change.

The task analysis provides the basis for selecting appropriate teaching tactics and strategies and formulating the objectives of teaching.

Various Types : The task analysis is classified into three types. These three categories of task analysis are quite different and they serve different purpose.

1. Content analysis or Topic Analysis,
2. Job Analysis, and
3. Skill Analysis.

Content Analysis: In this step of task analysis, the content or subject-matter is analysed into sub-topics and sub-topic into elements and these are arranged into a logical sequence. This type of analysis is purely educational and intellectual activity. For example, 'Density in Physics, Samas in Hindi, Fundamental Rights in Civics and Change of Season in Geography. This type of analysis is generally concerned with cognitive aspect of a teacher.

Job Analysis: This type of analysis concerns with tasks which are related to some professional and social activity. In involves psychomotor activities for example: Teacher-tasks, Doctor-task, Engineer's-tasks, etc.

Skill Analysis: This type of analysis is also related to the psychomotor activities but it concerns with the most specific skills. The skill analysis is included in job analysis. In Job analysis mainly skills are analysed, but skill analysis is done for specific activities for example: Questioning, Motivation and diagnosing, etc.

The pupil-teachers should have the knowledge and skill of content analysis. The content anslysis is the basis for preparing instructions and formulating the objectives of teaching. Therefore, detailed description of content analysis has been given below:

The Definition of Content Analysis : The term *'Content Analysis'* has been defined by I.K. Davies-

"It is the analysis of topic or content unit to be taught, into its constituents or elements and arrange them in a logical sequence."

A content is broken down into its element. Each element may be performed by using specific tactics and the specific objectives can be realized. The elements are arranged in a logical sequence so that positive transfer of learning can be facilitated. The teacher has to employ his imagination, creativity and insight in synthesizing the elements of the content.

There are various techniques (Glasser 1963, Homme 1962, Macnar 1965) of content analysis. Davies Matrix technique is most useful and practicable. A content is broken down into sub-topics and each sub-topic is further broken down into elements. The sub-topics are arranged in learning sequence. This has been illustrated with the help of a chart.

Content Analysis Chart

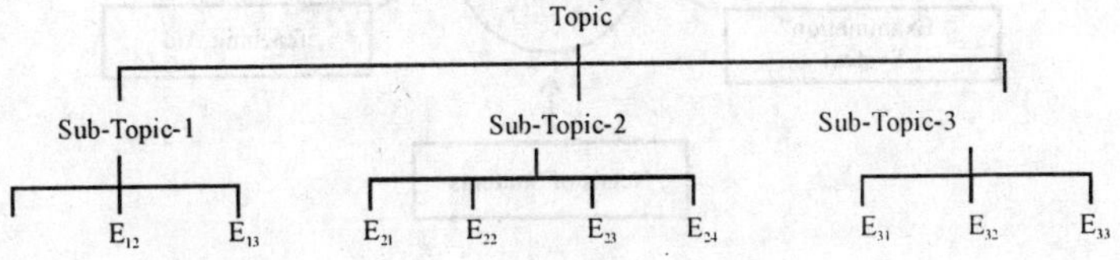

(E=Element)

Success of Content Analysis : The teacher has to make use of various sources for a content analysis, then he is able to present the correct structure of the content. The teacher should have the mastery over the content. The following sources are essential for content analysis:

1. Study of standard Text-Books.
2. Considering the needs of the learners.
3. Keeping in view the objectives of teaching-learning.
4. Considering the examination system.
5. Use of teaching aids, and
6. Teacher's own skills of teaching.

These sources have been shown in an integrated form with the help of a chart.

The mastery behaviour is determined in content analysis. It is based upon the needs of students of level or grade of education. The same content is taught at various levels but the structure of content is determined by considering the level of teaching. The teacher should consult and study the standard books available on the content so that appropriate content-structure can be determined. In addition to that, teacher should review the examination papers. The objective type questions require specific information about content. Therefore, new type content should be analysed in more small or specific elements whereas essay type requires the large elements of the content. The examination system helps in determining the size of elements of the content or structure of the analysing the content of his teaching.

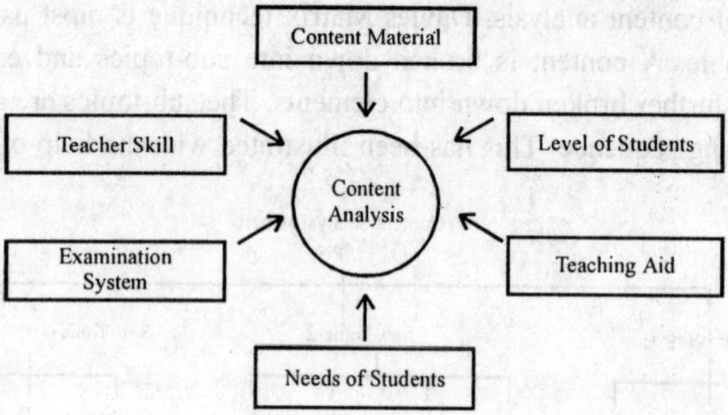

Integration of Sources of Content Analysis

Characteristics of Content-Element : The following are the chief characteristics of content element:

1. The student can exhibit by his activity that he can understand the element.
2. The comprehension of an element can be evaluated by a question.
3. The level of the element can be examined by behaviour of the student. The level of the element may be knowledge, comprehension and application, etc.
4. The understanding of various elements can be tested with the help of student's behaviour.
5. The emitted response for an element indicates the change in behaviour.

In this way every element is complete in itself. The knowledge and understanding of a concept for a fact may be given by arranging the elements in sequence.

Arrangement of Elements in a Sequence : The logical sequence of the elements can be made on the basis of the following rules:

(a) From Known to Unknown,
(b) From Simple to Difficult,
(c) From Concrete to Abstract.
(d) From Observation to Logical Thinking, and
(e) From Part to Whole.

The arrangement of elements based upon these rules increase the probability that logical sequence of the elements may be psychologically valid.

The concept of task analysis is practical in nature. Therefore, it has been illustrated with the help of an example. The pupil-teacher can observe an application aspect of this concept and can use to analyse his own content of teaching.

EXAMPLE

Topic-Management of Teaching Learning

Sub-Topic 1- Planning of teaching learning

Element	1.1	Task Analysis
"	1.2	Identification of objectives
"	1.3	Writing objective in behavioural

Sub-Topic 2- Organizing of teaching learning

Element	2.1	Selection of teaching strategies.
"	2.2	Selection of teaching tactics.
"	2.3	Selection of teaching aids.
"	2.4	Decision for rules and techniques of instruction

Sub-Topic 3- Leading of teaching of teaching learning

Element	3.1	Arranging for student's motivation.
"	3.2	Deciding the techniques of motivation,
"	3.3	Use of teaching skills.
"	3.4	Use of communication strategies.

Sub-Topic 4- Controlling of teaching learning.

Element	4.1	Evaluation of learning activities.
"	4.2	Evaluation of learning outcome.
"	4.3	Organizaing learning objective.
"	4.4	Providing the feedback to the earlier steps.

It is evident from the above example that managing teaching-learning topic can be divided into four units or steps. Each unit is meaningful and quite different from one another. The four units have been arranged in a logical sequence. This arrangement seems to be effective or workable psychologically. Similarly each unit has been further divided into elements. Every element of each unit has been arranged in a sequence so that learner may understand easily. In this way analysis and synthesis both type of activities are performed in task analysis.

The content analysis provides a guideline in determining and identifying the objectives of learning.

The Identification

The teaching objectives are identified after analysing the content to be taught because teaching is a meaningful and purposeful activity. The teaching objectives are determined in the planning step. The teacher can identify his teaching objectives with the help of his knowledge and understanding of educational objectives. Therefore, meaning and definition of educational and teaching objectives have been described here.

The Definition and Meaning : The objectives is a statement or a form of category which suggests any kind of change, the objective has the following characteristics:

1. It provides the direction to the activity which is designed for achieving an ultimate goal.
2. It helps for the planned change.
3. It provides the basis for organizing activities.

"The educational objectives imply the changes that we try to produce in the child."

The educational objectives are generally in the statement form. These are broad and philosophical in nature. The teaching objectives are specific and psychological in nature. The teaching strategies and tactics are selected on the basis of teaching learning objectives. B.S. Bloom has given a very comprehensive definition of educational objectives:

"Educational objectives are not only the goals towards which the curriculum is shaped and towards which instruction is guided, but they are also the goals that provide the detailed specification for the construction and use of the evaluative."

B. S. Bloom believes that education is a tripolar process:

The learning experiences are provided by teaching activities to achieve educational objectives and change of behaviour is evaluated in terms of educational/ objectives. Thus educational objectives are the basis for teaching activities and evaluation techniques.

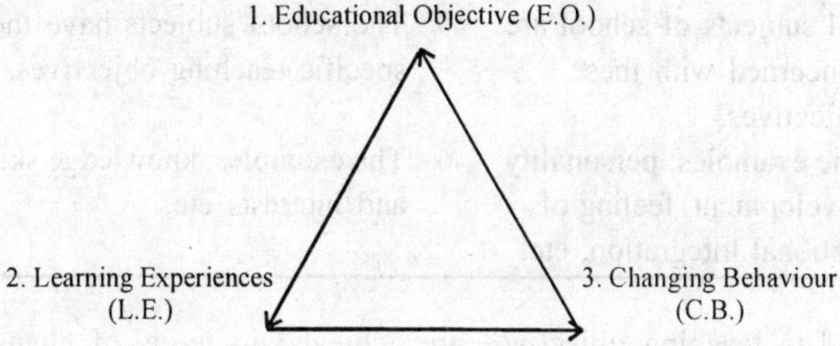

Type of Objectives- The objectives are classified in two major categories:

(1) Educational objective, and

(2) Teaching or learning objectives.

The educational objectives are broad and they are related to educational system and schools. The teaching objectives are narrow and specific and concerned with classroom teaching. The educational objective with the help of teaching or learning objectives. The educational objectives may be achieved by organizing teaching from primary to university levels whereas teaching objectives may be realized within a period of 40 minutes duration. For example: educational objectives are "to develop the feeling of national integration". This includes several teaching objectives—Knowledge, comprehension and application of national integration. The educational objectives may be achieved in a long period. The comparison between educational and teaching objectives has been given in the tabular form.

Comparison between Educational and Teaching Objectives

Educational Objective	*Teaching Objectives*
1. The are very broad.	1. They are very specific.
2. Social philosophy is the source of the objectives.	2. Psychology is the source of the objectives.
3. They imply the teaching objectives.	3. The educational objectives are achieved with the help of teaching objectives.
4. They can be achieved in a long period of duration.	4. They can be achieved within a period of classroom teaching.
5. All subjects of school are concerned with these objectives.	5. The school subjects have their specific teaching objectives.
6. The examples: personality development, feeling of National Integration, etc.	6. The examples: knowledge skills and interests etc.

The teaching objectives are achieved in terms of change of behaviour of learners. These are specific, direct and practical in nature. Therefore, these are most useful for teachers. The teaching objectives are related to learning outcome or change of behaviour of the learners. B.S. Bloom has classified the learning objectives in three categories:

1. Cognitive objectives,
2. Affective objectives, and
3. Psycho-motor objectives.

Thus, the change of behaviour is also of three type, cognitive, affective and psychomotor. Bloom and his associates on the university of Chicago, have produced a most important classification or taxonomy of cognitive educational objectives (Bloom 1969). The taxonomy arranges objectives in the domains into six categories. A useful way of looking at the domains is the cognitive domain, the teacher is interested in what the student will do, whereas in the affective domain, the teacher is additionally concerned with what he does to it or with it, and cognitive domain concerns with how he does it.

Each domain consists of six categories. These categories are in a hierarchical order. The first is the pre-requisite of the second and first five categories are the pre-requisite of the last category.

An old educational axiom states that 'growth occurs from within' and this inner growth is demonstrated in the two taxonomies by the way in which they are internally related.

Relationship between the Cognitive and Affective Domains: The cognitive and affective educational objectives are achieved in classroom teaching. The cognitive objectives are realized in military and other training programmes. Therefore, the detailed description of cognitive and affective domains has been given in the following paragraphs:

Taxonomy of Cognitive Educational Objectives and Learning Outcome

Cognitive Objectives	*Affective Objectives*
The lowest level in this taxonomy begins with the student's recall and recognition of KNOWLEDGE.	The lowest level begins with student's merely RECEIVING stimuli and passively attending to it. It extends for his more actively attending to it.
It extends through the COMPREHENSION of the knowledge.	Then his RESPONDING to stimuli on request, willingly responding and talking satisfaction in responding.
To his skill in the APPLICATION of the knowledge that he comprehends.	To his VALUING the phenomena or activity so that he voluntarily responds and seeds out further ways to take part in what is going on.
The next levels progress from his ability to make an ANALYSIS of the situations involving the knowledge, to his skill in SYNTHESIS of into new organization.	The next stage in his CONCEPTUALIZATION of each value to which he is responding by identifying characteristics or forming judgement.
The highest level lies in his skill in EVALUATION, so that he can judge the value of the knowledge in realizing specific objectives.	The highest level of the taxonomy in the student's ORGANIZATION of the values into a system is CHARACTERIZATION of himself.

Benjamin S. Bloom (1956) has written a handbook on taxonomy formulated to stimulate and systematize the assessment of objectives in cognitive domain. The cognitive domain of the taxonomy consists of six broad categories of cognitive learning arranged in an order to increase complexity: knowledge, comprehension, application, analysis, synthesis and evaluation. For each of these broad categories of cognitive learning, the taxonomy identifies specific learning outcome in behavioural terms and each of these educational objectives may be evaluated.

This taxonomy may assist the teacher in clarifying his educational objectives and modifying his teaching practices so that relevant, important outcome of learning are identified and realized.

(a) Preverbal percepts, (b) Factual information, (c) Concepts, (d) Generalization and principles, (e) Problem solving, (f) Creative thinking, (g) Theories, and (h) Systematized knowledge are the learning outcome of cognitive domain.

Condensed version of the taxonomy of educational objectives of cognitive domain:

Direction	Category
Low Level	1. Knowledge: (Remembering facts, terms principles in the form that they were learned),
	(a) Knowledge of specifics
	(i) Knowledge of terminology-
	(ii) Knowledge of specific facts
	(b) Knowledge of ways and means of dealing with specifics,
	(i) Knowledge of Convention.
	(ii) Knowledge of trends and sequences
	(iii) Knowledge of classifications and categories,
	(iv) Knowledge of Criteria,
	(v) Knowledge of methodology
	(c) Knowledge of Universal and absraction in a field
	(i) Knowledge of principles and generalizations.
	(ii) Knowledge of theories and Structures.
	2. Comprehension: (Understanding material student without necessarily relating it to other material).

Contd.

Direction		Category
		(a) Translation,
		(b) Interpretation, and
		(c) Extrapolation.
	3.	Application: (Using Generalizations or abstractions appropriately in concrete situations).
Medium Level	4.	Analysis: (Breakdown the material into elements).
		(a) Analysis of elements.
		(b) Analysis of relationship.
		(c) Analysis of generalization principles.
	5.	Synthesis: (Combining elements into a new structure).
		(a) Production of a unique communication.
		(b) Production of a plan or proposed set of operations.
		(c) Derivation of a set of abstract relations.
High Level	6.	Evaluation: (Judging the value of material for a specified purpose).
		(a) Judgement in terms of internal evidence.
		(b) Judgement in terms of external Criteria.

Cognitive Objectives

B. S. Bloom has divided the cognitive objectives in six categories. Their description has been given in the following paragraphs:

Knowledge: Knowledge objective involves the recall of specifics and universals, the recall of method and process, or the recall of a pattern, structure, or setting. The recall situation involves little more than bringing in mind the appropriate material. The teacher plans the situation for the learner to recall and recognize traditional, classification, criteria, principles and theories. The knowledge category includes the following three types of content:

(a) Knowledge of specifics, *i.e.,* facts and terminology.
(b) Knowledge of ways and means, and
(c) Knowledge of principles, theories and generalizations.

The material and problems may be of such a nature that little specialized and technical information is required. The pre-requisite of this category is still unknown.

Comprehension: This category indicates the lower level of understanding. It refers to a type of understanding as such that the individual knows what is being communicated and can make use of the material. The comprehension objective includes three types of activities.

(a) Translation of specifics: facts, principles and theories.
(b) Interpretation of the same specifics, and
(c) Extrapolation of the above content.

The translation is the lower level activity and extrapolation is the highest level of comprehension objective. The knowledge category is the pre-requisite of this category.

Application: This category includes the use of abstraction in particular and concrete situations. The abstraction may be in the form of general ideas, rules or procedures, or generalized methods. The facts, principles, ideas, rules and theories must be applied. This has also three levels:

(a) Make generalization of facts, principles and theories.
(b) Diagnose the weakness of these contents.
(c) Apply these contents.

This objective develops the predictive ability of the learner. It has the pre-requisite of both the earlier categories.

Analysis: This category involves to breakdown of a communication into its elements such that the relative hierarchy of ideas is made clear. The relationship among them can be expressed. This analysis is intended to clarify the communication. The analysis is attempted at three levels:

(a) Analyse the elements of communication.
(b) Establish the relationship among the elements.
(c) Formulate some principles to organize the elements. This category develops the reasoning ability of the learners. It has the pre-requisite of three categories.

Synthesis: This has pre-requisite of the earlier four categories. In this category all the elements are organized in such a way that they can form a unique whole. The elements are arranged and combined in such a way to form a pattern of structure not clearly observed before. The synthesis category includes the activities of three levels:

(a) Unique communication by arranging different elements.
(b) Suggest new plan by combining all elements.
(c) Establish an abstract relationship among different elements. This category of teaching and learning objective develops the creative ability of the learners.

Evaluation: All the earlier categories are pre-requisites of this category. It includes quantitative and qualitative judgement about the extent to which material and method satisfy criteria. The criteria may be those determined by the student or those which are given to him. It has two level:

(a) The internal judgement of the material and methods.

(b) The external judgement of the material and methods.

The two types of criteria: internal and external are used for judging the truthfulness of facts, principles, rules and theories. This develops the power of judgement.

Cognitive Learning Outcome

Teaching is organized to achieve these objectives. The different objectives are achieved by different cognitive leaning outcome. The following are the major learning outcome.

(1) *Pre-verbal Percepts:* In achieving knowledge and comprehension objectives.

(2) *Factual Information:* In realizing knowledge, comprehension and application objectives.

(3) *Concept Formation:* In attaining comprehension application and analysis objectives.

(4) *Generalization and Principles:* In achieving application, analysis and synthesis objectives.

(5) *Problem-solving and Creativity:* In achieving analysis, synthesis and evaluation objectives.

Identification of Cognitive Objectives: A teacher identifies his teaching objectives in terms of cognitive categories. There are three important considerations in determining the teaching objectives:

(a) Structure of the content,

(b) Needs of the students, and

(c) Level of entering behaviours.

The content analysis and entering behaviour of the students provide the basis and insight to the teacher to decide the level of learning outcome of students, the teacher can easily determine his teaching objectives in terms of cognitive category. The teacher should ensure the pre-requisites of the category that students have acquired in their entering behaviour. The teaching objectives may vary from knowledge to evaluation category under cognitive domain.

Taxonomy of Affective Educational Objectives and learning Outcome : Krath Wehl (1964) have produced a handbook and taxonomy designed to stimulate and systematise and assessment of objective in the affective domain, as Bloom's taxonomy has done in the cognitive area. The affective taxonomy is equally important as cognitive taxonomy for classifying educational objectives and learning outcome. The correct answer of an affective question depends upon the person queried and response in social situations, but the correct answer of a cognitive question is the same for all respondents. Situational factors of the examiner and an assessment context have a more significant influence on the results for affective measures than they do for ability measures.

(a) Interest (b) Appreciation, (c) Attitude, (d) Value, (e) Adjustment.

Condensed version of the Taxonomy of Educational Objectives in an Affective Domain

Direction	*Category*
Low Level	1. Receiving: (Pay attention)
	(a) Awareness
	(b) Willingness to receive
	(c) Controlled or selected attention.
	2. Responding: (Committed and actively attending)
	(a) Acquissence in responding
	(b) Willingness to respond
	(c) Satisfaction to response.
	3. Valuing: (Concepts are seen to have worth)
	(a) Acceptance of a value
	(b) Preference for a value
	(c) Commitment (Construction)
	4. Organization: (Construction of system of values)
	(a) Conceptualization of value
	(b) Organization of value system.
	5. Characterization of a complex value
	(Acceptance of value system)
High Level	(a) Generalized set.
	(b) Characterization

The teacher and instructions are appreciating the value of using such a taxonomy when they plan their objectives and examinations, perhaps the overall quality of the work accomplished in the classroom teaching and the examination system will improve and standards can be raised.

Affective Objectives

B. S. Bloom, Krath Wehl and Masia (1964) have classified affective domain in six categories. Their meaning and definitions have been given in the following paragraphs:

Receiving (Attending): The pre-requisite of this category is unknown. In this category the learner is sensitized to the existence of certain stimuli, *i.e.,* he may be willing to receive or to attend the stimuli. This is the first crucial step that learner is to be oriented to learn what the teacher intends to do. It includes three types of activities:

(a) Awareness about the stimulus or situation.
(b) Create willingness in the learner to receive it.
(c) Control the attention of the learner.

The level of affective domain increases the sensitivity towards human values.

Responding: The first category receiving is the pre-requisite of responding. At this level we are concerned with which go beyond attending to the phenomenon, the students should be sufficiently motivated to respond. This may be interested objective of teaching and instruction. It has three levels of responding:

(a) The learner's obedience for response.
(b) The learner's willingness to respond.
(c) The learner gets satisfaction in responding.

This level concerns with enjoyment of self-expression of music, arts and crafts, etc.

Valuing: The earlier two levels are pre-requisites for achieving this level. This category includes the worth of a thing, phenomenon or behaviour. The abstract worth is a result of individual's won valuing and assessment but it is a social product. The attitude is an objective of teaching. This level has also three type of activities:

(a) Acceptance of value,
(b) Preference of value, and
(c) Commitment of value.

The individual's commitment to the underlying value guides his behaviour.

Organization: The above three categories are the prerequisites of the organization category. As the learner successively internalizes values, he encounters situations for which more than one value is required. Therefore, necessity arises for:

(a) the organization of the values in a system.

(b) the determination of interrelationship among them.

(c) the establishment of the dominant value.

The organization category needs the conceptualization of values. It places the values properly. The appropriate organization of values can be done on the basis of conceptualization of them.

Characterization: The earlier four levels are the pre-requisites of characterization. At this level of internalization, the values already have a place in the individual's value hierarchy, are organized in some kind of internally consistent system. The acts are consistently in accordance with the values: (a); generalized set provides- the internal consistency to the system attitudes and values.

Affective Learning Outcome

The affective objectives range from receiving to characterization level. The various types of teaching objectives of this domain are achieved with the help of the following learning outcome:

1. Interest as learning outcome maybe obtained by achieving receiving and responding objectives.
2. Appreciation as learning outcome may be obtained by realizing, receiving, responding and valuing objectives.
3. Attitude as learning outcome is obtained by achieving, receiving, responding, valuing and organizing objectives of teaching.
4. Value as learning outcome is attained by realizing, valuing and organizing objectives of teaching.
5. Adjustment as learning outcome may be obtained by achieving the valuing, organizing and characterization of teaching.

Identification of Affective Objectives of Teaching : After task analysis, teacher identifies the affective teaching objectives in terms of above five categories. There are following crucial factors for identifying such teaching-learning objective:

(a) Structure of the content,

(b) Social needs of the students, and

(c) Level of students entering behaviours.

The task analysis, entering behaviour of the learner and their social needs are the basis for identifying the appropriate teaching objectives of affective domain. The objectives are achieved if lower objectives have already attained.

Writing Learning Objective

The identification of objectives in terms of taxonomic categories does not specify the form of teaching and learning activities. Therefore, it is essential to write these objectives in behavioural terms. The behavioural form of the objectives reveals the learning activities.

Need for Writing Objective in Behavioural Terms : The following are the main advantages of writing objectives in behaviour terms:

(1) Teaching activities are determined and delimited.

(2) Teaching and learning process may be integrated for effective learning outcome.

(3) The appropriate teaching strategies and tactics can be selected for effective learning.

(4) Teaching and testing can be made objective-centred. Thus testing may be based upon teaching.

Scafold states the following advantages of the behavioural objectives:

(a) Specification of objectives.

(b) Selection of items for preparing a test.

(c) Teaching can be related to learning.

(d) Integration between learning experiences and change of behaviour, and

(e) Selection of appropriate teaching strategies, tactics and teaching aids.

Methods of Writing Objectives in Behavioural Terms : There are various methods of writing objectives in behavioural terms. It is not a new concept and approach in the field of education but it is an old concept. It has five historical basis:

Drucker (1954) has given a new interpretation of management that it is changeable concept. The activities of management should be explained in terms of objectives, hence he has given emphasis on the hehavioural aspexcts of the objectives.

B. S. Bloom (1956) has shifted the emphasis from content to the objectives in examination system. He has suggested the reformation in examination system that achievement tests should be objective-centred rather than content centred. Each question should evaluate one specific objective. Thus, he has made an effort to write these objectives in behavioural terms.

Robert Mager's Approach (1962) is most popular in the development of programmed instruction. He concentrates on cognitive and affective objectives, in this approach he gives emphasis on action verbs rather than mental processes. The cognitive objectives can be best realized by programmed instruction strategy.

Robert Miller's Approach (1962) is used for writing psychomotor objectives in behavioural terms. The origin of this approach is from the military sciences. Thus, training objectives can be best written by Miller's approach.

NCERT (1972) (Regional College of Education Mysore —RCEM) has also developed an approach for writing objectives in behavioural terms. This approach is applicable for cognitive, affective and psychomotor objectives of teaching and training. It gives main emphasis on mental abilities for writing objectives in behavioural terms.

Mager's Approach

Mager (1962) considers that objectives should he written in the following manner:

1. First, identify the terminal behaviour by name; we can specify the kind of behaviour which will be accepted as an evidence that the learner has achieved the objectives.
2. Second, try to further define the desired behaviour by describing the inportant conditions under which the behaviour will be expected to occur.

3. Third, specify the criteria of acceptable performance by describing how well must the learner perform to be considered acceptable.

Although the three statements are not always necessary, it is a very good rule of thumb for beginners that they must follow the layout exactly.

Miller's Approach

Miller (1962) tackles the problem of writing objectives more from the point of view of skill-analysis, and according to him a clear objective should be preferably written in the following manner :

1. An indicator on which the activity, relevant-indication appear.
2. The indication or one which calls for a response.
3. The control objective is to be activated.
4. The activation or manipulation is to be made.
5. The indication of response should be adequate or feedback.

The level of detail, used in writing such descriptions is about the same as would be used for writing a set of technical instructions useful to no voice. Indeed, Miller has pointed out that a clear objective is written in the above manner and can be used as a procedure-manual for doing the job.

A comparison of the Miller and Mager's formats will show that they bear a marked resemblance; indeed, Mager sometimes prefers to follow the formats now associated with Miller. However, the layout and the grater detail of the Miller-type objectives does have a number of advantages for objectives in the psychomotor domain.

Stating the Behavioural Objective of Cognitive Domain : In describing the behaviour of man is required for a student when he demonstrates his mastery over the subject or the skill, it is an important to identify, in a very clear terms, exactly what will he do. This involves saying how will he recognise the cue or situation which will cause him to commence action or behaviour, as well as how will he recognise that the action have been successfully accomplished, the associated action verbs for different objectives have been summarized.

A list of associated action verbs for cognitive domain has been provided :

Cognitive Objectives and Associated Action Verbs

Objective			***Associated Action Verbs***
Knowledge	Define	Write	Underline
	State	Recall	Select
	List	Recognise	Reproduce
	Name	Lable	Measure
Comprehension	Identify	Illustrate	Explain
	Justify	Represent	Judge
	Select	Name	Contract
	Indicate	Formulate	Classify
Application	Predict	Choose	Construct
	Select	Find	Compute
	Assess	Show	Use
	Explain	Demonstrate	perform
Analysis	Analyse	Select	Justify
	Identify	Separate	Resolve
	Conclude	Compare	Break-down
	Differentiate	Contrast	Criticise
Synthesis	Combine	Argue	Select
	Restate	Discuss	Relate
	Summarize	Organize	Generalize
	Precise	Derice	Conclude
Evaluation	Judge	Support	Identify
	Evaluate	Defend	Avoid
	Determine	Attack	Select
	Recognize	Criticise	Choose

These action verbs should be used for defining the educational objectives of cognitive domain and also for examination questions.

There is no fast dichotomy among these domains, there is significant overlapping among these domains. The purpose of educational objectives is the development the child in desirable direction. The integration of learning outcome at different levels has been summarized in the tabular form. Robert Mager has used the taxonomy of cognitive domain of B.S. Bloom. The content of elements and taxonomic category as a teaching objectives provide the basis for selecting appropriate action verbs. The action verbs of each category indicate the level of teaching and learning activities. The objectives can be written in behavioural terms by combining action verbs with an element of action:

Behavioural objective=Element of content + Action verb of the objective category.

Example: Topic of teaching *Task Analysis',* objective of teaching; knowledge, comprehension and application,

(k) Behavioural form of knowledge objective: The learners are able to define the term Task Analysis,

(c) Behavioural form of comprehension objectives :
The learners are able to explain the terms Task Analysis,

(a) Behaviour form of application objective :
The learners are able to use or demonstrate the task analysis.

Similarly a pupil-teacher can write his teaching objectives in behavioural terms for his own subject in preparing lesson-plans. The examples of behavioural objectives have been given for the school subjects.

Subject Geography and Topic 'Climate'

The students are able to define the term climate.

(Knowledge Objective)

The student are bale to explain the term climate.

(Comprehension Objective)

The students are able to illustrate the concept of climate.

(Application Objective)

The students are able to analyse the factors of climate.

(Analysis Objective)

Physics Topic - 'Density' :

The learners are able to define 'density'.

(Knowledge Objective)

The learners able to explain or illustrate density.

(Comprehension Objective)

The learners are able to compute the density of given substances.

(Application Objective)

The learners are able to analyse the components of density.

(Analysis Objective)

Stating the Behavioural Objectives of Affective Domain : Robert Mager has also used the taxonomy of an affective domain. He develops-the action verbs for each category of this domain which indicate the behaviour which is required for a student to demonstrate. The list of action verbs for different objectives has been given below:

Affective Objectives and Associated Action Verbs

Objective			***Associated Action Verbs***
Receiving	Listen	Accept	Beware
	Attend	Receive	Favour
	Prefer	Perceive	Selset
Responding	State	Select	Record
	Answer	List	Develop
	Complete	Write	Develop
	Complete	Write	Derive
Valuing	Accept	Increase	Indicate
	Recognise	Develop	Decide
	Participate	Attain	Influence
Organization	Organise	Find	Associate
	Judge	Determine	Form
	Relate	Correlate	Select
Characterization	Revise	Accept	Demonstrate
	Change	Judge	Identify
	Face	Develop	Decide

These associated action verbs should be used in describing and formulation of the educational objectives at different levels of affective domain.

The element of a content and teaching objectives in terms of affective taxonomic category help in selecting the appropriate action verbs for demonstrating the learner's behaviour. The affective objectives can be written in behavioural terms by combining elements.

Behavioural objectives of *Task Analysis'*.

The students prefer task analysis in preparing his lesson-plan.
(Receiving Objective)

The students develop the task analysis of his teaching topic.
(Responding Objective)

The students accept the important task analysis in his lesson-planning.
(Valuing Objective)

Behavioural objectives of '*Fundamental Rights' in Civics.*

The learners accept the fundamental rights.
(Receiving Objective)

The learners are able to state the fundamental rights.
(Responding Objectives)

The learners are able to indicate the fundamental rights.
(Valuing Objectives)

The teaching objectives of other social-subjects can be written in behavioural terms on similar lines. This is the last term in planning teaching and learning because criterion test is developed before preparing the teaching instruction. Therefore, behavioural objectives are written usually in present tense. In lesson-planning these may be written in future tense.

Limitation of Robert Mager's Approach : Mager's approach is not a perfect method for writing objectives in behavioural terms. It has following limitations:

(1) It gives main emphasis on action verbs rather than mental process that involves in performing the actions.

(2) Mager is a behaviorist, therefore, he explains learning in terms of S-R whereas all human learning can not be explained by S—R learning.

(3) This method can be used for writing the lower level teaching objectives, higher level objectives can not be written clearly.

(4) The list of action verbs indicates that there is over lapping of action verbs in different categories. Thus, it may create confusion in the minds of teachers to use the appropriate action verb for specifying objectives.

(5) The psychomotor objectives cannot be written by Mager's approach. It is an applicable only for cognitive and affective objectives.

(6) There is also overlapping of action verbs provided in the list of cognitive and affective action verbs. For example, select, list, write, state, analyse recognize are common in both the lists.

(7) Mager's approach can be effectively used in writing teaching objectives in behavioural terms because teaching objectives are to three types.: knowledge, skill, attitude and interest. It can be effectively used in the development of programmed instruction.

RCEM Approach

The teachers of Regional College ot Educational Mysore realized the limitations of Mager's approach and they developed a new approach for writing objectives in behavioural terms.

The assumption regarding this approach is that human learning can be best explained in terms or metal process of mental abilities rather than behaviour. It has shifted the focus from product to process. This is very necessary indeed as the list of action verbs designating behaviour was to long and unwidely to have any meaningful application of classroom teaching. Having given a lot of thought to it and having discussed both the system at the Regional College of Education Mysore, the education and content cum behavioural outcome.

The RCEM approach has used the Bloom's taxonomy of Educational objectives with a little modification. The system has converted into four categories. The last categories—analysis, synthesis and evaluation, are denoted by one category, *i.e.,* 'creativity'. These four categories have been further divided into seventeen mental abilities or processes. These abilities or processes are used for writing the objectives of cognitive affective and psychomotor domains in behavioural terms. These seven mental processes have been summarized in the following table:

Taxonomy of Educational Objective in the RCEM Approach

Bloom's Taxonomy of Objectives	***The RCEM Taxonomy of Objectives***	***Mental process or abilities***
Knowledge	Knowledge	Recall
		Recognize
Comprehension	Understanding.	Seeing relationship
		Cite example
		Discriminate
		Classify
		Interpret
		Verify
		Generalize
Application	Application	Reason out
		Formulate hypotheses
		Establish hypotheses
		Infer
		Predict
Analysis	Creativity	Analyse
Synthesis		Evaluate
Evaluation		Evaluate

It is evident from the above table that there are seventeen mental process or abilities, two for knowledge, seven for understanding, five for application and three for creativity. The comprehension category is termed, as understanding. An outline has been given here for writing objectives in behavioural terms.

Writing Objectives in Behavioural Terms : This method also requires the structure of the content and objectives are identified in taxonomic category considering entering behaviour of the learner. An appropriate mental process is selected and the element of content is combined with the mental abilities to produce the behavioural form of the objectives. The following seventeen forms can be used for this purpose:

Knowledge Objectives

The learner is able to recognize.......

The learner is able to recall.......

Understanding Objectives

The learner is able to see relationship between....and .....

The learner is able to cite example of.....

The learner is able to discriminate between.....and.....

The learner is able to interpret.......

The learner is able to classify.....

The learner is able to verify.....

The learner is able to generalise......

Application Objectives

The learner is able to reason out.......

The learner is able to formulate hypothesis for......

The learner is able to establish hypothesis for.......

The learner is able to infer about........

The learner is able to predict about.......

Creativity Objectives

The learner is able to analyse......

The learner is able to synthesize......

The learner is able to to evaluate......

The objective of all school teaching subjects can be written with the help of seventeen statements. After identifying the objectives, the elements of the content may be placed in blank space of the statement to obtain the behavioural form of the objectives. This method seems to be easy and useful for this purpose. This can also be illustrated with examples.

Topic-Task Analysis of Teaching Technology

1. The learner is able to recall the definition of task analysis. (Knowledge)
2. The learner is able to cite the example of task analysis. (Understanding)

3. The learner is able to predict about the element of task analysis.

(Application)

4. The learner is able to analyse the task analysis into its elements.

(Creativity)

Topic- 'Density' of Physics

1. The learner is able to recall the definition of density.

(Knowledge)

2. The learner is able to see the relationship between mass and Volume.

(Understanding)

3. The learner is able to predict about the density of a substance.

(Application)

4. The learner is able to analyse the density in its climate.

(Creativity)

Topic- 'Climate' of Geography

1. The learner is able to recall the definition of its climate.

(Knowledge)

2. The learner is able to discriminate between weater and climate.

(Understanding)

3. The learner is able to infer about the climate of a region on the basis of data.

(Application)

4. The learner is able to analyse the climate in its factors.

(Creativity)

Topic- 'Fundamental Rights' of Civics

1. The learner is able to recall the meaning of fundamental rights.

(Knowledge)

2. The learner is able to discriminate between rights and duties.

(Understanding)

3. The learner is able to infer about the fundamental rights from various activities of citizen.

(Application)

4. The learner is able to analyse the fundamental rights its type and elements.

(Creativity)

Topic- 'Functions of Leaf' of Biology

1. The learner is able to recognize the functions of leaf.

(Knowledge)

2. The learner is able to discriminate between 'respiration and 'carbon assimilation.'

(Understanding)

3. The learner is able to predict the function of leaf by seeing its form.

(Application)

4. The learner is able to analyse the elements of 'carbon assimilation' function.

(Creativity)

Similarity of the objectives of teaching of other school subjects can also be written in this way.

The Characteristics : It has the following advantages in writing the objectives in behaviour terms—

(1) This method is very easy and useful.

(2) This method is more specific and definite than the Robert Mager's approach.

(3) It does not have any doubt or confusion in preparing criterion test items.

(4) This method is applicable for cognitive, affective and psychomotor objectives.

(5) The method explains the human learning in terms of mental processes or abilities.

(6) It has shifted focus from product to process in writing objectives in behavioural terms.

(7) This method has been developed in Indian situations, therefore, it seems to be most useful for writing objectives in behavioural terms in our schools.

The Limitations : The following are the main disadvantages -

(1) All behavioural objectives can only be written in seventeen mental abilities where as Guilford has extracted 120 mental abilities.

(2) These seventeen mental processes are employed in writing the behavioural objectives in all the three domains. Hence it is difficult to differentiate among cognitive, affective and psychomotor objectives.

(3) It is generally very difficult to select appropriate mental process for a content element.

(4) There are seven mental processes for understanding, two for knowledge, five for application and three for creativity, in this way, there is no proper balance in mental abilities assigned to different categories.

(5) Micro are only three mental abilities in creativity objective, whereas, Torrence and others have given five type of activities.

The teaching is organised for the development of a child. The child's development is concerned with cognitive, affective and psychomotor domains. Therefore, Mager's approach can not serve the purpose of writing teaching objectives in behavioural terms. It can be used in planning instructional material. The RCEM approach is useful for writing teaching objectives. There is no last dichotomy among the three domains. The higher objectives of teaching and learning outcome are complex and integrated in these domains.

QUESTIONS

1. Define the term Task Analysis'. Differentiate among Job Analysis', Skill Anlaysis and Content or Topic Analysis'. Give an example of content analysis.
2. Define the term 'Objectives'. Differentiate between educational objectives and teaching objectives. Illustrate with examples.
3. Discuss the taxonomy of educational-objectives of cognitive, affective and psychomotor as given by B. S. Bloom and his associates.

4. What things should be kept in mind while writing instructional objectives?
5. The Robert Mager's approach is best fitted for writing behavioural objectives of programmed instruction.' Discuss this statement.
6. Discuss this RCEM approach and its uses for writing objectives in behavioural form. Give examples five each of Mager's approach and RCEM approach.

5

Teaching-Learning

The main focus on teaching is to facilitate learning, where there is teaching learning must be there. Teaching activities are designed to produce change in the behaviour of the learners. Therefore, a new concept of teaching-learning has emerged out in the field of education. The concept of teaching is incomplete without learning.

The Concept

B.O. Smith (1961) put it like this 'Learning does not necessarily issue of teaching that teaching is one thing and learning is quite another. It enables us to analyse the concept of teaching without referring the process and conditions of learning. Smith suggests a definition, "Teaching is a system of actions intended to induce learning."

Learning is often defined as a relatively "permanent change in behaviour"; this usually includes the influence of growth, motivation and emotions.

Clark suggests a definition of teaching activities that are designed and performed to produce change in student-behaviour. *B. S. Bloom* (1956) states that teaching activities: lecture, question answer, discussion, discovery and assignments aim at achieving cognitive, affective and psychomotor goals.

N.L Gage (1969) considers that the process of teaching and learning must be adapted to each other so as to make whatever combination of procedure pay off best. We should conceive teaching-learning as process for effective learning.

These definitions indicate that learning is essential for teaching and the learning structure should be considered for effective teaching. Now, the greater emphasis has been laid on the concept of teaching-learning.

Thomas F. Green has argued differently in his book entitled 'Activities of teaching', that 'there is no learning without teaching and teaching may not be without learning'. He puts it like this, 'teaching intent or goals may be learning but all teaching may not facilitate learning. He has further illustrated that pleading a case may be the purpose to win it but there is no surety to win the case. Similarly the doctor gives a treatment to cure the patient but every patient is not cured by the treatment. Teacher designs teaching to induce learning but every student is not able to learn. One the other hand learning is the change in behaviour through situations and activities. The purpose of teaching is to create appropriate situations which facilitate learning in the broader sense. Thus, no learning is possible without teaching and all teaching may not result in learning.

Nature of Teaching

The following are the important characteristics of teaching:

1. Teaching is a social and professional activity.
2. Teaching is an observable through teacher-behaviour or pupil-teacher interaction.
3. It is measurable and quantifiable by observational techniques.
4. It is modifiable by the use of mechanism or feedback devices.
5. It can be analysed into the following ways:
   (a) Types of teacher-activities.
   (b) Types of educational objectives.
   (c) Types of learning conditions or structure.
   (d) Types of learning components.
6. It is a linguistic process (communication by the use of a language).
7. It is therapy for learners.
8. It is a prescription to the students.
9. It has telling, showing and doing functions.
10. It is an interactive process or face to face encounter.
11. It involves encouraging, harmonizing, expressing and balancing functions.

12. It is a continuum from conditioning to indoctrination through training and instruction.

Teaching is considered art as well as science: Silverman (1966) has expressed:

To be sure, teaching—like the practice of medicine—is very much an art which is to say, it calls for an exercise of talents and creativity. But like medicine, it is also—a science, for it involves a repertoire of techniques, procedures and skill that can be systematically studied, described and improved. A great teacher, like a great doctor, is one who adds creativity and inspiration to the basic repertoire."

The, word 'teaching' is used in various ways, but there are three major uses of this word in general condition:

First, It refers to a body of knowledge, a body of ideas and a system of beliefs.

Second, teaching is referred to as an occupation or a profession in which teacher instructs and educates.

Third, teaching refers to ways of marking something known to others, usually in the routine of a school.

Teaching is a system of actions which are varied in form and are related to content and pupil's behaviour.

Role refers that teaching is a task which involves certain activities. The task of teaching has a focus to facilitate learning. Teaching task can be performed skilfully, carefully, and successfully.

Teaching is behaving in a social context and is therefore, amenable to scientific observation and analysis.

Types of Teaching

There are various ways to classify teaching. The following are the main types of teaching:

(1) Teaching involves different functions which can be classified into three categories:
   (a) Telling
   (b) Showing
   (c) Doing.
(2) Teaching is organised at three levels:
   (a) Memory level of teaching.
   (b) Understanding level of teaching, and

(c) Reflective level of teaching.

(3) Teaching is formed by employing three types of behaviour—

(a) *Authoritarian* teaching behaviour,

(b) *Democratic* teaching behaviour, and

(c) *Laisess faire* teaching behaviour.

(4) Teaching is usually organized in three phases:

(a) Diagnostic phase of teaching,

(b) Prescriptive phases of teaching, and

(c) Evaluative phase of teaching.

(5) Teaching is formal as well as informal.

The description of these categories have been given in other chapters of this book .

Relating Teaching to Learning

William H. Burton (1958) has made an attempt to investigate that relationship between teaching and learning and he gives the following reasons:

(1) Teaching can be made effective by relating it to learning.

(2) Teaching objectives can be identified in behavioural terms and appropriate learning situations may be created to realize these objectives.

(3) The appropriate teaching conditions or structures may be generated for effective learning.

(4) The effective teaching aids may be selected for creating learning situations.

(5) The teaching strategies and tactics may be selected to achieve the optimal objects of learning.

(6) The concept of relationship of teaching and learning will be an aid to understand the nature of teaching and teaching theories may be evolved.

(7) The knowledge of the relationship will be helpful for teacher-education to produce effective-teachers.

Psychological Forces

N.L Gage (1967) believes that 'teaching' should be central point of educational psychology but its central point is 'learning'. Teaching cannot be improved by studying the nature and factors of learning because this knowledge is not sufficient to solve classroom problems. The psychological forces may be an aid to teaching to bring desirable change among the students. Gage classifies the psychological forces under the following categories:

(1) Forces for the change behaviour.

(2) Learning conditions as force, and

(3) Cognitive force.

Forces for the Change Behaviour : Teaching is oriented for the desirable change among learners. The reinforcement is very important for any type of change in students-behaviour. It is a general statement that there is no learning without motivation. The motivation releases the energy for the learner. The reinforcement is also a condition or force which increases the probability of desired response or behaviour. The external motivation is useful for small children or lower level of learning and achieving the knowledge objectives. The internal motivation is effective for adults or higher learning and achieving higher objectives (analysis, synthesis and evaluation). The internal motivation is an important psychological force for the permanent change of behaviour. In classroom teaching, the teacher uses verbal praise for excellent performance and assigns the grades for home work. At university and college level the teacher raises the level of aspiration of the student and involvement in subject. It is the third external condition of learning.

In designing instructions, the teacher makes the provision for providing reinforcement to the learner. The research studies have yielded that extroverts learn better through intermittent schedule of reinforcement whereas introverts learn better through continuous schedule of reinforcement. Teaching and instruction can be made effective in terms of learning codes by using appropriate type of motivation and suitable schedule of reinforcement.

Learning Conditions as Force : *William H. Burton* and *N.L Gage* believe that learning theories are not complete in themselves, but the experimental situation of learning is most important to understand the nature of learning. A learning theory is nothing but an explanation of a learning condition or situation. The teaching and learning conditions are much more useful than the learning theories.

The concept of learning conditions is given by Robert Gagne. I.K. Davies employs five conditions of learning in teaching and instruction.

The teaching activities are designed and performed for creating appropriate learning conditions for the learner so that desirable change can be brought about. Thus learning conditions function as psychological forces for teaching and learning situations.

Cognitive Force : The student behaviour and learning objectives may be classified into three domains: Cognitive, Affective and Psychomotor. The change of behaviour may be related to one of these domains. All the teaching activities are designed to develop the three domains. Thus, learning and teaching strategies may be of three types:

Objective	*Teaching*	*Learning Type*
1. Cognitive	Lecturing	Knowing
2. Affective	Dramatization	Feeling
3. Psychomotor	Experimentation	Doing

It is evident from the above presentation that teaching activities are of three types to achieve the three of objectives and facilitate three types of learning. The cognitive force are basic for planning and organizing the teaching tasks. The teaching is organized from memory to reflective level to develop the cognitive domain from knowledge to evaluation level.

Conditions of Learning

Robert Gagne (1965) believes that learning can not be explained comprehensively with the help of learning theories alone. He argues that learning theories are the generalization of experimental learning conditions based on the observations which are not based on measurement and most of the experiments on learning have been conducted on animals (rats, cats and dogs, etc.). Thus, learning conditions are basic to understand the concept of teaching.

Gagne assumes that simple behaviour requires some pre-requisite. There is a continuum of learning conditions and behaviours. Teaching acts are also on a continuum from memory to reflective level. It means that memory level to reflective level. It means that memory level is the pre-requisite for understanding level of teaching. Gagne has defined the term teaching:

"Teaching means arranging conditions of learning that are external to the learner. These conditions need to be constructed in a stage-by-stage, each stage is the just acquired capabilities of the learner, the requirement for retention for these capabilities."

There are eight different types of situations in which human learning conditions have been identified. These set of operations or conditions which change the capabilities of the human learner are brought about. Robert Gagne (1965) distinguishes varieties of learning as follows—

1. Signal learning, 2. Stimulus response learning, 3. Chain learning. 4. Verbal association, 5. Discrimination learning, 6. Concept Learning, 7. Rule learning, and 8. Problem-solving.

The implication is that there are eight corresponding kinds of changes in the nervous system which need to be identified and ultimately accounted for. Each of these may require different prerequisites for their initial states or different structures.

Gilbert (1962) and *Mechner* (1965) recognize the three structures: 1. Chain Structure, 2. Multiple-discrimination, and 3. Concept structure.

Every task by every definition, must process like unique structure or organization. *I.K. Davies* recognises five basic learning structures out of which classes of Gagne: learning conditions as these are useful and meaningful to the teacher and learner.

1. Signal structure,
2. Chain structure,
3. Multiple discrimination structure,
4. Concept structure, and
5. Principle structure.

Gagne's hierarchy of learning makes it possible to relate learning situation to teaching activities.

Signal Learning: A signal involves as specific response of verbal or motor to a specific stimulus. The learner acquires a precise response to a discriminated stimulus what is learned is a connection *(Thorndike* 1998), or discriminated operant *(Skinner* 1938) or conditioned response *(Pavlov* 1927) sometimes called instrumental response *(Kimble* 1961).

Teacher or learning signals involve the simple tactics. These may be of three types:

(1) Establishing contiguity in stimulus and response (close proximity).

(2) Constant practice and rehearsal of stimulus and response connection.

(3) Reinforcing the correct response by its confirmation and wrong response is ignored.

Chain Learning: What is acquired in a chain of two or more stimulus-response connections is the chain learning. The conditions for such learning have been described by *Skinner* (1938) and *Gilbert* (1962). The chaining of behaviour is a common class of learning. It consists of a sequence of verbal or motor actions. This type of learning has the pre-requisite 'signal learning' for its initial structure.

Teaching learning chain involves establishing contiguity between successive links. Three types of teaching tactics can be used:

Progressive Changing: In this type, the chain starts from first chain and then second and so on or at the end last, *i.e.,* mastery behaviour, *e.g.,* linear programming.

Retrogressive Chaining: It is a backward chain starting with the last act (mastery behaviour) and then moving retrogressively towards first act at the end, *e.g.,* mathematics.

Rote Learning: The chain can be learnt by rote memory like reciting a poem.

In teaching practice and repetition are always useful to facilitate this type of learning structure.

Multiple-discrimination Learning: The individual learns to make different identifying responses to as many different stimuli, which may resemble each other in physical appearance to a greater or lesser degree (Postman 1961). It has the prerequisite signal and chain structures. It involves distinguishing one category of phenomena from another (Underwood 1964).

The teaching-learning of multiple discrimination involves the following two tactics:

Distinctive Conditions: Both, stimuli and responses must be made as distinctive as possible.

Simultaneous Presentation: All conditions should be presented together in the same time and force before student to discriminate.

Practice seems to be important in learning the multiple-discrimination.

Concept Learning: The learner acquires a capability of making a common response to a class of stimuli that may differ from each other widely in physical appearance. He is able to make a response that identifies an entire class of objects or events *(Kendler* 1964). Concept learning involves the student making a generalization about a whole class of phenomena that may differ from each other in physical appearance.

The tactics of teaching may be two types for creating concept learning structure.

Generalise within the Class: The student should be presented with a set of related but different stimuli, to each of which he make the some response.

Discrimination between Class: The student should learn to discriminate between the concept and all other concepts.

Davies (1967) found that practice or repetition are not much useful concepts for learning structure.

Principle Learning: A principle is a chain of two or more concepts. Its function is to control behaviour. It is a kind of learning that requires thinking ability. The pre-requisite of principle learning is the concept of learning structure.

The conditions of this type of learning may be generated by two types of teaching tactics:

Recalling the Concepts: The concepts should be made as distinctive as possible and student should recall the concepts which are required for making the principle.

Chaining the Concepts: The concept should be chained together after recalling them.

When student has learnt the principle, he should be asked to state the principle in his own words.

Teaching activities are organized to create these learning conditions or structures in a hierarchical order to achieve the taxonomy of objectives. The learning structure provides the guide for preparing instructions and planning of the teaching activities. Thus, teaching acts are closely associated with learning operations.

Theories of Teaching

The efforts are being made to evolve a theory of teaching because learning theories have failed to provide substantial solution for the classroom teaching problems. Educational Psychology should shift its central activity 'learning' to teaching.

Cronbach (1963) suggests that theories of teaching can be based on theories of learning. An old theory helps in developing a new theory. Similarly, learning theory can be helpful in formulating theory of teaching Cronbach's ideas are not theories, but theorizing in the form of statements of the elements of learning. He has presented seven elements of learning which express in miniature a theory of behaviour. These seven elements may be used as the base for theory of learning.

Situation: The first element of learning is called situation, and it involves content, teacher, student, teaching methods, teaching aids and objectives. The content is analysed and arranged in a sequence to facilitate transfer of learning. A variety of situation is selected and arranged in a sequence so that pupils may learn responses that are appropriate to the objectives of learning.

Personal Characteristics: The second element of learning consists of pupil abilities. The personal characteristics of pupils are assessed by administering aptitude tests and other datas to judge for what method and material is the pupil ready. Teaching activities are organized by considering the individual variations of the students.

Goal: The third element is called goal. The learner intents to bring about change in behaviour as a consequence of his efforts and that change of behaviour forms his goal. A skilled teacher attempts to achieve these goals by his teaching activities. The teacher provides a kind of reinforcement to his pupils to orient them towards the goal. Teaching and learning have the same goal.

Interpretation: The fourth element is known as interpretation. The element directs attention towards first element, *i.e.,* situation. This element calls for prediction about future course of action on the basis of past experiences. It is closely related to the element goal. The interpretation may be made with or without conscious awareness.

Action: It includes the initiation and response of the student. If learner is not aware about interpretation in a new situation, he acts tentatively. This is termed as creative activity of the learner. If learner finds a new solution of the problem, it is known his original thinking. The acts of the pupil help him to learn new behaviour. The teacher encourages pupils for active responses.

Consequences: The sixth element is known as consequence. The teacher observes the pupil's performance and diagnoses the pupil's weakness and locates the defective method and technique. It has two functions, first is to revise or improve the method and technique of teaching and second is to provide the feedback to the teaching system. The teacher should help the learner so that he may observe the consequence of learning.

Reaction to Thwarting: The last element is reaction to thwarting. If learner is not able to achieve his goal, he is thwarted, as may be busy in adaptive behaviour. If he reaches his goal, his emotional tension is reduced. The teacher should assist the pupils to interpret and identify courses of difficulty.

These seven elements of learning are related to some generally recognized problems of teaching. Cronbach has stated that the organizing curriculum materials, motivating the pupil evaluating the performance and provision for individual difference are the essential problems of teaching. These seven elements are common in both, teaching and learning.

Teaching Principles

In the teaching process, teaching strategies and tactics are selected to achieve specific objectives of learning. Therefore, it is essential to evolve principles of teaching which can be used for designing effective teaching acts and developing effective teaching strategies. But no set of principles has emerged that may truly be called principles of teaching. Hilgard (1956) made an attempt to prepare a list of some generalizations about teaching which are acceptable to most of learning theories.

William H. Burton (1958) and his associates have discovered principles of teaching. Burton's principles may be tentative and need verification. Burton has suggested that a number of theories of learning may be reviewed in order to develop the principles of teaching. According to him no theory of learning is comprehensive in all respect. He has found only two summaries of principles of teaching that are in agreement with theories:

(1) Hilgard (1956) principles of teaching.

(2) L.R. McConnell (1958) principles of teaching.

Teaching Principles Based on Hilgard's Learning Principles : *Burton* has prepared a list of learner's characteristics considering Hilgard learning principles and determined learning situations for developing these characteristics. These learning situations are termed as Burton's principles or teaching. A list of these principles based on Hilgard's learning principles is as follows:

Learner's Characteristics	***Principles of Teaching***
Intelligence	Bright student can learn things in a better way and dull student can not learn.
Motivation	A motivated pupil learns more readily than one who is not motivated..
	The excessive motivation may be less effective than moderate motivation for learning discrimination.
	Learning through reward or success motivation is more effective than punishment.
	Learning under intrinsic motivation is preferable to learning under extrinsic motivation.
Aspiration Level	Learner's require practice in fixing realistic goals for themselves. These goals should not be too high or too low.
	Tolerance for failure is best taught by giving a backlog of success.
Learner's Attitude	The personal history of a teacher may hamper of enhance learner's ability to learn.
	Active participation of learner is more effective than passive reception.
Learning Conditions	Meaningful material and meaningful tasks are learned more quickly than non-sense material.
	Practice and repetition is much more useful for permanent learning.
	Knowledge or correct answers relationship between new and old task, the transfer of learning will be better.
	If learner himself discovers relationship between new and old tasks, the transfer of learning will be better.
	The retention can be encouraged by spaced or distributed recall of learnt material.

Teaching Principles Based on Learning Principles of T.R. McConnell : Burton has another source for teaching principles, *i.e.,* McConnell's learning principles. Burton (1958) has used these Principles to develop his own position is the paper entitled 'Basic principles in a Good Teaching-learning Situation.' Burton has prepared a list of learner's abilities considering McConnell learning principles and he has evolved setting for learning as principles of teaching. The learner's characteristics and teaching principles have been summarized in the following table:

The learner's Characteristics	***Teaching Principles***
The learner is a living organism a unitary integrated whole.	The learning experiences should be provided for natural integration of feeling, doing and thinking aspects.
The learner always seeks to maintain equilibrium or balance by satisfying his needs.	The learning experiences should be provided in meeting the needs of learner.
The learner is goal-seeking organism to satisfy his needs.	The setting of learning should be purposive or goal oriented. An appropriate guidance may be given to a learner to achieve his goal.
The learner is an active behaving exploring individual.	The learning situation should provide freedom to develop creative contributions.
Notable differences exist between individual in speed of learning.	Different types of learning experiences should be provided for satisfying the needs of each and every learner.
The learner is a social being who brings with him a personality and set of values. He needs a social environment.	The family background and individuality of the learner should be taken in account while establishing learning experiences for him.

Contd.

The learner's Characteristics	*Teaching Principles*
A learner may be quite immature so he needs guidance.	Learners need sympathetic guidance while building an awareness, and personality development.
The learner is a social being and seeks activities involving with other person or Group work.	The whole range of classroom interaction should be the cooperative group process to develop the socialized personality.

Burton has drawn this conclusion that above eight learner characteristics are basic for designing learning situations or developing principles of teaching.

The two sets of teaching principles are quite different. In the first set of teaching principles Burton has given main stress on psychological forces whereas second set involves the needs of the learner for creating learning settings.

Bloom's Objectives

The objectives of learning and objectives of teaching are the same. The objectives are the causing factors for the relationship of teaching and learning. The taxonomy of objectives, conditions of learning and levels of teaching are on the same continuum. The lower objectives or conditions of learning or level of teaching are the pre-requisites for the higher one. The testing can be based on teaching by making them objectives-centred. It has been illustrated specifically in the following table.

Objectives as factors for Teaching and Learning Relationship:

Bloom's taxonomy Objectives	*Gagne's Conditions of Learning*	*Bigge's Level of Teaching*
Knowledge	Signal learning	Memory level of teaching
Comprehension	Chain learning	
Application	Multiple descri-mination learning	Understanding level of teaching
Analysis	Concept learning	
Synthesis	Principle learning or Problem solving	Reflective level of teaching

The table indicates that teaching levels and learning conditions are closely associated due to objectives. The understanding level of teaching requires the pre-requisite of memory level. Similarly multiple discrimination has the prerequisite as signal and chain learning. The comprehension objective needs the knowledge as the pre-requisite. Thus, objectives conditions and levels are on the same continuum.

QUESTIONS

1. Indicate the conditions of learning which are basic to teaching.
2. Enumerate the principles of teaching based learning.
3. Indicate the cognitive categories which are given by B.S. Bloom.

6

Designs of Instruction

Teaching broadly consists of instructional designs. The development of educational engineering has provided the scientific basis of instructional system. Educational technology has the main assumption that teaching is not only an art but also a science; teachers are not only effective by birth but they can be made effective through training institutions.

Glaser (1968) states that professional skill and efficiency can be developed with its help of instructional designs. The experts and specialists are attempting to investigate the level of professional skill to be developed. *L. Carter* (1966) found in his investigation that instructional designs were effective for developing group professional efficiency than an individual. Glaser has enumerated the following functions of instructional designs:

(1) It emphasizes on structure of the task. The content is analysed for its structure and ascertaining its characteristics.

(2) The learner's responses are analysed in view of objectives and levels of learning. The entering behaviour is considered for providing new stimuli to have desired responses of the learner.

(3) The appropriate teaching strategies, techniques and tactics are selected for presenting content so that desired learning structure may be generated. The techniques of motivation are employed for leading the teaching.

(4) The measuring instrument is constructed for evaluating the performance level of the students and decision may be taken about the objectives of learning.

The desired objectives could not be achieved on the basis of learning theories. Therefore, teaching learning structure, teaching theories and structure of the content have been developed. Instructional designs are the sum of these things.

The Definition

Unwin (1968) have given a comprehensive definition of instructional design.

"Instructional design is concerned with an application of modern skills and techniques for the requirements of education and training. This includes facilitation of learning by manipulation of media, methods and the control of environment so far as this reflects on learning."

Such type of thinking was introduced in 1950 and the different approaches have been evolved for the problems of education and training but the following three approaches are most popular:

(1) Training Psychology,

(2) Cybernetic Psychology, and

(3) System Analysis.

The three approaches of *Instructional Designs* are not contradictory but supplementary to one another in solving the problems of education and training. They are closely related to deal with the input, output and process aspects of educational technology.

Training Psychology emphasizes on task analysis and design of interrelated training components. Cybernetic Psychology focuses on dynamic feedback and self-regulation. System Analysis focuses on System.

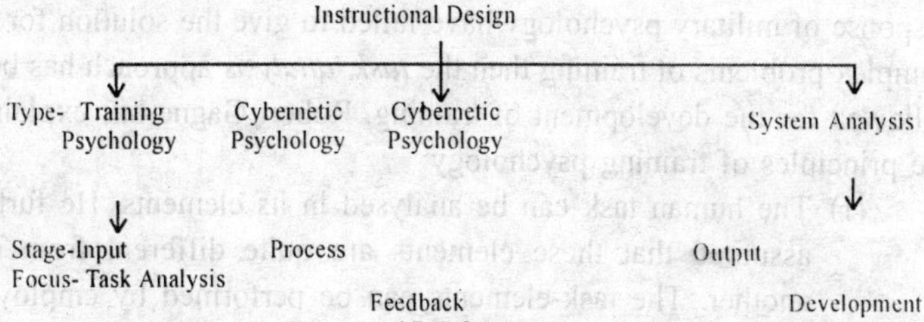

The above chart indicates that training psychology concerns with input aspect and its main function is task analysis. It evolves the structure of teaching and learning. The second approach cybernetic deals with the process aspect of education and its major function is to provide reinforcement for leading the teaching. The third approach system analysis concerns with the development of organization and administration on the basis of output aspect of education. The meaning, principles, procedure and application of these approaches are being described in detailed in the following paragraphs.

Training Psychology

Training psychology is mainly concerned with the problems of teaching, learning and training. This has come up through investigation on complex problems of training. Its origin is taken from military training. The main objectives of training psychology is to improve the activities in which learner performs function. The learning outcome could not be improved by learning theories, therefore, training psychology prepares an outline for task by analysing its components. The task components are organized in such a way that desired objectives may be achieved. The crucial aspect of training psychology is the *'Task Analysis.'*

It is an approach to teaching and training. It employs learning-conditions in teaching learning process rather than learning theories. The main assumption of this approach is that learning is dependent variable whereas teaching is the independent variable. The learning can only be improved by developing teaching tasks.

Our training institutions can not produce effective teacher with the help of learning theories. Moreover, they have failed to provide substantial solution for teaching and training problems. Training psychology is an approach for these problems.

Principles of Training Psychology : The principles of stimulus-response of military psychology have failed to give the solution for the complex problems of training then the *task, analysis* approach has been followed for the development of training. Robert Gagne has explained the principles of training psychology:

(1) The human task can be analysed in its elements. He further assumed that these elements are quite different from one another. The task-elements can be performed by employing different-tactics.

(2) The task-elements function as a mediator for last task. The functions of an element are helpful in the transfer of learning

and training. The shortage of task elements reduce the transfer to zero. Training psychology is based on three principles:

(i) The elements are identified and analysed for the performance last task.

(ii) It is assured that every task elements can be performance effectively.

(iii) The elements are organised in such a sequence which may generate appropriate learning conditions.

These statements convey the meaning to the principles of training psychology. These principles are broadly associated with task analysis.

Models of Teacher-Education

The teachers are prepared by determining the nature of training tasks which they are to perform in classroom teaching. The development of teaching concept is based on teacher-education model. The large amount of work has been done in this area during 1960's. The number of teacher-education models have been developed and these models are based on the principles of training psychology. The teacher-education models can be classified in three groups because B.O. Smith and Clark have given three types of teaching tasks. On the basis of teaching tasks, the following classification of teacher-education models has been made:

Presage Factors

(1) Michigan State Model
(2) Florida Model
(3) Syracuse Model
(4) The Wisconsin Model

Process Factors

(1) Teacher College Model
(2) The Georgia Model
(3) Regional Laboratory Model
(4) The Toledo Model

Product Factors

(1) Teacher for the Real World Model
(2) The North-West Regional Laboratory Model. .

The presage factors models training tasks are organized in such a way that their focus is or the development of the internal abilities and efficiency of teachers. The main emphasis is given on the mastery of content and development of right-type of attitude of teaching.

The second type of teacher-education models orient the training task for developing teaching skills or teacher-behaviour in the classroom interaction. The Georgia and Toledo models are the examples of this type of model. Pre-service and in-service programmes are organized in Indian conditions for developing process factor.

The third type of teacher-education models are based on output system. These models are used for improving the outcome of learning. The Real World and Regional laboratory models are the main examples of product-factors. Such type of teacher-education internship in teacher-education programme may be employed for this purpose.

Training Psychology and Instruction : The principles of training psychology are not only useful for developing teacher-education models but also for developing instruction. *Norman A. Crowder* has propounded branching programmes main stress is given on task analysis and difficulty of the elements is identified.

The diagnosis done for the difficulty of elements and remedial instruction is designed for such difficult elements.

The branching programme is originated from human training and from psychology principles. The task-elements are performed by each learner according to his own needs. This strategy fulfils their own requirements for each and every learner.

Application of Training Psychology : The training psychology has been developed for the practical problems of training and training. It has a great scope of application in the area of education and training. The principles of training psychology are being used for improving present training programme by developing modeis of teacher-educational in our country. The principles of training psychology may be helpful for student teachers:

— To analyse the teaching task and developing competency.

— To identify the goal of training programme and specify learning objectives.

— To plan and prepare educational programmes for actual teaching.

This lesson-planning and presentation in the classroom may be greatly improved by using the spirit of training psychology.

The principles of training psychology can provide scientific basis for designing individualized or remedial instructions and development of curriculum. The curriculum and instructional material can be made specific and relevant to the objectives, to the competence and skill to be developed in the learner.

Various Types

Instructional designs can be classified by viewing teaching-learning process as related to teaching skills, instructional objectives, competencies or performances, teaching strategies, teaching, teaching models, specific technology, and learning styles. The following will be discussed in the chapter.

The Classifications : Instructional Designs have been classified in five categories:

1. Objective-based
2. Skill-based
3. Competency-based
4. Model-based
5. Learning style-based

Competency Based Education

Competency-based education, also known as performance based education is a new approach to teaching, having as its core, the ideas of accountability and competencies. With regard to accountability it is argued that teachers should be held 'accountable' for their products. This accountability is accomplished by breaking teaching into discrete competencies or behaviours which can be stated as objectives competencies or behaviours which can be stated as objectives. Mastery of these competencies is then possible (Unwin and McAllese 1978).

Competency-based education rests upon few assumptions which are generally shared by educationists. They are of six Types as follows.

1. Learning takes place through changes in the behaviour of learners and that teaching aims at facilitating these changes.
2. Individuals achieve similar objectives but at different rates.
3. Teachers should be accountable for the learning that takes place in their students.

4. Continuous evaluation of teaching is used as a feedback for revising the instructional programme and this in turn promotes effective teaching.
5. The objectives of any educational programme bears close relationship to the educational goal.
6. Systems approach can be applied to education, especially to instructional planning and designing.

In competency- based education, competencies are spelled out so that it is possible to assess student learning through direct observation of student behaviour. The student knows in advance the extent and level of competencies to be mastered by him. The accomplishment of the learning objective can be observed and measured in the form of specified learner behaviours. In order to facilitate this, performance goals are specified and agreed to in great detail much in advance of instruction. The teacher is held accountable, not for his students 'obtaining a passing grade' but for attaining a given level of competency in performing the essential tasks of learning. Student's progress rate depends on demonstrated competencies. The emphasis is laid on exit and not on entrance requirements. Further the focus is being on acquisition of specific competencies by all the students. Time becomes variable and depending on the needs and capabilities of the learner, he is allowed to attain the competencies at his own rate and space.

Elam (1971) explains five basic features of competency-based programme:

1. Competencies to the demonstrated by the students are derived from explicit conceptions of teachers' roles and are publically stated in such a manner that students' learned behaviours are related to specified competencies.
2. Criteria to be employed in assessing competencies are stated in terms of expected levels of mastery under specified conditions.
3. Assessment of competency depends on students performance as the primary source of evidence and strives for objectivity.
4. Student's rate of progress is determined by demonstrated competencies rather than time or course completion.
5. Instructional programme is intended to facilitate the development of specified competencies.

Competency-based education is, therefore, unique in the sense that it focuses on the student's acquisition of pre-specified, agreed-upon competencies and demonstration of these specified competencies through objective assessment. Learning or instructional objective are explained and the achievement of these objectives are made explicit and the achievement of these objectives are observed in the modification of learner behaviour. Minimum levels of achievement of these objectives are the established criteria of success.

Meaning Module

Instruction is presented in modules, a module being a set of learning activities with objectives, per-requirements, per-assessment, instructional activities, post assessment and remediation. Modularization helps in self-pacing, individualisation, and independent study. The use of modules allows a much greater variety of experience than standard courses and provides a far better basis for personalised construction. Many competency-based education programmes make use of self instructional modules.

Criterion-referenced testing is an integral part of competency-based teacher education. Criterion-referenced tests are those kinds of tests that indicate whether the learner has achieved the goal specified for the learning tasks. They do not make a reference in comparison to the performance of other learners. It is considered that the criterion-referenced tests are more sensitive than norm-referenced test for the purposes of detecting instructional efforts. They can provide the only relevant information on students' learning excellence or deficiency.

Competency-based education is unique in the sense that it shifts the emphasis from testing the memory to the demonstration of required competencies and thereby emphasizes outputs. They are not teacher-oriented but student-oriented. The principal, staff member of a concerned discipline at a particular level, undergraduate or post-graduate should evolve the academic scheme. The first step is the preparation of instructional modules suited to the level of a target group. Time is not a factor but the possibility of attaining the competencies specified by the working term, be all students at that level is more important. The prepared modules can be tried out with a small group of students. Implementation of the modules with supporting materials such as books, booklets, and cassette, slides and film strips, if necessary, will form the second stage. Students will not be permitted to proceed to the next unit of a module unless they master the competencies in that unit. A criterion-referenced test based on the pre-specified competencies should be conducted to ascertain the proficiency of the students. If the performance of the student is satisfactory they are allowed to proceed to the next lesson unit. When it is found that some of the students are lagging behind in mastering the competencies, time may be given for attaining the competencies. In some cases a different set of instructional package is needed as students have different patterns of learning and communicating. In case the instructional objectives or the competencies based on them are found to be unsuitable for that particular group the whole programme needs recasting. There may be non-academic reasons such as emotional and personal problems of the students that could hinder the mastery of the competencies. The different competencies students will acquire can be more accurately reflected by a well-defined criterion-referenced test in contrast to its counterpart, the norm-referenced tests.

The difficulties experienced by such students can be identified and referred to a teacher or some other qualified person for guidance and counselling. Since the personal and academic problems are intertwined and mutually interacting, cooperation between the class teacher and the counsellor when the help of such a person is requisitioned, is essential for redressing the problems the student faces.

Realising the vital role that the competency-based education could play in cognitive development of college students, teachers could make a modest beginning in preparing competency-based modules on specific topics and try them out on small groups. The instructional design, based on competency-based education is yet another approach to efficient learning at college level.

Learning Style-based Education

Of recent origin is the research studies on the styles of learning adopted by the learners. Students use different approaches when faced with learning tasks and problems. The way in which the students approach the learning tasks, and the behaviour in learning situations determine their learning style, Rosenberg (1968) defines learning style as referring to 'an individual's characteristic pattern of behaviour when confronted with a problem'. It is pointed out that the learning style of an individual has relation to factors such as prior learning experiences, openness to interpersonal and extra-personal information, physical facilities, and learning environment.

On the basis of the work of researches on learning, *Rosenberg* has arrived at four general learning- patterns which are rigid-inhibited style, undisciplined style, acceptance-anxious style and creative style. It should be noted that when categorizing an individual as belonging to a given learning style because he exhibits the characteristic of that style, he should be considered first and foremost as an individual person rather than a member of a particular category.

Learners with a rigid inhibited style of learning require constant supervision as they get confused easily. They tend to give unrelated response to questions put forward. Changes in the class routine easily upsets them and they also exhibit signs of nervousness. They depend on the support given to them by the teacher. The behaviour of the rigid-inhibited learner is, therefore, a problem to himself and his teacher.

The 'undisciplined' learner exhibits characteristics such as refusal to obey commands, showing disrespect to teachers, deceiving, stealing, bullying, etc. Such learners invariably leave their learning task unfinished due to lack of tolerance. They concentrate on what gives them pleasure at the moment.

The fourth type of learning style according to Rosenberg is creative style. Learners of creative style are self-confident, and able to evaluate their own performance with objectivity. They are prepared to learn from their mistakes and show divergent thinking ability. Anxiety stimulates their functioning, specially during the learning process rather than impair it. A creative learner continues with the learning task until he completes it, which gives him satisfaction. He performs well on a divergently and, therefore, also prefers to work independently.

There are several other approaches to classifications of learning styles, depending on how a person looks at the whole problem. Kagan (1965) discusses about impulsive-reflective dimensions of learning style. Teachers tend to group students as obedient or disobedient, timid or outgoing, bright or dull rather than as reflective or impulsive. A reflective individual may be categorised as a dull student and impulsive quick individual as bright. Both reflectiveness and impulsiveness are related to the individual's conceptual thinking. Impulsiveness may lead to meeting with difficulties such as proceeding to work out a problem without understanding it, starting an experiment without following the instructions properly, completing a reading passage without understanding the major concepts, etc. Reflectiveness is indicated in trying to comprehend material that has a variety of complex concepts in a passage above the level of students or in going over remedial work. Impassivity can result in developing anxiety and consequently being punished, and ridiculed by teachers and classmates, specially when it is associated with the speed of response.

There are also learning styles characterised as dependent-independent, co-operative-non-cooperative, anxiety-free, anxiety-prone, competitive-noncompetitive; study habits oriented-trial students' learning styles by probing into their learning patterns some of which can be indicated indirectly in the classroom through teacher-students' learning styles by probing into their-learning patterns some of which can be indicated indirectly in the classroom' through teacher-student interactions in the evaluation of academic performances and in the specific behaviour patterns.

Form the above classifications, the college teachers surmise first, the existence of different styles of learning adopted by students and secondly, the effect of these styles on the learning process. Consequently the instructional design could be based on learning styles, where the planning, preparation and conduct of a lesson emphasizes learning styles of the students. The teacher's design of instruction should provide opportunities to the students who use different learning patterns. Teachers should also make an attempt to reduce the factors that do not encourage good learning styles such as anxiety, frustration and emotional instability, dependence on teachers and parents, rote memory and convergent thinking.

Teaching Strategies

Teacher strategies aim at establishing relationship between teaching inputs and learning outcomes, mainly in terms of realising the learning outcomes. Teaching strategies include teaching methods, approaches and techniques such as lecture method, tutorial approach, case study technique, demonstration method, term-teaching approach, programmed instruction, etc. In planning and instructional design, the teacher selects a particular essential factor to base he design such as objectives, skills, competencies, models or learning styles. In doing so, he focus attention to the type of design he is going to prepare. The teaching strategies used to elaborate the content or subject-matter of that unit or topic have to be spelled out in that particular design. Teaching strategies have been introduced in this book for large groups, small groups and individual instruction.

Teaching strategies when designed with clearly spelt-out objectives, and effective means of achieving them with inbuilt evaluation techniques is known as educational technology. Application of technology will ensure the achievement of objectives with the minimum effort and time required. When teaching result in effective learning of all the students taught, then any strategy that is applied to achieve this can be called educational technology. Educational technology is not deterministic, in the sense that if 'x' is done, 'y' will certainly happen. It only says that the probability of 'y' happening is very high if 'x' is done. The teaching strategies suggested have the high probability of effecting effective learning in students. Practising teachers may have to bring about some modifications, minor changes and adapt them to further increase the probability of their success in helping students learn more and better. And that is what educational technology, and for the reason, and technology is for.

Cybernetic Psychology

The second approach of instructional designs was evolved in the World War II. The term cybernetic has come to denote discipline which is associated with the research of communication and control'. It suggests concern with component elements of a system and they may function together to produce the most effective integrated system. The term cybernetic is used by Norbest Wiener (1948) associated with the physical system and physics.

Meaning of Cybernetic

The term cybernetic has been coined from the Greek word for steerman and thus, calls to mind and first importance cybernetic concept is that of feedback.

Cybernetic is defined by W. Wiener as "the science of control and communication in the animal and the machine."

Cybernetic is the sciences communication and control. In any system control is basic and key element. Control, here, means connectiveness and regulation, and system is a dynamic state.

Consider our school system, when the error between what the parents want their children to learn in school and they actually receive to become too great, the school policies are changed by the force of public opinions. In this way, the school systems are regulated by the modes of community. All regulatory bodies throughout of our entire society are the feedback control system.

Cybernetic Theory : *Cybernetic,* can be considered as a branch of training psychology. It conceptualizes human beings in engineering terms considering him like an electric machine which used the process of sensory feedback to control and modify its behaviour.

Cybernetic theory views an individual as a feedback system which generates its activities in order to detect and control specific stimulus characteristics of the environment. It analyses intrinsic mechanism by which control is established an maintained of sensory feedback mechanism. The focus of the whole theory is the dynamic feedback and self-regulation.

All system include atleast three basic elements: Input, process and output.

The input unit provides some process by which material or information is entered the system.

The process unit acts on the material or information to modify it in any way.

The output unit consists of some techniques for discharging the results of process from the system.

The output from a system which returned as input to control future output is called feedback.

The system can be of two types-an open loop system and a closed loop system. The closed loop system is often referred to cybernetic system. In the open loop system the output is returned to the system and consequently affects future output of the system is one which places a boundary around the system.

The essence, then, of Cybernetic psychology rests on its principles of sensory-oriented feedback which are intrinsic for the individual (he 'feels' the effect of his decision) and are the basis of self corrective devices.

Cybernetic System : Instruction also can be considered as a cybernetic system. The instructional system also has three major elements. A cybernetic instructional system would also include knowledge of results to the learner and some record of students responses. Its input also consists of library material, subject-matter content, learner characteristics and objectives. Students responses function as feedback for input. The procedure controls the presentation and modifies the presentation of display and knowledge of results on the basis of student's responses correspondence to the objectives. In the cybernetic system of instruction, following is the order of input, output and procedure.

The first essential input is the content or material to be presented, *i.e.* library material or library input which is inclusive of any written material or audiovisual material, programmed instruction, diagrams, charts, etc.

The most important input for an instructional system are the objectives (performance standard) by which the system is designed to accomplish.

A third input for a cybernetic instructional system is the formation concerning with the individual characteristics of the students.

Because this is a cybernetic system so the fourth type of input consists of the feedback for the learner in the form of his responses. This is an important pre condition. Without this an instructional system is not able to adjust the presentation and to produce the change in behaviour specified by the objective input. It may be noted here that in most of the instructions in schools, the input of students responses is ignored.

The first essential output for an instructional system is the display of the learner which may be oral such as lecture explanation, visual, written, and so on. A display is any stimulus situation structured and presented to the learner for the purpose of establishing some responses.

In a cybernetic system, a second output presented to learner is in form of knowledge of results.

If student's response is input to the system, a third type of output which may or may not be used in a particular instructional situation will be the record of each student's response.

The procedure is the selection mechanism which presents and displays in a linear fashion, one following the other. Movie or filmstrip presentation are good examples of such a system.

Feedback theory evaluates the techniques of self instruction according to how well they are conform to principles of cybernetic design. In order to optimize feedback control of symbolic knowledge and skills original presentation should be more varied and flexible than a permitted by most of the teaching machines and programmes. Specially organized systems of reference are also important. However self instructions is useful for drill and review in specific details.

The mechanism of feedback devices are most effective for the modification of teacher-behaviour. These mechanism are based on the principles of cybernetic.

Application in Education : Most useful concept in the cybernetic is that of feedback which has far reaching implications for teaching learning and training. The following are the major implications of cybernetic:

(1) The principles of cybernetic are applied for classroom instruction, group as well as individual learning.

(2) It enables the teacher to understand some of the fundamental mechanism that control learning.

(3) It provides the basis for self-education. The feedback control is used to develop programmed instructional material.

(4) Cybernetic principles are used for developing remedial instruction or individualized instructional material.

(5) Teacher-education programme can be improved by employing the mechanism of feedback devices for the modification of teacher-behaviour.

(6) The innovative practices in teacher-education programme such as micro teaching, stimulated social skill teaching and interactional analysis are based on the theory of feedback.

(7) The input, output and process units of teaching enable the teacher to understand and analyse teaching in more scientific manner.

(8) The teaching activities can be made highly structured and well organized in view of learning objectives.

The classroom instruction, a school or the programme of teaching can be considered as a dynamic system. This stresses on the principle that teaching is a resultant activity of the combination or forces, factor and conditions. The teacher has to take in consideration all these factors to generate appropriate teaching situation. Thus, cybernetic concept is most useful for developing design of training programmes for complex behaviour.

QUESTIONS

1. Define the term instructional designs and enumerate its major approaches and their purpose.
2. Explain the term Training Psychology' and its contributions to education and teacher training.
3. Enumerate the types of Instructional Designs. Describe competency based education.
4. Explain the term 'Cybernetic'. Describe the applications of cybernetic in education.

7

The Approaches

Curriculum is the most important component of educational process. It is a dynamic process which plays significant role in shaping the society. The term curriculum has been defined in various ways. The review of available definitions, indicates the changing emphasis in the structure of the curriculum. Various approaches and models of curriculum have been used in the transaction of curriculum and designing curriculum.

The following are the main approaches to curriculum construction:

1. Herbartian Approach
2. Morrison Approach
3. Evaluation Approach
4. Management Approach
5. Integrated approach

The details of these approaches have been provided in the following paragraphs.

Herbert Approach

Memory level teaching and learning is that kind of learning which supposedly embraces committing factual materials to memory and nothing else.

Assumptions - The following are the assumptions of memory level of teaching:

(1) The more meaningful material is to be learned easily ; it is to memorize. The more meaningful learnt material tends to be retained.

(2) The capacity of memories and retain material probably bear no positive relationship to the capacity of intelligent behaviour.
(3) The memory level teaching contribute indirectly to intelligent behaviour and for the problem-solving.
(4) The memorized facts usually contribute little to effective students-growth.

In any ordinary school situation on occasions even the most imaginative teaching is applied. Mathematical table, spellings, Sanskrit grammar symbols and formulaes may be taught through a process of straight memorization by using drill procedure. However, much more study will be required to develop method for teaching all the fundamental skill objects in ways which will go away from rote memorization. In this direction some new innovations have been done, new mathematics is an example for the some in which main stress is given on concept formation rather than to memorize the facts. But these experiments have not yielded the fruitful results. Thus, memory level of teaching plays a significant role in development of a child.

Model of Teaching : The model of teaching is originated by Herbert. It consists of five main aspects:

1. Focus, 2. Syntax, 3. Social system, 4. Support system, and 5. Evaluation system.

Focus: The teaching at memory level aims at causing learning that may enable the student—

1. To train the mental discipline.
2. To acquire factual informations.
3. To retain the learnt material for longer time.
4. To recall or produce and recognize the learned material.

Syntax: The structure of the model is developed with the help of five formal steps of Herbert. These steps form the paradigms of teaching. Preparation, Presentation Comparison and Abstraction, Generalization, and Application.

Preparation: The function of this step is to bring into consciousness relevant ideas of the subject-matter. The Teacher plans about the presentation of the content.

Presentation: The new ideas or knowledge of content is imparted in such a way that it may be linked with earlier knowledge of the students. The presentation at this stage involves the following activities:

(a) Teacher should have a definite work.

(b) Teacher should have a definite structure of teaching activities.

(c) Teacher should impart specific content.

The kind of presentation in teaching-learning has three characteristics -

(i) Definiteness, (ii) Predictability, and (iii) Observable specified knowledge structure.

Comparison and Abstraction: In this step, the teacher attempts to compare between new system, new facts and new ideas to identify similarities among new facts.

Generalization: In this step teacher generates the situations so that students are able to point out similarities of elements of new ideas and knowledge. The changing of learning aids in generalization. The rhythm and recitation methods are used at this stage.

Application: Teacher creates situations or problems so that student may use memorized facts for the further facts. The mathematical tables are used in multiplication and division.

Social System: This model consists of authoritarian behaviour. The teacher is more active and his main job is to structure and to present the content systematically and logically in the class.

The learner is like a passive listener in classroom. He has to memorize and reproduce the content. The students' activities are directed by the teacher. The students have to carry out instructions of the teacher and they can not initiate in the classroom. The social system is such that teacher can teach even wrong things to students.

At this level the form of motivation is purely extrinsic. The teacher provides motivation through reward verbal praise and punishment. It the learner is motivated or reinforced continuously then he learns better.

Support System: This model requires some supportive devices to make it more effective. More meaningful material should be used to present at this level. The subject-matter should be made definite in its structure. The audio-visual aids may be used to involve more sense and make the content interesting for learner. The content should be specified and presented in an observable form.

Evaluation System: The evaluation is an indispensable aspect of teaching because it produces evidences about the realization of goals of the teaching model.

Usually oral tests are given to measure the retention of learned material. The objective tests of recall and recognition type are administered to evaluate the knowledge of students.

Morrison Approach

The term 'understanding' has been used so ambiguously by psychologists and educators that teachers are likely to use it rather vaguely without being able to define it clearly.

Dictionary meaning includes the following definitions of the verb 'understand'-

(1) To perceive the meaning, grasp the idea; comprehend the meaning.

(2) To be thoroughly familiar with, approached clearly the character or nature of a term of concept.

(3) To comprehend by knowing the meaning of the word employed as a language.

(4) To grasp clearly as a fact or realize.

A student of education is not satisfied with the meaning or definition. He refers the meaning of the term 'understanding' as given below-

(a) Understanding is as seeing relationship.

(b) Understanding is as seeing the tool use of facts.

(c) Understanding harmonizes well with cognitive field outlook.

(d) Understanding is as seeing both relationship and tool use.

(e) Understanding is a generalized insight.

The term 'unresisting' is used in psychology and education for the above meaning.

The 'understanding' may be of three types-

(i) Full understanding - it refers the factual information.

(ii) True understanding- it conveys the meaning of a concept.

(iii) Functional understanding- it means an application of facts, principles and concepts.

The Meaning: Understanding level of teaching is that teaching which seeks to acquaint students with the relationship between generalization and particulars—between principles and solitary facts—which show the uses for which the principles may be applied.

Teacher is trying to keep his introduction on an understanding level, if he succeeds, his students will be able to identify cases in which a given rule applies and then use the rule as a guide. The same kinds of results are obtained when we teach rules or spelling rules for dividing fractions or rules repairing a motor or theories of physics and chemistry.

Model of Teaching: This is also known as Morrison's model of teaching. Morrison has developed this model of teaching. The paradigms of teaching consist in five aspects: focus, syntax, social system, support system and evaluation system.

Focus: The main focus of understanding level-teaching is to have the mastery over the concept. This model is idea-centred. It provides substantial knowledge to subject-matter and to encourage adaptive responses or true adaptation.

The memory level teaching is the pre-requisite for achieving these objectives.

Syntax: The structure of understanding level teaching involves five steps—exploration, presentation, assimilation, organization and recitation.

Step I. Exploration: It consists of three operations:

(a) It involves testing, questioning to explore initial learning of the students. It provides apperceptive sequences, where he should start.

(b) It intends to assist teacher to arrange subject-matter in psychological sequence.

(c) A third role of exploration is orientation of teacher to decide how a new unit is to be approached or presented.

Step II. Presentation: It includes three activities:

(a) Teacher presents the new content into small units, he attempts to maintain continuous rapport with the students in the class.

(b) The teacher tests the students to diagnose or observes how many students fail to grasp the presented content.

(c) If necessary, the presentation is repeated. Teacher should not proceed towards the new unit until most of the students fully understand. Some material can be presented three times. Teacher is more active in this step.

Step III. Assimilation: At the end or presentation a test is administered when students have passed out the test of presentation. Teacher moves to assimilation.

(a) The purpose of assimilation is thoroughness of subject-matter.

(b) The students are active in this step, they do much work in library, laboratory, field work, assignments and to consult source material.

(c) The work of the student in this step is highly individualized.

(d) The assimilation period basically is the time of supervised study. The teacher and students are more active.

(e) The main objective of assimilation period is for students to see numerous particulars in relation to the generalization on which the unit is based.

(f) A mastery test is also administered at the end of assimilation. If students can not pass the test, they are asked for further assimilation.

Step IV. Organisation: An organization provides an apperceptive sequence, when student passes a mastery test and thus terminates a period of assimilation and moves towards the organization step. It involves the following operations:

(a) Organizations step is to determine whether he can reproduce the essentials of the unit in writing without any help. Morrison refers to the written reproduction of the unit as the period of organization. The final step in the mastery of any understanding is taken when we write ourselves clear handed about it.

(b) This step is especially essential in subjects of extensive content which include a large number of elements in one learning unit. In certain subjects such as arithmetic, mathematics and grammar the written reproduction of an unit is possible. The student can move directly from assimilation to recitation.

Step V: Recitation: A student can move up to the last step directly from assimilation in certain subjects and also when the period of organization terminates. It includes the following activities :

(a) Each student presents orally before the teacher, his classmates in condensed version of the understanding taught in the unit.

(b) Morrison plans for mastery recitation. He plans daily recitation.

(c) Recitation may take the form of a written paper.

Social System: Teacher should be active enough to see that he should not be authoritarian. He should be democratic in teaching in the classroom. He has to act as a leader of the group. His main job is to guide and to motivate the students. His efforts should be of discovering and mastering the truth. His behaviour should be flexible, dynamic and full of human touch. He should have full faith in the learners. These are the essential qualities of a teacher who intends to organize teaching at this level.

The source of motivation at this level of teaching is not only extrinsic but also intrinsic and personal involvement of a teacher. Teacher's job is to create a need among the students to acquire understanding of new concepts. In presentation and assimilation step the teacher should encourage the students with verbal praise and approval of their correct responses. Teacher can raise the level of aspiration of students as well as the class as a whole.

Support System: This system is helpful to make this model more effective and goals may be achieved. The teaching aids should be used at presentation stage so that it may not be repeated several times. The audio-visual aids and other, devices may be used for an effective presentation.

This system is much more useful at assimilation stage. The subject-matter can be gathered from various sources. The programmed instruction material may be provided to the learners, because this stage is highly individualized. The teacher's proper supervision is very essential at the stage of assimilation. The learners should be given an, opportunity to practice the learnt material according to their own.

Evaluation System: The organization and recitation provides an evidence about the effectiveness of this model. The essay and objective type tests are used for evaluating the outcomes of this model. The multiple choice and analogy type items are best items for measuring the understanding of the students. Mastery recitation is an evidence for the workability in support of this model of teaching.

The Criticism : This model of teaching has the following advantages and disadvantages:

1. Morrison paradigm of teaching is really a psychological and functional for effective learning.
2. This paradigm is helpful for thoroughness or true learning or mastery over the subject-matter.
3. It is apparent failure of this model to pay due attention on human behaviour.
4. The teacher should motivate students through promoting their personal involvement in the subject-matter. It would be more effective if it would provide a greater place to psychological motivation.
5. Morrison has talked too much on reflection on the part of the students. In reality he has laid great emphasis on answers rate than on issues.
6. The idea of mastery teaching with its emphasis on students relating individual fact-to principles and its attenuations thoroughness, represents a vast improvement over much of the instruction now is given in our public school.
7. Morrison seems to have ignored the use of teacher's motivation the students for promoting their personal involvement with subject. The teacher should make the effort to promote 'level of aspiration' of the class, so that the learners may develop the structure on their own.

Evaluation Approach

The concept of evaluation approach is given by B.S. Bloom. His main emphasis was that testing should be based on teaching and both these activities should be objective-centred. Today teaching is organized by using the evaluation approach. Under this approach yearly-plan and unit plan are prepared. The education process is considered as tri-polar process. There are three fundamental elements: (1) Education objectives. (2). Learning experiences and (3) Change of behaviour of evaluation approach.

The evaluation approach and educational process are closely related to each other. The effectiveness and appropriateness of educational process is ascertained by evaluation approach. All the activities of teaching are evaluated in terms of student's performance, which is known as change of behaviour. In this approach criterion test is used rather than achievement test. A criterion test is always objective centred. Therefore, in the present chapter main feature of evaluation approach have been described in detail.

Meaning and Definition : The evaluation approach is a new concept in the discipline of education, which has revolutionalized the process of education.

In this approach main emphasis has been given in realising the objectives of education in behavioural terms.

Quillen and Huna have defined the term evaluation approach in the following manner :

"Evaluation is the process of gathering and interpreting evidences on changes in the behaviour of the students as they progress through school." In evaluation approach teaching and testing activities are performed side by side. The term evaluation is used in broader sense. It does not confine only upto student achievement but it includes the total process of teaching and learning. All the activities of teacher and students are evaluated qualitatively and quantitatively. The evaluation of a student performance does not confine to cognitive domain but it also includes the affective and psychomotor domain. The total change of behaviour of student is evaluated. In the school different type of learning experiences are provided to the students for developing their personality. The term change of behaviour includes cognative affective and psychomotor behaviours. The educational process is evaluated in terms of change of behaviour of students. Three types of activities are evaluated in terms of change of behaviour of students. Three type of activities are done in the evaluation process—

(1) How far have the teaching objectives been realized?

(2) How far the learning experiences are effective?

(3) What changes of behaviour have occurred in the students?

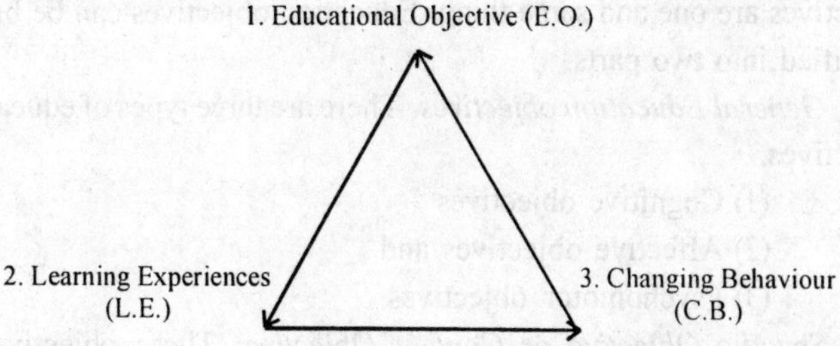

B. S. Bloom has stated that education is tri-polar process. This process has been shown as follows.

The following three steps in using evaluation approach—

First step - Education objectives.

Second step - Learning experiences.

Third step - Change of behaviour.

These three steps are closely related to each other and are performed in a sequence. The teaching and testing activities go side by side and these are objective-centred. It is the main assumption of this approach that failure of the student is due to the in appropriateness of learning experiences of teaching. Because it is main responsibility of teacher to bring desirable change among the students. Thus the change of behaviour and evaluations in terms of teaching objectives.

All the school subjects which are taught to them for providing learning experiences. Other activities which are organized in the school, are meant for learning experiences, but these should be directly related to the teaching objectives. In the following paragraphs an example has been given for using evaluation approach in teaching Geography.

The Application : The following steps are used when teaching is organised with the help of evaluation approach :

(1) Formulation of teaching objectives.

(2) Providing learning experiences for realizing the teaching objectives.

(3) Evaluating change of behaviour of the student in the light of teaching objectives.

Formulation of Teaching Objective : In this step teacher has to identify his teaching objective development of a student and teaching objectives are one and same thing. Education objectives can be broadly classified into two parts.

General Education objectives: There are three types of educational objectives.

(1) Cognitive objectives

(2) Affective objectives and

(3) Psychomotor objectives

Specific Objective or Content Objective: These objectives are written in behavioural terms, which are related to the content of a subject such as Hindi, Maths, History, Geography etc., These specific objectives are also known as teaching objective. Teaching objective are psychological in nature whereas education objectives are philosophical in nature. The education objectives are achieved with the help of teaching objectives, in teaching process main emphasis is given in realizing behavioural objectives. The behavioural objectives are classified in the following parts :

Knowledge Objective: In this objective the awareness and understanding of concept, fact principles, Laws and theories is provided. The students are able to recognise, to recall and to evaluate these things.

Skill Objective: It is the second teaching objective in which the learning experiences provided to enable the students for solving the problem related to their life situation. Student will be able to identify the causes and effect relationship of human activities or situations.

Development of Attitude Objective: It is the third objective of teaching in which right type of attitudes are developed towards the personal, social and national problems.

Knowledge Application: It is the fourth objective which concerns with the application of acquired knowledge in his life situations.

Development of Values: It is the main focus of education. That desirable values should be developed among the students, so that the students will be able citizen of nation. It is the highest objective of education.

The behavioural objectives are used in organizing both teaching and testing activities. The following are the main behavioural objectives:

(a) The student is able to comprehend facts, principle and theory.

(b) The student is able to solve the day to day life problems

(c) The student is able to understand and observe the facts, realities of life.

(d) The student is able to evaluate and appreciate the elements of human life.

(e) The student is able to understand the emotional integration and internationalism.

Learning Experiences : It is the second step of evaluation approach. Those experiences which are helpful in achieving the teaching objectives inside the classroom and outside the classroom are known as learning experiences. Thus all the learning experiences cannot be called as learning experiences. The following are the main aspects of the learning experiences—

(1) Teaching objectives related to the topic.

(2) Outline of the courses.

(3) Teaching methods and techniques.

(4) Maxims of teaching and teaching aids.

(5) Text-books and home works.

(6) Role of teacher and relationship between teacher and students.

The teaching objectives are achieved objectives by providing learning experiences to the students. The learning experiences are controlled by teaching objectives and text books of the subject. Teaching can be effective by creating appropriate learning experiences. These experiences should provide the appropriate learning experiences. These experiences should provide the opportunities to do some activities themselves. The teaching activities should be objective centred, and student should be involved in some activities. John Dewey advocated that a major task of teacher is to generate learning situation, which will motivate to the students for performing, certain activities, which are related to the objectives. A teacher's role is to organise and control all the teaching activities.

A teacher has to organise and create learning situations for providing experiences to the students according to their available resources. Teacher should behave to the students like philosopher, instructor and friends.

The learning experiences vary subject to subject. The different schools have the different resources. Therefore teacher has to plan according to his subject and available resources and prepare a out line of his teaching activity. A teacher has also to plan about the evaluative techniques for ascertaining the teaching objectives. In presentation of teaching content and preparing test for evaluation purpose, a teacher has to consider the needs and level of students in view of his teaching content.

He has to develop a sequence of teaching activity so that appropriate learning situations can be generated for providing learning experiences to the students. A teacher prepares his lesson plan for learning experiences. Some models of lesson plans have been given in the lesson plan chapter of this book.

Change of Behaviour : It is the third step of evaluation approach. The change of behaviour takes place with the help of learning experiences. The change of behaviours are related to all aspects of his personality. It includes both internal and external behaviour. There are three aspects of change of behaviour of students—cognitive, affective and psychomotor. The student achievement is of two types—cognitive achievement and non-cognitive achievement. The non-cognitive achievement includes interest attitude, values and certain skills. These changes of behaviours are evaluated in terms of teaching objectives formulated in the first step. A criterion test is used for this purpose.

There are three limitations of present examination system—

(1) The examination tests are not related to learning experiences and change of behaviour. The main emphasis is given on note memorization.

(2) The tests do not cover total teaching content, usually sampling is done.

(3) The tests are not objective. They are highly subjective.

In the evaluation approach these limitations are taken into consideration and following things are considered in preparing test—

(1) The table of specification is prepared in which the content and objectives are outlined.

(2) The table provides a guideline for preparing a test on the content and teaching objectives.

(3) An objective as well as Essay type test and other techniques are used.

Managing Approach of Curriculum : The concept of teaching, levels of teaching models of teaching and learning, strategies of teaching provide theoretical knowledge of teaching to teachers and pupil-teachers. But this awareness of teaching does not orient the pupil teachers how to plan and organize their teaching and about managing teaching-learning. This knowledge and understanding is very essential during the training period of the understanding and skill for managing teaching-learning process effectively. The training institutions are providing knowledge about Herbartian steps of teaching: Preparation and Presentation. Herbartian approach of teaching gives too much emphasis on presentation but it does not focus on the purpose and goals of teaching while teaching is considered as purposeful activity. The teaching is organized to achieve some specific goals of education. Now, the present approach of teaching gives main emphasis on objectives.

I.K. Davies considers that teaching is a noble profession. He has given a new concept Managing teaching-learning in the field of education. The concept provides the practical steps for planning and organizing teaching activities in classroom situation. The pupil-teacher can make use of these steps in organizing his classroom teaching.

Davies has borrowed this concept of managing teaching-learning from other human organizations. This chapter deals with the origin source and steps of managing teaching-learning process.

[This approach is discussed in detail in Chapter Curriculum Transaction and Research]

Integrated Approach

The experiments were conducted in psychology in the beginning of 20th century. Gestalt psychology, was also introduced. It was proved that mind in an unit. Mind receives the knowledge as a whole not in parts. Whole knowledge is stable in the mind.

These researches and inventions have also influenced education. An integrated curriculum was introduced in U.S.A. This type of curriculum is based on the unification theory. The ideas and activities will be useful only when these can combine in an unit.

The project method is used in an integrated curriculum. It is an activity-centred curriculum. Group-controlled instructions are employed in this type of curriculum. It is also known as activity-oriented curriculum. The knowledge of all subjects is imparted by relating it to some social activity. The activity should be related to life. The main focus is to develop social efficiency among the students. These is no compartment of subject. The knowledge is considered as an unit. The subject contents are the parts of an activity. An activity is assigned to a group of students, the required knowledge of the subjects for performing the activity are given to the students. The learning by doing technique is used in this type of curriculum. The school subjects are integrated and correlated. The courses of study should be related of real life situations.

According to Henderson, there should be no barrier or compartmentalization among the subject. It provides such experiences to the students which are easy to understand and easy to use it.

The approach is given by pragmatic philosophy. Kilpatric has employed the project-method and introducing integrated approach to curriculum. It employs group-controlled instruction which must be activity oriented method of instruction.

The Characteristics : The following are the main characteristics of this type of curriculum.

1. The knowledge of subjects is given in the integrated form.
2. The students learn the various subjects simultaneously.
3. This type of curriculum is activity oriented and experience-centred.
4. This type of curriculum provides knowledge of the subject which is useful in real life.
5. The students' interests are taken into considerations.
6. It employs group-controlled instruction therefore duties and responsibility are assigned to the students.
7. It helps in developing spirit of team work and feeling of cooperation.

The Difficulties : The following are the difficulties in the construction and using this type of curriculum :

(1) It is not possible to include the interest of each every student.

(2) It is used in group-controlled instruction therefore individual interest can not be developed.

(3) There is no definite outline or structure of the content.

(4) There is no sequence in the subject-content.

(5) It is very time consuming.

(6) It is not possible to integrate all the subjects on an activity.

(7) There remain gaps in the knowledge while using integrated curriculum.

(8) The project is designed for the task not for providing the knowledge of the subjects.

(9) An outline of subject can not be prepared before the project.

(10) The knowledge of the subject depends on the need of project not the need of the students.

The concept of integrated curriculum approach is good but scope is narrow. The sequence of the content is not followed.

The Limitations : The following are the major limitations of this approach :

(1) It is very costly from time, money and energy point of view.

(2) There is no definite structure of content.

(3) The sequence of subject-content is not followed.

(4) It can be used at lower level but can not be used for higher level.

(5) The higher objectives of education can not be achieved by this type of curriculum.

(6) It is similar to basic education but vocational courses are much more useful.

(7) It does not consider the individual difference of the student.

(8) All the subjects can not be taught by this approach.

QUESTIONS

1. Explain the term approach and model of curriculum. Describe the need and scope of approaches and models of curriculum.

2. Explain the term Management Approach to Curriculum. Describe major features of management approach to curriculum.
3. Enumerate the main approaches of curriculum. Describe evaluation approaches of curriculum.
4. Enumerate the main models of curriculum. Describe the Saran Model of Curriculum.
5. Differentiate between approach and models of curriculum. Describe the integrated approach of curriculum and indicate its disadvantages.

8

Curriculum Aims

Education is the process of development, in which efforts are made for the all-round development of a child. Education involves three processes—Teaching, Training and Instruction. The learning experiences are provided with the help of the activities for bringing desirable behavioural change among students. The content is the mean for organizing teaching activities. The learning situations are generated by teaching tasks in which student gains new experiences and has to do something , this is the objective of teaching-learning. An outline of the content in the narrow sense is known as curriculum or syllabus. The teaching structure is based on the format of curriculum, and the pivot of education is the curriculum. The curriculum is based on the social philosophy which is a changing phenomenon. Thus, the meaning and format of curriculum is also changing according to the need of the society as well as nation. Under this book and an attempt has been made to answer three basic questions what, why and how? related to curriculum.

The Meaning

An old concept of curriculum was to consider it as merely syllabus or an outline of courses of study.

The curriculum word is of Latin language. It means 'race course'. In education it means 'work field of student' or race course of the students. It consists of two words-race and course. The word 'course' means curriculum and race refers students' experiences and activities. A teacher performs his teaching activities in view of curriculum.

The new concept of curriculum is very broad-based. It consists of the totality of experiences that a pupil receives through the manifold activities that go on in the school, in the classroom, library, laboratory, workshop and playground, and in the numerous contacts between the teachers and the pupils. It is neither dogmatic nor rigid in its form and structure. It is neither uniform nor standardised to conform to a prescribed pattern. It is characterised by variety and flexibility and is tailored to the needs of the students at different age levels. It gives the students an increasing awareness of the environment around them so that they may fit in more efficiently in the mileu of community life. It thus secures more integrated group relations. *Munroe* says, "Curriculum embodies all the experiences which are utilised by the school to attain the aims of education." The curriculum from this point of view may include the syllabus which is the detailed statement of subject-material, the programme which determines the way in which material taught is to be inter-related and ordered and to some extent the methodology which determines the way in which material is accurately presented in the classroom." The Secondary Education Commission has also pointed out clearly the nature and conception of the desired curriculum: "It must be clearly understood that, according to the best educational thought, curriculum does not mean only the academic subjects traditionally taught in the school but it includes the totality of experiences that a child receives at school. In this sense, the whole life of the school becomes the curriculum which can touch the life of the students at all points and help in the evolution of a balanced personality."

Curriculum is, therefore, something which is related to the life and the needs of the pupils of different age levels. It includes both what they should learn and also shaw they should learn it. It includes all the experiences that child undergoes the guidance of school authorities. It is the result of the interaction between and among many people. Many influences affect its quality and may material conditions affect its functioning.

The Definitions

The term 'Curriculum' has been defined by the scholars and educationists. Some the definitions have been provided here to understand the nature and characteristics of curriculum.

B. Rudyand and H. Henry

"Curriculum, in its broadest sense, includes the complete school environment, involving all the courses, activities, reading, and associations furnished to the pupils in the school."

Curriculum includes, physical, social and academic environments of a college.

Cunninghous

"It (curriculum) is a tool in the hands of the artist (teacher) to mould his material (pupil) according to his ideal (objective) in his studio (school)."

Froebel

"Curriculum should be conceived as an epitome of the rounded whole of the knowledge and experience of the human. race."

Munroe

"Curriculum includes all those activities which are utilised by the school to attain the aims of education."

Horne

"Curriculum is that which is taught to the students. It is more than reading and writing. It includes practice, activities, industry, vocation and acquiring knowledge.

Caswell

"The curriculum is all that goes in the lives of children, their parents and teachers. The curriculum is made up everything that surrounds the learner in all his working hours. In fact the curriculum has been described as the environment in motion."

Secondary Education Commission

"Curriculum does not mean the academic subject taught in the school but it includes total experience that a child receives at a school."

John F Kerr

"All the learning which is planned or guided by the school, whether it is carried on in groups or individually, inside or outside the school, is known as curriculum."

Taylor

"The curriculum consists of content, teaching methods and purpose. These three dimensions interacting are operational curriculum."

Philip H. Taylor

Philip H. Taylor has defined curriculum operationally. He has indicated three dimensions of curriculum - content, teaching method and purpose.

Paul Hirst

Paul Hirst has given a comprehensive definition of the term curriculum-

"A programme of activities designed so that pupils will attain, as far as possible, certain education ends or objectives is known as the curriculum."

The Characteristics

The above definitions indicate the following characteristics of the concept of curriculum.

1. Curriculum is a tool in the hands of the teacher which is used to realize the objectives.
2. It is pivot, around it whole human knowledge concentrates.
3. It includes those activities which are used by the school to attain the purpose of education.
4. It is more than teaching and learning and includes practice, activities, industry vocation and acquiring knowledge.
5. The curriculum is made up of everything that surrounds the learner in all his working terms.
6. It has been described as the environment in motion (physical, social and psychological).
7. Curriculum includes total learning experience that a child receives at a school.
8. All the learning inside or outside the school which is planned and guided by the curriculum.
9. It includes content method of teaching and purpose of education.
10. A programme of activities designed to realize the objectives is know as curriculum.

Curriculum and Syllabus

A syllabus or courses of study, which relate to different subjects only, indicate the frame-work and amount of knowledge and facts which will be imparted to pupils of different age levels. They are generally verbal, bookish, and theoretical. But the modern concept of curriculum and its scope, as described above, fully explains that curriculum is a wider and broader term. Its stress is not on memorisation and learning facts by rote. The emphasis is on the child and the primary consideration is to develop his personality to the fullest. It includes all that will affect the behaviour pattern of the pupils, how the responses could be organised and directed towards desirable modes of behaviour. *Courses of study* are thus a part of the curriculum. We should never think syllabus, and courses of study and curriculum as synonymous terms. Curriculum embraces, besides academic courses, co-curricular and extra-curricular activities of the pupils, community relationships, work experiences of the pupils, and the study of their growing needs and their planning, coordinating and executing of diverse measures and means to satisfy those wants, giving them as high a sense of achievement as possible. "The understandings, attitudes, and appreciations, abilities and skills which pupils needs now in the solution of his current problems, turn out to be similar to those which, he will need later in solving adult problems. Understandings, attitudes, and abilities needed in adult life begin their growth in nursery and are developed through continuing by experiences until the learner emerges into an adult replaced by a wealth of suggested materials and experiences."

Caswell has very aptly laid down the scope and nature of curriculum. According to him "The curriculum is all that goes on the lives of the children, their parents and their teachers. The curriculum is made up of everything that surrounds the learner in all his working hours in fact, the curriculum has been described as "the environment in motion."

In India, we have never planned and conceived curriculum in its broad sense. Curriculum and syllabus have always been taken to be in synonymous terms. This has naturally circumscribed the scope and content of education. The emphasis has subsequently been on imparting factual knowledge, pertaining to different subjects. The courses of study prescribed hardly pay and attention to foster among children right attitudes and behaviour patterns, which may give students social efficiency to live fuller and more gainful lives. No effort is made to cultivate among the pupils' knowledge of essential skills and basic understandings, which may give them capacity to apply the knowledge of learnt facts to new situations.

The Scope

Curriculum is, therefore, very comprehensive in its scope. It touches all aspects of the life of the pupils-the needs and interests of pupils, environment which should be educationally congenial to them, ways and manners in which their interests can be handled and warmed up, the procedures and approaches which cause effective learning among them, the social efficiency of the individuals and how they fit in with the community around. It is intimately related with the individual as a member of the society. It embodies the educational philosophy, the values which it aims to achieve, the purposes it wants to realise and the specific goals that it wants to achieve. The emphasis is on the child. In the total education of the child, all the subjects like history, geography, science, and language are but tools. They are the means, and therefore, the children must not be made to fit in such frame of study.

The Development

This concept is usually written and spoken as *"curriculum development"* the term curriculum is considered as incomplete. Curriculum development means a continues process or never ending process. It is difficult to trace out the origin. The out come of teaching is known through students' achievement and learning. The assessment of objectives are done on the basis of change of behaviour of the learners.

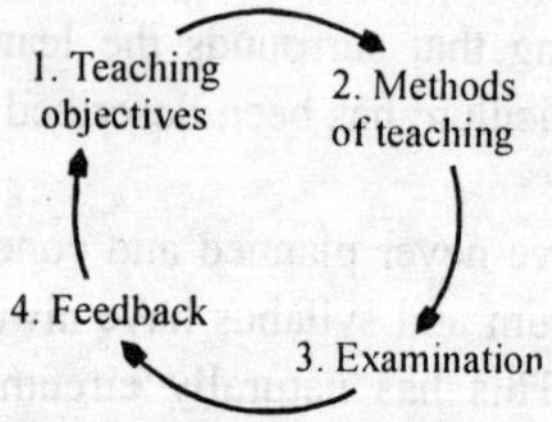

The learning experiences provide the desirable change of behaviours of the pupils which are evaluated with help of examination. Therefore, the term is known as *'curriculum development'*. The main focus of the curriculum is to develop the students. The curriculum is designed to realize the objectives in terms of change of behaviours. Therefore it is a cyclic process—1. Teaching objectives 2. Method of teaching 3. Examination or testing and 4. Feedback. These elements have been described in brief.

Teaching Objectives - Three types of teaching objectives cognitive, affective and psychomotor are identified in view of subject-content to be taught. These objectives are written in behavioural terms. All learning experiences are organized to achieve these objectives.

Methods of Teaching - The most important aspect for providing learning experiences is the teaching strategies. The objectives are realized in terms of behavioural changes of the learners. The content is the means to select the method of teaching and level of the pupils.

Process of Evaluation - The evaluation of change of behaviour is done to ascertain about the realization of the teaching learning objectives. The level of pupils' performance indicates the effectiveness of method of teaching and learning experiences.

Feedback - The interpretation of performance provides the teacher to improve and modify the form of the curriculum. The curriculum is developed and teaching objectives are also revised. The methodology of teaching is changed in view of the curriculum and objectives are to be achieved.

Objectives of Development

There are three components of educational process—teacher, students and curriculum. It has three type of objectives, cognitive, affective and psychomotor. Educational process involves three major activities—teaching training and instruction. According to B. S. Bloom it is considered as tripolar process- (1) Educational process (2) Learning experiences and (3) Change of behaviour. It is also a cyclic process, shown with the help of the following diagram.

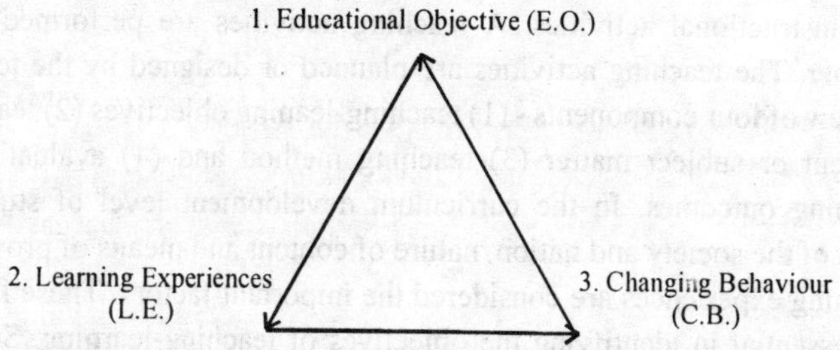

The teaching process is done through interaction between teacher and students in view of the curriculum or course of content. Thus, the curriculum is basis for the interaction between teacher and taught. The following are the major objectives of curriculum development.

1. Curriculum provides the means for the all-round development of a child. Teaching is organized with the help of curriculum.
2. Curriculum involves the human experiences, culture and civilization which is to be transferred to new generation.
3. Curriculum is the means to develop the moral character, discipline, honesty, cooperation, friendship, tolerance and sympathy with others.
4. It helps in developing the ability of thinking, wisdom, reasoning, judgement and other mental abilities.
5. It considers the stages of growth and development of child for development attitude, interest, values and creative ability.
6. It provides the awareness and understanding of physical and social environment and its components.
7. Curriculum develops the right type of feelings and beliefs towards religions, new values and traditions.
8. It helps to develop democratic feeling and democratic way of life among students.
9. It integrates the knowledge of various teaching subjects in view of their future life.
10. It determine the mode of interaction between teacher and students in school. The mode of teaching is also decided by the nature of curriculum.

Basic Elements

The educational process is done with the help of teaching, training and instructional activities. A teaching activities are performed by a teacher. The teaching activities are planned or designed by the teacher in view of four components - (1) teaching-leaning objectives (2) teaching content or subject matter (3) teaching method and (4) evaluation of learning outcomes. In the curriculum development level of students, need of the society and nation, nature of content and means of providing learning experiences are considered the important factors. These factors are essential in identifying the objectives of teaching-learning. Several types of teaching objectives are attained by the same content. Thus, a content has its own structure. Teaching is organized from memory to effective level on the same content of subject-matter. The specific objectives or behavioural objectives are realized by organizing specific teaching tasks and activities. Thus the curriculum development involves four basic elements - (1) Objectives (2) Content (3) Method of teaching or strategies of teaching and (4) Evaluation. These elements are interdependent as shown in the figure

Objectives - The subjects content structure, levels of students, and type of examination components are considered in the identification of objectives of teaching and learning. These objectives are specific and are written in behavioural terms so as to develop learning structures and conditions.

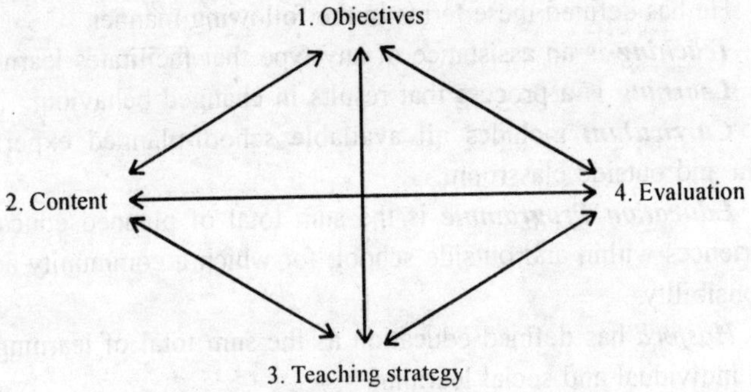

Relationship among the Basic Elements

Content or Subject-Matter - The content of any subject is usually broad. It is analysed into sub-content and faster into its elements. These elements are arranged in a logical sequence. The behavioural objectives are written with the help of these elements of the content. It is also known as logic of teaching.

Strategy of Teaching - The specific objectives of teaching are attained with the help of appropriate teaching strategy. The behavioural objectives provide the awareness and insight about the specific learning conditions. The strategy is employed for providing learning experiences and bringing desirable behavioural change.

Evaluation - The level of students' attainment is evaluated by employing criteria referenced test. It shows the effectiveness of strategy of teaching and other components. The interpretation of evaluation provides the feedback to the curriculum and its components. These components are improved and modified in view to attain the objectives of teaching and learning. It is an empirical basis for the 'curriculum development'.

The Relationship

Curriculum is closely related to other educational elements, though the curriculum is an important element of educational process.

Philip L. Hosfor mentioned four major areas of education in his book titled 'Instructional Theory.'

(a) Teaching, (b) Learning, (c) Curriculum and (d) Educational programme.

He has defined these terms in the following manner.

Teaching is an assistance of any type that facilitates learning.

Learning is a process that results in changed behaviour.

Curriculum includes all available school-planned experiences within and outside classroom.

Education Programme is the sum total of planned educational experiences within and outside school, for which a community accepts responsibility.

Hosford has defined education as the sum total of learning with both, individual and social learning.

There is an interaction among the four areas of education which have been illustrated diagrammatically.

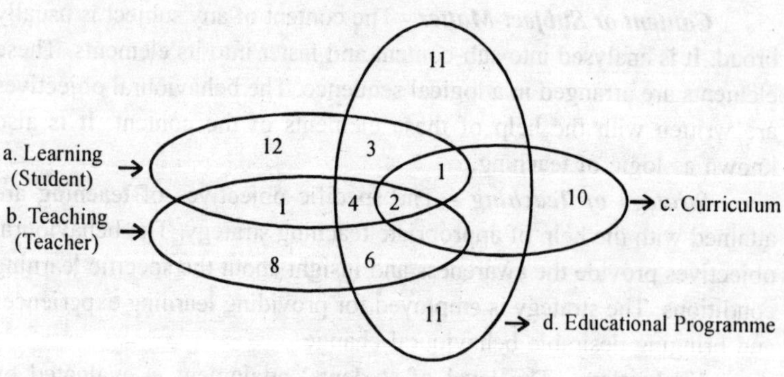

Interaction Areas of Education

The interaction areas of education as shown in the above diagram may be interpreted in the following manner—

1. That part of curriculum in the educational programme which impinges on the learner without teacher involvement, the student uses materials.
2. Teacher, student, curriculum interaction.
3. Student interacting with educational programme without teacher or curriculum involvement.
4. Spontaneous teacher-pupil interaction within the framework of the educational programme without the curriculum.
5. Teacher curriculum interaction is the planning phase of teaching.
6. Teacher and educational programme interaction.
7. Teacher-behaviour influencing the learner outside the educational programme.
8. Ali other teacher-behaviour without curriculum and educational programme.
9. Curriculum in the educational programme but teaching of learner.
10. Curriculum is not in the educational programme. It may be due to lack of school funds.
11. All other aspects of educational programme which have not been enforced in the school.
12. All learning of pupil is not attributable to the educational programme. The learner's change of behaviour which is other than curriculum, educational programme and teacher influence.

It is evident from the above interpretation of interaction areas of education that teaching and learning are related due to curriculum, educational programme and teacher-behaviour.

Need and Importance

The need of education determines the importance of curriculum. The review of literature in this content reveals that there has been changing emphasis in the process of education. Thus the need of curriculum has evolved the concept of *'Curriculum development.'* The needs of the curriculum have been merited as follows.

1. The human can acquire knowledge while other species can not acquire knowledge. It is an important aspect of human beings.

2. The mental aspects are trained and developed, thus mental faculties are trained by teaching various school subjects.
3. The vocational and technical education prepare the students for different jobs. During British period, clerks were prepared through educational curriculum.
4. The interests and attitudes are developed according to the students' potentialities. Curriculum is designed as child-centred.
5. The good citizens are prepared by developing democratic way of life. It also develops the ability and capacity of teachership.
6. The ability of self-realization is also developed by education and to make good man.
7. It also develops the feeling of appreciation and sound judgement.
8. The education is given always for future life so that he can earn his leaving.
9. It also prepares for scientific inventions and technical development.
10. It brings perfection in child. It helps in allround development.

It is a powerful instrument for social change as well as social control.

Influencing Factors

The curriculum is the educational and social concept, but is based on the social-philosophy of life. Therefore, the social and educational factors influence the curriculum development. Some of the important factors are given in the following parts.

1. Management of education 2. Examination system, 3. Form of government, 4. Board of studies, 5. National commission and committees and 6. Social change. A brief description of the factors is as follows—

Management of Education -The curriculum and its management are closely related to each other. These have been influencing each other since very beginning. Now education is the state subject. Thus every state of our country has own curriculum and education system. At primary stage education is child-centred and at secondary stage it is subject-centred. Now there is main emphasis on vocational courses and technical education. The major approach of education is objective-centred, so the curriculum is also objective-centred.

Examination System - The nature and structure of curriculum is based an the examination system. The are two type of examination systems. Essay type and *objective type.* The essay type questions are based on the broad aspect of the content while objective type questions are based on specific elements of the contents. The higher objectives are assessed with the help of essay type examination and lower objectives are measured by using objective type examination. Thus the curriculum and methods of teaching are influenced by the examination system.

Form of Government - The needs of nation and society are fulfilled by education and its curriculum. The form of government has direct influence on education process. An autocratic form of government employs teacher-centred instruction (TCI) in school, where as in democratic form of government considers interactive-process or learner-centred instructions (LCI). In our country we do not have national system of education. Every state has its own system of education and form of its curriculum.

Board of Studies - The form of curriculum is developed by board of studies. There are different board of studies for the different stages of education. Every university has various board of studies for different subjects. The members of board of studies employ their experiences, interests, attitude and mental abilities. Usually the convener of board of study designs the outline of the course which is approved by the members of the committee.

National Commission and Committees - After independence, several commission and committee have been established at national level for the improvement and modification of education at various levels of education, primary, secondary and college and university education. The commission and committee have designed and suggested course of studies. National policy of education has emphasized on the vocational and technical education after +2 level. The curriculum has been designed in view of these recommendations.

Social Change - The social change is very slow and economic change is very rapid. The economic changes influence the courses of studies. Today there is wide scope of computer-education. An outline of computer-education has been designed for various level of education. There is great scope of distance-education and use of multimedia approach in our education system. Apart from these factors, there are several other factors which have great influence on curriculum development.

(1) Social tradition (2) State government (3) Central government (4) Society (6) School. These factors are related to each other as shown in the figure.

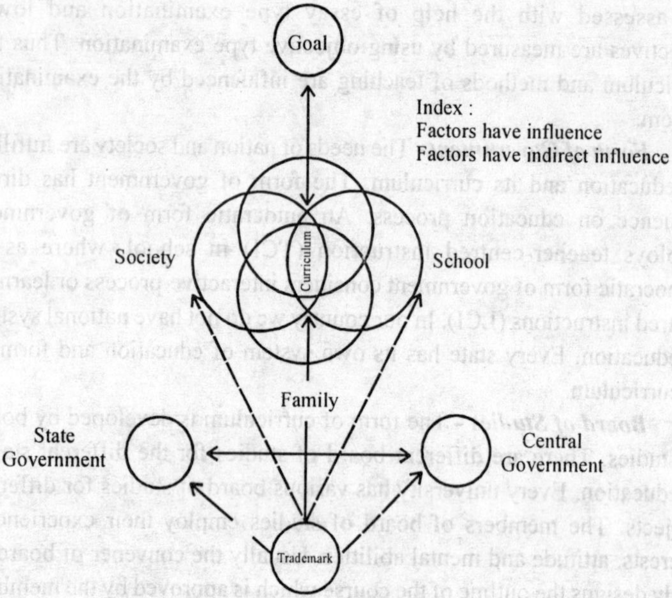

Factors Affecting Curriculum Development

Various Types

There are different views regarding the curriculum management. There has been changing emphasis on the components of education which has influenced the types of curriculum. Some of the important types of curriculum are enumerated as follows.

(1) Subject-centred curriculum, or Teacher-centred curriculum,
(2) Child-centred curriculum, or Learner-centred,
(3) Task-centred or Activity-centred curriculum,
(4) Objective-centred curriculum,
(5) Experience-centred curriculum,
(6) Correlated-curriculum,
(7) Core-curriculum and
(8) Integrated curriculum.

Subject-centred or Teacher-centred Curriculum - The curriculum is greatly influenced by social philosophy. Therefore ideas or subject content should be given emphasis in developing curriculum. Herbartian approach gives emphasis on presentation of content in classroom teaching. It is also known as content-centred curriculum or teacher centred-curriculum. This type of curriculum is unpsychological as it does not consider the students' needs interest and abilities. It is not helpful in developing democratic outlook of the students. This type of curriculum is easy to design and easy to understand by the teacher. It can be easily revised and modified. It depends on the social and educational thinking. It helps to test the students performance easily. This type is preferred by teacher, students and parents.

Child-centred Curriculum - The curriculum is designed and based on the nature of child. It considers the need, interests and abilities of the learners. It considers the stages of growth and development of children. This type of curriculum is used in Montessori and Kindergarten education.

Task-centred Curriculum - John Dewey has suggested this type of curriculum. Kelpetrik has given project-method teaching for this curriculum. Mahatma Gandhi emphasized on basic education i.e. 3H education - hand, head and heart.

Objective-centred Curriculum - B. S. Bloom has suggested evaluation approach to education. It is tripolar process - Educational objectives, Learning experiences and Change of behaviour. The curriculum is the major component of learning experiences which should be objective-centred. In the formation of objectives-national, social and students' needs are considered. The evaluation of students is also made objective-centred. The curriculum is designed in view of the objectives of education. This type of curriculum is used in the present system of education.

Experience-centred Curriculum - In this type of curriculum main stress is given on the learner experiences. This type of curriculum is given by pragmatism. It is same as activity centred. The learning by doing device is used for this curriculum.

The experience-centred curriculum establishes the relationship between school and society. It helps in developing creative aspect of the students and develops the leadership qualities.

Correlated Curriculum - In this type of curriculum different subjects of school are taught by correlating each other. All the school subjects have same purpose. It assumes that knowledge is an unit. All the subjects should be taught with the help of correlated curriculum. It is difficult to design this type of curriculum. The content of different subjects should have same level of students comprehension.

Core Curriculum - This type of curriculum includes compulsory and optional course of study. The compulsory courses have to be studied by every student. Hence it is also termed as core-curriculum. The core-curriculum is related to student and social needs. It helps in preparing good citizen. The optimal courses are offered to student according to his need and interest. Thus, it is also learner-centred curriculum.

Integrated Curriculum - There has been a great controversy about the integration of the curriculum. Some people advocate that curriculum should achieve integration among different subject-areas. There are others who plead that the curriculum should steadily integrate the goals which a particular society sets before itself. There is a third group of those, who convincingly assert that the source of essential integration should be the expanding experiences and environment of the child. According to them, a model curriculum will be integrated into two dimensions. Needs and experiences of the child should lead to horizontal integration, the common purposes of education should integrate it vertically throughout to meet the needs of different children and their diverse environment. It is for this reason that a different curriculum is postulated for boys and girls for rural and urban areas and for the exceptionally bright and mentally retarded children.

Principles of Curriculum

The educational programme as whole is governed by the form of government. Our education system has been developed for democratic form of government. Thus, the curriculum development should be based on the following principles-

(1) It should be clearly understood that according to the best educational thought "the curriculum does not include only the academic subjects traditionally taught in the school but it includes the totality of experiences that a pupil receives through the manifold activities that go in the school, in the

classroom, library, laboratory, workshop playground, and in numerous informal contact between teachers and pupils." It should be objective-centred.

(2) There should be enough variety and flexibility in the curriculum to allow for individual differences and adaptation to individual needs and interests. Any attempt to impose on the student, subjects for which they have neither any liking nor interest, will be unproductive and ungainful. There are, of course, certain broad areas of knowledge skill, and appreciations with which all children must come into contact, and these must find a place in the curriculum.

(3) The curriculum must be vitally and organically related to community life, interpreting for the child its salient significant activities. In order to be effective and socially useful, it must be dynamic in nature and be suited to the needs and exigencies of new circumstances. Now, when the country is free and independent, it must reflect our new democratic ideology of a secular welfare state, which has opened equal opportunities for all its citizens. Our curriculum in secondary schools must prepare the youths of tomorrow with a sense of robust citizenship so that they make the best use of their educational opportunities. The curriculum framed must be capable of adaptation to local needs and life-situations of students. Today, when the whole world is also closely knit together, it must foster in them a sort of understanding.

(4) The curriculum should not be narrow but broad based in its scope. It should be designed to train the students not only for work but also for leisure. Sport activities should be introduced to realize this objective. It should also provides them with cultural pursuits and afford them better and more wholesome opportunities for the creative utilisation of their leisure.

(5) Our curriculum must present knowledge in an integrated way unified and correlated with the other branches of knowledge. Its numbers are isolated and uncoordinated watertight subject. Different subjects should be interrelated and within each subject, the content should be envisaged as far as possible as

"bread-fields." Units of teaching should be correlated better and functionally with the life and environment of pupils rather than with narrow bits of information.

(6) At the high school stage, there is still another criterion which will have to be observed. At the end of this stage, may students leave schools to enter life. So our curriculum must make provision for vocational and technical courses of study. Courses of technical, industrial, and agricultural base should be introduced. Along with this, a reasonable amount of general education should be given to make the students more informed and cultured. The opening of the multi-purpose schools now envisages to overcome this limitation of the curriculum. It will provide for certain core subject as well as certain optional subjects catering to the aptitudes and capacities of children.

(7) For the successful functioning of democracy, it is essential that people acquire social efficiency, and they learn to live co-operatively, contributing their mite to the welfare and betterment of the society of which they are integral parts. Curriculum, through its varied educational programmes, must afford our children concrete opportunities to live their lives democratically so that they learn to subordinate their personal interests to the over all good of the community.

Co-curriculum

Today, extra-curricular activities are not thought as a mere 'side-show' or 'extra' but they constitute an integral and inescapable part of the curriculum. The aim of education is not only to impart a series of facts pertaining to different subjects, but is to ensure the fullest and manifold development of the individuality of children, along with enabling them to acquire social efficiency so that they can live in group life, co-operatively and jointly. Co-curriculum activities are acquiring increasing significance in modern practices.

Teacher's Role

With the planning and formulating of the curriculum, the teacher should be closely associated.

Even an ideal curriculum falls in the hands of an unimaginative and lethargic teacher. A resourceful teacher will not treat the curriculum as an end in itself but will make in the basis of all-round education.

(1) To carry out the objectives and spirit underlying the curriculum. It is the main role of a teacher.
(2) To given equitable treatment to different subjects' areas and to finish them within the allotted time.
(3) To provide proper learning situations to children.
(4) To develop the curriculum from known to unknown and from concrete to abstract, and further to relate it to the physical and social environment of children.
(5) To secure interaction between the personalities of children and his own personality.
(6) To direct proper educative experiences among them-activities chosen should be well-selected and suitable for children.
(7) To seek the co-operation of the parents.
(8) To encourage active learning among them and to make children actual participants in the learning process.
(9) To ensure confidence in the pupils by affording them educative freedom and to let them function democratically.

Defects in Present System

The present curriculum has the following weakness or defects:

(1) It is not useful to attain the goals of education.
(2) It has neither served the interests of the students nor it is geared to the needs of the community.
(3) It is narrowly conceived.
(4) It is bookish and theoretical.
(5) It is unwieldy, bulky and overcrowded.
(6) It makes inadequate provision for practical activities.
(7) It does not cater to the needs and capacities of pupils.
(8) It is examination-dominated.
(9) It makes no provision for vocational and technical training.
(10) It does not prepare students for life.
(11) It merely prepares students for university education. It does not give them knowledge of fundamental concepts nor does it build proper and healthy attitudes in them.
(12) It has neither social relevance nor it has a graduated content within the class, or with the classes following or preceding it.
(13) It does not secure the all-round development of their personalities. The entire range of pupil's experiences and

capacities intellectual, physical, emotional, aesthetic and social-is not covered.

(14) Its basis is neither active nor productive.

(15) It is far removed form the real course of life. It is unable to adapt itself fruitfully to the exigencies of new circumstances.

(16) Its load is very heavy. Subjects to be studied are too many and their study is comparmentalised. In its organisation, there is no integrated approach.

(17) It does not make provision for meeting differences in abilities and aptitudes of different pupils. There is no diversification of courses to channelise and capitalise different interests.

(18) It does not afford any interaction between the personality of the teacher and his pupils.

(19) The curriculum, consequently, does not train pupils for life and for their prospective responsibilities.

(20) It does not consider the local need and requirement of local community.

Curriculum in Democracy

Our attention is now drawn towards curriculum planning and evolving methods of instruction for the realisation of the democratic ideal of education. It may be stated that for the attainment of democratic objectives, we shall have to revise our conceptions of curriculum and also evolve dynamic methods of teaching rather than to stick to rigid, stereotyped, and inflexible instructional procedures. Education, in a democracy, is for life adjustment and the traditional methods of organising the curriculum will not serve the needs of the individual and the society. In a broad sense today, "curriculum does not mean only the academic subjects traditionally taught in the schools, but it includes the totality of experiences that a pupil receives through the manifold activities that go on the school, in the classroom library, laboratory, workshop, playgrounds, and in the numerous informal contacts between teacher and pupils. In this sense, the whole life of the school becomes the curriculum which can touch the life of students at all points and help in the evolution of a balanced personality."

Formerly, the curriculum of our schools was narrowly conceived. It was confined merely to informational contents and its main emphasis was on isolated learning. With the change in the conditions of life and in the context of our existing socio-economic and political conditions, our curricula for children have to be broad-based to equip them to meet the challenges of the newly emerging social and political life. Today curriculum is regarded as pertaining to all such matters as the purpose of instruction. The methods of teaching, materials of instruction, organisation of instruction, selection of out of classroom activities, their organisation, programmes of social service, community survey, etc. "Curriculum programmes should be concerned with living and learning conditions in the school and in the community with living and learning conditions in the school and in and the interests of pupils. Education programmes should emphasis moral responsibility and prepare children for the complexities of modern life." Curriculum change "should be devoted to improve democratic processes, using what is known about learning and growth, working with community and using its resources in improving curriculum planning and teaching, evaluating the curriculum, the teaching and educating for international understanding and defence of freedom."

With the increase of enrolment in our schools and the enormity of the task of catering for the needs of children with different interest and abilities, it has become necessary to make provision for a diversified curriculum in schools. "The task of educating so many children at so many different educational levels with such a variety of abilities, needs, and goals, requires an completely different apporach. With this increase in a diversified school population, broader curricular programmes are needed. Emphasis should be placed on the total development of the person as being equally important as the intellectual and the academic. Such a curriculum will acknowledge that the social responsibilities of education must present situations where problems are relevant to the problems of living together, and where observation and information are calculated to develop social insight and interest."

With the changed conception of curriculum, the methods of instruction will also have to be changed. Teachers in a democracy will realise that only those methods will help them in handling the youths and initiating them into the activities of the society which are "psychologically and socially sound and raise the whole quality of their (children's) life." In an essentially dynamic and evolving society, rigid and fixed systems and methods will be misfit. Our methods of instruction, therefore, will have to be flexible and progressive so that boys and girls receive the necessary motivation to participate effectively in individual and group projects. The traditional methods and instruction will help little to raise the tone to the individual's life and social environment.

No phase of secondary education in a democracy is more significant than the selection and organisation of the curriculum and its presentation to pupil in a way that they get real stimulus and incentive for learning things. It is not possible within the limits of the chapter to analyse in detail the weaknesses of the curriculum of our secondary school today, which is largely bookish, rigid, examination-ridden, narrowly conceived, bulky, unwieldy, unbalanced, and too much academic, having little provision for vocational and technical proficiency.

The Principles : It is necessary to enumerate some general principles of curriculum development for school in democracy.

(1) Curriculum for schools in a democracy should include the totality of experiences that a child receives at school.

(2) It should be sufficiently broad-based and flexible enough to meet the needs of children of different interests and abilities.

(3) It should be vitally related of the needs to the community and should make full use of local resources.

(4) It should train children not only for work but also for leisure.

(5) It should be an integrated system, unified in approach, and correlated with the experiences of learners and their environment.

(6) It should be vocational and of technical base. Curriculum should have a balance between general and vocational education.

(7) It should be flexible and be not either standardised nor of a set pattern.

(8) It should maintain balance between the needs of learners and those of the society.

(9) There should be co-ordination among teaching learning and testing situation.

(10) The curriculum construction should be done in view of the educational objectives. It should be means, not end.

(11) The curriculum should take into consideration of local needs and requirements of the community.

Kothari Commission

The secondary education commission (1952) suggested the framework of curriculum. It had several defects maintained in the above paras. Therefore Kothari commission recommended curriculum from lower primary to higher secondary level.

Lower Primary Level - The commission has suggested curriculum from first class to fourth class. It should have language, maths, work experience, creative activities, health education and social-service subject. These subjects should be given due weightage.

Higher Primary Level - This level is considered from fifth class to seventh class. The curriculum for this level should include two languages, science, maths, social studies, craft and physical education subjects.

Lower Secondary Level - From class VIII to class X is known lower secondary level. The curriculum for this level was suggested by the commission that it should involve three languages, science, maths, geography, civics, work experience, physical education moral and value education subjects.

Higher Secondary Level - This is, also known as plus two level. It has recommended the following subjects :

(a) Two languages - one Indian and one foreign language.

(b) Any three subjects from the following :

Additional language, geography, history, economics, civics, sociology, psychology, physics, chemistry, biology, home-science and geology.

(c) Work experience and social service.

(d) Physical science,

(e) Craft and art, and

(f) Moral and value education.

The Utility

In planning of education curriculum development is an important and necessary activity. It has the following uses :

Realization of Education Objectives - An organization of education is based on the curriculum. The curriculum development is done in view to realize the objectives of education. Thus the curriculum is a means for achieving the educational objectives.

Proper Use of Time and Energy - It provides the guideline to the teachers as well as to students, what a teacher has to teach and the students have to learn.

Acquisition of Knowledge - The curriculum is the means for acquiring knowledge. Actually human knowledge is one but is divided into subjects for the convenience and organization point of view. Thus the curriculum is designed for the different subjects.

Determining the Structure of the Content - Every subject content has its wide structure which is to be taught from lower level to the higher level. Thus, the main task of curriculum development is to determine structure of content for a particular stage of teaching. Thus, the curricula of different subjects are designed from primary level to university level.

Development of Personality - The curriculum is also important and significant for personality development of the student. The curriculum is designed which helps in developing the good qualities of the students. It helps in developing physical, social and moral qualities of the learners.

Preparation of Textbooks - The curriculum provides the guideline and bases for preparing text-books for the use of students and subject teacher. If the curriculum is changed or modified, the test books are also changed. A good text book has wide coverage of curriculum-content of a subject.

Conducting Examination - Our education is examination-centred. The students have forces to obtain good mark in the examination. Thus examination papers are prepared as per curriculum of the subject senility students also prepare the content for the examination. Thus, curriculum is basis of teaching, learning and testing.

Organizing Teaching-Learning Situations - The teaching-learning situations are organized in view to the curriculum. Teaching work is also assigned with to help of the curriculum.

Decision about Instructional Methods - The instructional methods are selected and used inview of the curricular. The same content is taught from memory to reflective level. It may be teacher-centred or learner-centred instruction.

Development of Knowledge, Skills and Attitude - The nature of curriculum provides the basis for developing knowledge, skills, attitude and creative ability. It also helps in developing leadership qualities.

QUESTIONS

1. Define the term curriculum and enumerate its characteristics. Explain the cyclic process of curriculum.
2. Enumerated the objectives of curriculum and indicate its basic elements and their roles.
3. Indicate the need and importance of curriculum. Point out factors affecting curriculum development.
4. Give the types of curriculum and indicate the defects of present curriculum. Indicate the principles of curriculum development in democracy.
5. Describe the recommendations of Kothari commission for the curricula for the various stage of education and indicate the scope of curriculum.

9

The Models

The Curriculum models are very useful for teachers for planning and organizing educational process. The can make its use in the transaction of curriculum and preparing an outline for guiding students' activities and developing instructional procedure for realizing objectives.

Curriculum models are just as instructional design. It brings competency in educational process and teaching learning. It is the best way to proceed in formulating theories of teaching learning and instruction is to begin with what is known about learning and instruction. Teaching models are the basis of teaching theories. Curriculum models and approach are very close to models and approaches to teaching. In the second part of the chapter some model of curriculum are provided. The following are the main models of curriculum.

1. Hilda Taba Models of Curriculum
2. Saran Model of Curriculum
3. Mukhopadhayaya Model of Curriculum

Hilda Taba Models

Hilda Taba has developed Inductive Teaching Model. This model provides the backbone to social studies curriculum.

Focus: The main focus of this model is to develop the mental abilities and gives emphasis on concept formation. This involves cognitive tasks in concept formation.

Syntax: The teaching is organized in nine phases. The first three phases are concerned with the concepts formation by involving enumeration, grouping and labelling categories. The second three phases are related to the interpretation of data by identifying relationship, explaining relationship and drawing inferences. The last three phases are concerned with an application of principles by hypothesizing, explaining and verifying the hypothesis.

Social System: In the all nine phases, the classroom climate is conductive to learning and cooperative. A good deal of freedom should be given for pupil-activities. The teacher is usually the controller and initiator of information. The teaching activities are arranged in a logical sequence in advance.

Support System: The teacher's job is to help the students in dealing with more complex data and information. The teacher has to encourage the student in processing the data. It has been basically designed to develop thinking capacity. A particular mental task and cognitive task require specific strategy to improve thinking.

Classroom Application: Taba has designed the model to create inductive thinking among learners. It helps to organize social studies curriculum so that cognitive, process may be facilitated. The learning experiences are the basis of information to arrange the content in an effective sequence. The first three phases are useful in dealing with elementary classes and the last three phases are useful for higher especially for science and language curriculum.

Comprehensible Evaluation : Hilda Taba has developed teaching model as well as curriculum model. This curriculum model is based on the evaluation concept. This concept is given by B.S. Bloom who has also defined the term evaluation.

"Evaluation is the process of gathering and interpreting evidence on the changes in behaviour of all the students as they progress through school."

B.S. Bloom has introduced the concept of evaluation in the context of examination refer. He made educational process objective centred and given three steps - (1) Educational objectives (2) Learning experiences and (3) Change of behaviour. The curriculum plays significant role in developing learning experience. The whole educational process is based on the curriculum which is designed for bringing desirable change in the behaviour of the learner.

An evaluation plays significant role in designing the outline of the curriculum. Hilda Taba has given four steps for curriculum construction—

1. Identification of objectives.
2. Evidences for teaching-learning operation.
3. Evidences on factors affecting learning.
4. Evidences on pupil behaviour pertaining to objectives.

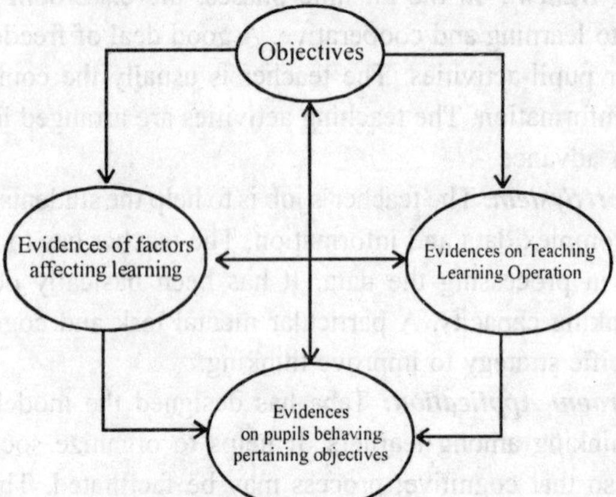

Comprehensive Evaluation Curriculum Models
[Hilda Taba]

The details of these steps have been given in following paras.

Step 1: The curriculum is evaluated in the light of educational objectives identified for preparing learning experiences. These objectives include-cognitive affective phychomotor creativity and perceptions. The evidences are collected for the identification of the objectives.

Step 2: Under this step appropriate teaching method, teaching technique and audio-visual aids are used for generating appropriate learning situations, so that desirable objectives can be achieved. Evidences are collected for the learning experience.

Step 3: The evidences are collected for teaching-learning operations such as motivation reinforcement which help in learning of the student. This factors influences the learning exercise. Audio-visual aids make learning experiences interesting. The students do not memorize the content.

Step 4: The utility of the curriculum is evaluated on the basis of pupil change of behaviour. The change of behaviours are evidences for realizing the education objectives. The examination system is objectives centred. It is both qualitative and quantitative. An attempted is made to assess the total change of behaviour.

These four steps, as suggested by Hilda Taba, are used in curriculum construction or developing the outline of the curriculum. He has suggested the following four stages for this purpose i.e., for curriculum development :

Stage 1: Deciding the kinds of evaluation data needed.

Stage 2: Selecting or constructing the needed instruments and procedure.

Stage 3: Analysing and interpreting the data to develop the hypothesis regarding needed change.

Stage 4: Converting hypothesis into action.

Hilda Taba curriculum model is virtually on the evaluation approach of B.S. Bloom designed for examination reform.

On the basis of evidences collected in different stages are used to diagnose the weaknesses of the curriculum. These evidences are further used for formulating hypotheses. The structure of the curriculum is modified on the basis of verification of the hypotheses. Thus an empirical approach is used for the curriculum development. The hypotheses indicate the type of modification needed in curriculum development.

The above steps and stages are used in a sequence. This model of curriculum is highly empirical. The modification is done on the basis of evidences.

Evaluation Model

This model of curriculum has been developed in Indian conductions. This model is similar to Hilda Taba model of curriculum. This model is also based on B.S. Bloom evaluation approach. The term evaluation is used in this model as defined by B.S. Bloom. Under this model evidences and data are collected and these are interpreted in the light of curriculum.

The learning process is based on teaching. The relationship is established between teaching and learning, both are objective-centred. The teaching activities are performed with the help of content to be taught. Thus there are two stages of curriculum development process. These stages are divided into five steps.

Stage I: Curriculum Development (Phase 1)

Step 1: Identification Initial objectives .

Step 2: Writing specific objectives, Organization of content and Instruction aids, Instructional procedure to be decided.

Step 3: Use of available material in the school by the student or for teaching learning situations.

Stage II: Curriculum Development (Phase 2)

Step 4: Sources of development and teacher experience are used for the modification of curriculum.

Step 5: Continuous observation and evaluation of teaching learning activities. To make this process cyclic.

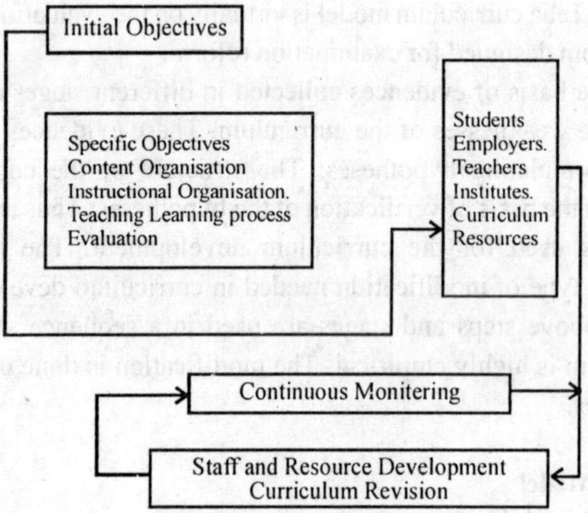

Models of Curriculum Evaluation
[Mukhopadhaya]

The details of the steps have been provided in following paragraphs :

In the first step needs of the students are identified. The specific objectives are identified and written in behavioural terms. These may be cognitive, affective, phychomotor and physical. The taxonomy of educational objectives is used for this purpose. The level of teaching is also decided at memory level, understanding level and reflective level.

In the second step specification is done for the instructional procedure. The structure of the content is also developed for organization teaching activities and creating learning experiences for bringing variable behavioural change in the students.

Third step includes all the available sources and material in school so that the available sources can be used in learning experience. The content is the basis for providing learning experiences or creating learning instruction. The sources of school and experiences of teachers play significant role in curriculum development.

Fourth step makes use of above informations in the modification and improvement in the curriculum. This requires continuous observation and evaluation. Evaluation is also objective centred and criterion-test is used for this purpose. The collected data are interpreted in the light of the objectives. The process is helpful to diagnose the weaknesses of curriculum.

Fifth step provides the basis for using cyclic process of curriculum development. It needs continuous evaluation and observation of the activities organised in school. The significance and utility the sources and material are also evaluated.

Under this model the above stages and steps are used continuously to make the curriculum upto date. Thus this model makes use of the cycilc process.

Saran Model

This model was developed by *Y. Saran* in 1976. It is most popular and commonly used model of curriculum. It was developed through system analysis approach which is very scientific and empirical. It is based on technological components. The model is influenced by instructional designs. The main emphasis is given on specific or behavioural objectives. The input, process and output are analysed, modified and improved. It has the following assumptions :

Assumptions : The following are the main assumptions

(1) No curriculum is complete and perfect in itself. Every curriculum needs improvement and modification.

(2) New curriculum is also not complete in itself. Therefore it is essential to analyse the old or traditional curriculum to diagnose its weaknesses which can be improved and modified. Thus, curriculum development should be based on system analysis which is most practical and effective approach.

(3) All the three aspects, input, process and out-put help in evolving an effective model of curriculum.

Aspects of Curriculum Model: It has three main aspects (1) Input (2) Process and (3) Output. The main stress is given on output aspect to diagnose and evaluate the workability of the curriculum system. The details of these aspects have been provided in the following paras.

Curriculum Model As Onput

Input	*Process*	*Output*
Expertise	Formulation	Curriculum
Needs	of Objectives	Development
Material Resources	Selection of Content	

Input Aspect: This aspect has been divided into three components (a) Sources of content, need and views of the subject experts (b) Selection of content and formulating objectives (c) Deveiopment of the format of the curriculum. In the first component sources of content are located with the help of subject experts. The need of the content is also emphasized by subject experts.

The objectives are identified on the basis of need and structure of the content. The form of content is decided on the basis of objectives. There is a taxonomy of objectives in each domain. The objectives and subject content are employed in curriculum construction.

Output Aspect: Input and output aspects are equally important in curriculum construction. The curriculum is the basis for preparing instructional procedure and organizing learning experiences. The process aspect is a link or bridge between input and output aspects of educational process; the output aspect includes several factors along with the evaluation. The input and process aspects are decided on the basis of evaluation or out-put of the evaluation is always objective-centred and criterion referenced task are used. The evidences and data are interpreted in the light of objectives whether these could be achieved or not. It also functions as feedback. The causes of weakness or not achieving objectives are identified for improving the whole system i.e. input, process and output. The diagnosis is also the main function of evaluation. It provides a guideline for improving the curriculum. Thus, system analysis is used in the model of curriculum.

On the basis of input, process and output analysis, the steps are identified for curriculum development.

Procedure for Development

The following nine steps are used in input process and output aspects :

1. Survey is done for need assessment.
2. Assessment is done for future needs of the society and students.
3. Identification of objectives (input aspect).
4. Writing objectives in behavioural terms i.e. specification.
5. Selection of content with the help of experts of the subjects.
6. Designing or preparing evaluation system (output aspect).
7. Resources of development of curriculum.
8. Empirical tryout of new model of curriculum to examine its workability.
9. Review of system analysis.

The main emphasis is given on the objectives in this model of curriculum. It is based on objective-centred approach of curriculum. The details of these steps have been given in the following paras.

Survey for need Assessment: There are several basis for need assessment, most of these have been provided in the earlier chapters of this book. Some important basis are as follows.

(1) Philosophical (2) Sociological (3) Psychological (4) Scientific (5) Political (6) National needs (7) Students needs and (8) Cultural needs are surveyed. Social change, economic and technological changes should also be taken for need assessment. The new tendencies of the society and social philosophy should also be considered. It requires the survey techniques, such as questionnaire, interview and observations. The need assessment should be explored objectively. It is the foundation of curriculum and education.

Assessment of Future Needs: The education and curriculum are planned for future needs of society as well as nation. Education is the creator of the future society. It prepares the future citizens. Education and curriculum always plan and prepare for future life. Therefore, future needs of the society, nation and students should be explored through various sources. National Policy of Education (1986) was prepared for preparing students for the 21st century.

For example the students are entered into primary school, will come out after 20 years. We have to educate the child of future needs after 20 years. It is the most difficult task to assess the future needs. It includes the following aspects :

(a) Social and national future needs.
(b) Students' future needs.
(c) Trend of changes of tendencies.
(d) Technological advances.
(e) Advancement of knowledge.

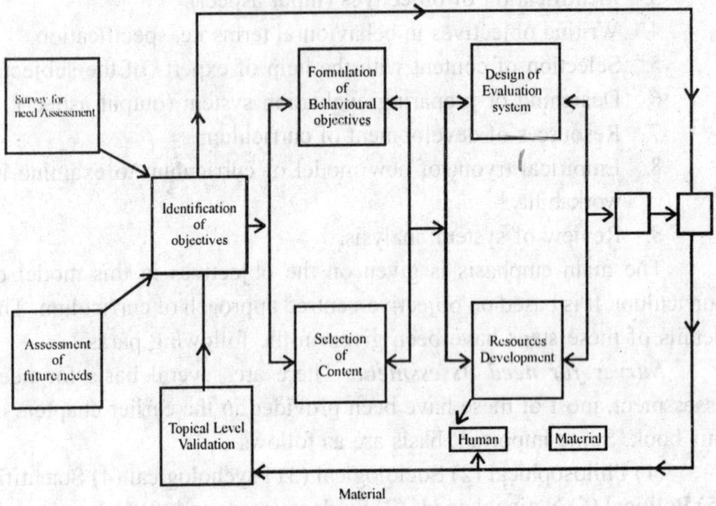

Saran Curriculum Model
[By Analysis System]

The expert opinions in this context are essential. The facts are considered in identifying the objectives.

Formulation of Specific or Behavioural Objectives: The output is assessed in terms of change of behaviour. The child growth and development is important factor. Teacher generates the situations for providing learning experiences. The objectives are within by employing Robert Mager techniques. Measurement and evaluation become easier task. Criterion-referenced tests are used for assessing change of behaviour.

Selection of Content: Generally a content structure is very broad. The same content is taught at different levels of education. The same content is used from memory to reflective level teaching. The structure of content is based on the objectives and comprehension level of the students. The content is means to realize the objectives.

Designing the Evaluation System: The significance of curriculum requires the evaluation of learning outcomes. There are two purposes of evaluation—

(a) Decision about the realization of objectives.

(b) Diagnose the weakness, because objectives could not be achieved.

The second function of evaluation provides the basis for diagnosis and improving the curriculum or subject-content. The evaluation should be objective-centred rather than content-centred. The criterion referenced tests should be used. The obtained evidences should be interpreted in the light of the objectives.

Resources Development: In developing and modifying the curriculum, available means and resources in the schools should be taken into consideration. Curriculum of agriculture requires agricultural lands. Science curriculum needs laboratory, library and reading room literature. These resources should be taken into consideration while developing curriculum for specific subject-centres.

Trial of New Curriculum: The newly designed curriculum should be tried out to assess the workability and utility. The assessment can be done empirically as well as logically. The experts opinions can also be collected about the new curriculum. The system analysis technique should be used for this purpose. The final form of curriculum should be based on the try out, both logically and empirically. The objectives should be kept in mind during try out process. The curriculum can be further improved and modified the basis of tryout evidence.

Review of System Analysis: The above steps and activities are reviewed which provide the direction for the improvement. Thus, there is need for curriculum development to make it uptodate. Final form should be designed on the basis of experiences, tryout and experts opinions.

Saran model of curriculum is prepared by employing above steps and activities. It is a practical model of curriculum. The scientific approach system analysis is used for designing the model curriculum ; it is very broad and comprehensive model of curriculum.

Criteria for Evaluation

The review about literature related to curriculum indicates that there are four major criteria for assessing the workability of the curriculum.

Subject-Content: In the curriculum, various subjects are included such as—Hindi, English, Sanskrit, History, Geography, Social Science, Physical Sciences, Bio-Science, Home science, Maths, Economics, Psychology, Sociology, Physical education Art, and Drawing etc. The structure of content of these subjects is determined for the curriculum development.

Experiences: The curriculum provides the following type of experiences to the students, social, historical, geographical (time and place sense), physical, political, civics senses, religious, spiritual and reactive experiences, expression of ideas facts and events.

Skills: Some curriculum provides the situations for developing skills or psychomotor actives- languages reading writing. Speaking, observations, perception use of different type instrument in the workshops and field works communication skills, craft work. Verbal and non-verbal communication skills. It is related to psychomotor objectives.

Attitude and Values: This type of curriculum provides the experiences for developing affective domain of the learners. The feeling, beliefs, attitudes and values are developed. It develops self confidence, honesty, sensitivity sincerity, morality, objectivity, character and adjustment.

These factors are given due weightage in good curriculum. These factors are related to cognitive, affective and pshcyomotor domains.

QUESTIONS

1. Enumerate the main models of curriculum.
2. Indicate the stages and steps of Saran model of curriculum.
3. Describe the role of evaluation approach in designing models of curriculum.

10

Various Researches

The concept of teaching, levels of teaching models of teaching and learning, strategies of teaching provide theoretical knowledge of teaching to teachers and pupil-teachers. But this awareness of teaching does not orient the pupil teachers how to plan and organize their teaching and about managing teaching-learning. This knowledge and understanding is very essential during the training period of understanding and skill for managing teaching-learning process effectively. The training institutions are providing knowledge about Herbartian steps of teaching: Preparation and Presentation. Herbartian approach of teaching gives too much emphasis on presentation but it does not focus on the purpose and goals of teaching, while teaching is considered as purposeful activity. Teaching is organized to achieve some specific goals of education. Now, the present approach of teaching gives main emphasis on objectives.

I.K. Davies considers that teaching is a noble profession. He has given a new concept *Managing teaching-learning* in the field of education. The concept provides the practical steps for planning and organizing teaching activities in classroom situations. The pupil-teacher can make use of these steps in organizing his classroom teaching.

Davies has borrowed this concept of managing teaching-learning from other human organizations. This chapter deals with the origin source and steps of managing teaching-learning process.

The Meaning

The human beings have tried hard to make their lives good. They have made maximum use of their resources to overcome their problems and difficulties. The appropriate use of means and resources, is termed as 'Organization.' "The use of means and resources for realizing the specific objectives is known as organization." These main techniques are used in an organization—

1. To establish the integration between means and resources,
2. To classify the activities and processes, and
3. To determine the hierarchy between rights and duties.

Scott has also defined the term organization. He assumes that ultimate objective of an organization is to resolve or minimize the conflict.

The organization reduces the value and importance of a thing or person which creates hindrance in success of organization. An effective organization establishes the stability and reduces the instability of the situation. A prediction can be made about the actual outcome on the basis of an organization. For example, text books, curriculum, and programmed instruction texts are designed to achieve the specific learning objectives. But these things provide minimum information about internal structure of the content and behaviour structure of the students. Teaching technology gives main emphasis to understand and to determine these structures.

The management and industry are highly influenced by stability, prediction and structural aspects of a concept of an organization. This type of thinking is very useful or understanding the concept of educational technology. A prediction can be made about educational outcome and appropriate tactics may be selected for generating the desired learning structures. A stability can be maintained in teaching learning process.

The concept of organization is directly related to human beings. Thus, the nature of man has influenced the concept of organization. The nature of man be understood with the help of the following assumptions:

Human Nature

March and Sinion (1958) have worked on industrial management and they have described the theories of organization. They have explained three they are :

1. Classical Theory of Organization: (Task-centred).
2. Human Relation Theory Organization (Relationship centred).
3. Modern Theory of Organization (Task and Relationship centred).

The nature and assumptions of these theories have been described in the following paragraphs.

Classical Theory : The main assumption regarding human nature is that the members of an organization have the capacity to work and to carry out the orders. But they have not a capacity to initiate and take decision about the problem of organization. They can not influence the working system of the organization. They work like a machine. It is task-centred theory of organization.

This theory has influenced educational system. According to this theory, the teacher controls all activities of the students. The students are the passive listeners in classroom teaching and they follow the instruction of the teacher. Teaching is task-centred and teacher-centred. The main emphasis is given on presentation.

The knowledge and skill are developed in the interest of organization. No opportunity is provided to develop the student's abilities. Thus, the lower type objectives may be achieved by this type organization.

The major limitation of this theory is that it does not consider the interests, attitudes, and values of the members of the organization, while it is very essential for effective functioning of any organization.

Human Relation Theory : It is relationship-centred theory of organization. This theory is based upon the assumption that members of an organization bring their interests, feelings, attitudes, values and goals. Therefore, due weightage should be given in organization to their feelings. Generally there is difference between goals of organization and goals of members. An organization should encourage and reinforce the behaviour of the members. The real organizational behaviour requires the level of attitude and morale of the members.

The present system of training and education is highly influenced with the relationship-centred theory of organization. This theory has been formulated against the classical theory of organization. The system of training and education does not consider the individual variation of the students in the classical organization theory but this theory considers the students, abilities, attitudes, interests and feelings. This may be helpful in the all-round development of the students. The teacher has to play several roles: friend, guide and counsellor. Teacher's main duty is to give an opportunity to students to participate and he has to encourage and reinforce them. There should be equal participation between teacher and pupils in teaching-learning-situation. The teaching process make use of maximum use of teaching aids. The learning is based upon the theory of behaviour sciences. The structure of content and its sequence is so arranged that they facilitate students' learning. It does not stress on role memory learning. It does stress on more meaningful activities which are performed in teaching- leaning process, e.g., project work, discovery games and sports etc.

The classical and human relation theories are contradictory to one another and they have distinct assumptions regarding human nature. There is also a third theory which functions as a bridge between the two.

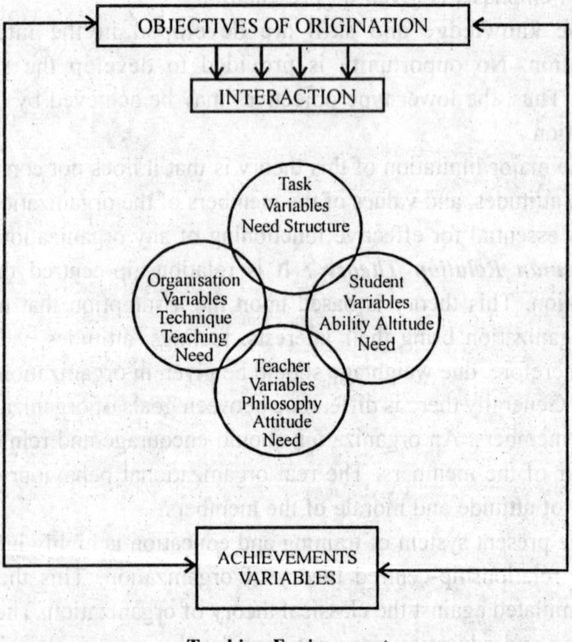

Teaching-Environment

Modern Theory : It is task and relationship-centred theory of organization. It may be termed as eclectic theory of organization. It gives emphasis on both task as well as human relation of the members of an organization. This theory is based upon the assumption that members of an organization have the capacity for problem-solving and taking decision. The behaviour of an organization is based upon the perception and thinking system of the members.

These three theories are based upon the human nature, therefore, they are not actually contradictory to one another but supplementary to one another. These have different goals. These theories have been formulated from industrial and administrative organization point of view but they are applied in education system. The education is child-centred. This has been illustrated with the help of the diagram.

According to this theory, education is objective-centred. In planning the teaching and training tasks, need of students and objectives are considered. The teachers make efforts of integrate students variables, task considered. The teachers make efforts to integrate students variables, task variables and organization's variables. This results in students performance.

The theory concerns with independent study, instruction system, structure of the instruction and instructional technology. According to Davies, it is an aspect of educational technology. It is called third educational technology. The teaching and training are based upon system approach.

Concept of Teaching-Learning

Davies and Thomas have given the new concept of management of teaching-learning. This concept is based upon modern theory of organization. It is task and relationship-centred. This has two type of teaching activities—

First activity is to organize teaching-learning situations and second activity is to perform teaching-learning tasks. Betrand Russel has pointed out these two teaching activities in the following manner—

"First altering the position of matter at or near the earth's surface, relative to other such matter; second is to tell other people to do so."

Davies calls the teacher as a manager because he has to organise teaching activities first, and then he has to perform these activities in the teaching process. He has described the four major activities which he performs in four steps: Step I-Planning, Step II-Organizing, Step III-Leading, and Step IV-Controlling or Evaluating. The design of teaching-learning system is prepared with the help of these steps. These steps include the following activities—

1. Analysis of the whole system.
2. Task analysis.
3. Entering behaviours the learner.
4. Specification of knowledge, skills and attitudes of the students.
5. Identifying the students' needs.
6. Formulation of learning objectives.
7. Organizing learning resources.
8. Selecting appropriate teaching strategies.
9. Encouraging and motivating students' activities.
10. Evaluation of teaching system.
11. Learning and teaching system.
12. Observing the learning system.
13. Modification in teaching- learning system.
14. Planning for the criterion test, and
15. Construction of criterion test.

These activities can be put under four steps of teaching-learning process.

First Step: Planning: Before going to the classroom, teachers analyse the content or topic into its elements which are arranged in logical sequence. He formulates his teaching objectives in behavioural terms. He selects the appropriate teaching strategies. This step consists of 1, 2, 3, 4, 5, 6, 14 and 15 activities of teaching-learning process as given above. Teacher must have knowledge and skill about these activities, then he may be able to solve the problems of learning system and can make his teaching effective. The planning is an important step of managing teaching-learning.

Second Step: Organizing: This is the second step of managing teaching-learning process. The learning sources and organized by the teacher so that he can achieve the objective successfully. The effective and economical resources are used. In this step learning environment and learning structures are generated by the teacher for realizing the learning objectives. The teacher has to take decision about teaching strategies, teaching aids and tactics of teaching. In this way, this step includes two major activities: I. organizing learning resources and II. learning and teaching system. This step requires the training of teaching skills and practising teaching skills, then the teacher can make his teaching effective. The main problem of this step is to integrate teaching and learning resources.

Third Step: Leading: The teacher's task is to tie the students-activities. In managing teaching-learning process, the teacher encourages and praises the students activities and behaviour so that they can learn by being active and learning objectives can be achieved. Leading is an individual activity. The most important aspect is that how a teacher motivates his students in leaning process. The main task of teacher is to encourage, to guide and to observe the students' activities so that the learning objective may be achieved.

The leading step involves various type of instructions and teaching tactics. The appropriate teaching tactics are selected by considering the learning situations. The teacher has to make use of his imagination, creativity and experiences.

In this way the leading step includes: activities I. Selecting appropriate teaching strategies and II. Encouraging and motivating the students behaviour activities. The teacher should have practical knowledge and understanding about the theory of motivation and techniques of motivation. The students needs are considered about taking decision for strategy of teaching and technique of motivation.

Fourth Step: Controlling: Controlling is also the duty of a teacher. Teaching is incomplete without this step. The teacher takes decision about the success of organizing and leading steps that how far these activities of teaching can be achieved, the learning-objectives. If they can not achieve the objectives successfully the teacher has to revise or modify the activities of these steps and has to apply again in teaching process.

This step includes: activities 10- evaluation of teaching system, 12 observing the learning system and 13-modifying the teaching-learning system. This step requires practical knowledge of measurement and evaluation strategies. Only then the teacher evaluate the workability of organizing and leading activities. He should have the knowledge and skill for developing the criterion test.

Davies has given four steps of 'managing teaching learning system' which include the following activities.

Step	*Activities*
I Planning	1 System Analysis
	2 Task Analysis.
	3. Entering behaviour.
	4. Specification of knowledge, skills and attitudes.
	5. Identification of needs.
	6. Formulation of objectives.
	7. Criterion test.
	8. Construction of criterion test.
II Organizing	1. Organizing learning resources.
	2. Implementing teaching activities.
III Leading	1. Selecting Communi strategies.
IV Controlling	1. Evaluation of teaching system.
	2. Observing learning system.
	3. Modification in teaching system.

John P. Dececco has designed his book 'The Psychology of Learning and Instruction': 'Educational Psychology' on Glaser's 'Basic Model of Teaching'. The chapters of this book deal with the activities involved in the above four steps. Similarly Davies has also written his book 'Management of Learning', which provides the detailed description of the four steps of the concept of 'Managing Teaching-Learning'.

The paradigms of four steps of Davies provide practical outline of organizing teaching activities for classroom. The teacher can easily use these steps for teaching different subject to realize the different objectives of learning. This model is more practical for classroom teaching than Glaser's Basic model of teaching. The Basic Model of teaching is highly theoretical in nature.

Robert Glasser' (1962) has developed a 'Basic Model of Teaching' which also consists of four steps. These steps are quite similar and involve the following activities:

Step	***Activities***
I Instructional Objectives	1. Formulation of instructional objectives.
	2. Preparation-list of activities.
	3. Task analysis.
II Entering Behaviour	1. Defining entering behaviour.
	2. The development and Measurement of intelligence.
	3. Identification of motivation level.
	4. Identifying social and learning conditions.
III Instructional procedure	1. Determining the basic learning conditions.
	2. Establishing integration between teaching and learning activities.
	3. Selection of teaching principles.
	4. Solution for teaching problems.
IV Performance Assessment	1. Determining criterion behaviour.
	2. Construction of criterion test.
	3. Evaluation of the characteristics of criterion test.
	4. Providing the feedback to I, II, II steps.

The Transaction

The term curriculum development is most popular while *Transaction of Curriculum* is very recent concept introduced in education. The transaction of curriculum means 'management of curriculum; I.K. Davies has used the term managing teaching-learning and teacher is a manager. Davies approach has initiated and introduced the term 'Management' in education process.

The Definition

The term management has beep defined by the experts of other disciplines e.g. industry, business and politics etc. The following definition is very close to the concept of Management of curriculum :

"Management refers to conscious preference from variety of alternative plus proposals and further more that such choices involve purposeful commitment to recognize and derived objectives. Management employs strategies to achieve the objectives.

It is a functional definition of management which indicates the various activities which are performed under the transaction of curriculum.

(1) Planning a Curriculum.

(2) Formulating Educational Objectives.

(3) Organizing the Tasks.

(4) Employing Strategies and Techniques.

(5) Selecting and Appointing Workers.

(6) Executing and Coordinating among works.

(7) Evaluating and Controlling the Tasks.

(8) Encouraging and Providing Feedback.

This concept relates management technology and broad outline is developed under 'Instruction design'. The basis of 'management' involves the following five activities: 1. Planning 2. Organization 3. Administration or Execution 4. Guiding 5. Controlling or Feedback. ,

Education is a system which has various sub-systems. It is assumed that no system is perfect. Therefore, every system or sub-system needs improvement or development. The term 'curriculum development' refers the improvement in the curriculum.

There are various approaches which have been used in educational management. The most popular approach is evaluation approach which is designed by B.S. Bloom. He considers that education is tri-polar process—

(1) Education objectives (2) Learning experiences and (3) Change of behaviours (evaluation).

The most important component of 'Learning experiences is the curriculum or subject content. It is a cyclic process in view of improving the system of education so that objectives can be realized.

Similarly I.K. Davies has designed and introduced 'Managing Teaching-Learning Approach' which involves four steps in educational process—

(1) Planning of Teaching,

(2) Organizing Teaching,

(3) Leading of Teaching, and

(4) Controlling of Teaching.

The last step in known as 'controlling teaching'. It means evaluation of objectives which provides the feedback for improving these steps. The planning includes managing curriculum and implementing curriculum. The transaction curriculum means the basic model of curriculum which depends on the objectives of education.

The Bases

The transaction of curriculum is the commitment for realizing desired objectives of education. The objectives are based on various considerations and factors. The same considerations are equally important in planning or deciding the basic structure of curriculums. The following are the bases of transaction of curriculum—

1. Social philosophy of the society.
2. National needs or State needs.
3. Nature of course of study.
4. Type of examination system.
5. Form of the government.
6. Theory and assumptions of human organization.
7. Growth and development stage of students.
8. Recommendations of national commissions and committees of education.

The above basis of curriculum management and educational objectives are theoretical and practical. The last basis is more practical in transaction of curriculum. After independence several commission and committees have been established in Education-University education commission 1949, Secondary education commission (1952), National commission of education (1964-66) and National Policy of education (1986) etc. These commissions have given the recommendations for managing curriculum or courses of study for different stages.

Role of the Board

In our country national commission and committees have been established and these have given recommendations for education at national level. But we do not have national system of education. Education is on the state list. Every state of our country has its own system of education and state board of education. It is the responsibility of state board of education (SBE) to plan and prepare curriculum or courses of study. The state university and central university have the academic autonomy plan and prepare courses of study for degree and post graduate level for various subjects. There are some boards of education such as CBSE (Central Board of School Education) and ICSE (Indian Council of School Education). These boards plan and prepare the courses of study for school and + 2 level.

Management or Transaction of curriculum is a broad concept which includes the courses of study at school and + 2 level for different subjects for different stages pre-primary, primary, secondary and higher secondary. It is the function of CBSE board, ICSE Board, and State Boards of education.

Similarly for degree and postgraduate level courses of study are planned and prepared by the board of studies of universities. The following are the agencies which plan and prepare or manage curriculum.

1. State Board of Education at State level.
2. CBSE Board of Education at National Level.
3. ICSE Board of Education at National level.
4. Universities Board of Studies for higher education.

Technical and vocational courses are managed by the councils. National council of teacher-education has been functioning since 1995 and managing courses and programmes for teacher-education i.e. B.Ed. and M.Ed. courses of study. Some of such councils are mentioned which are managing courses and programmes for technical courses—

1. N.C.T.E - National Council of Teacher-Education.
2. The Council of Medical Sciences i.e. for MBBS, MD and MS at National level.
3. ICSR and IARI Social Science and Agriculture Science.
4. The Law Council for LL.B. and LL.M.
5. The Council of Engineering Science B.E.; M,E. B.Tech, M.Tech.
6. National Council of Educational Research and training (NCERT).

Transaction of curriculum concerns with broad area of courses of study of different disciplines. There are boards of education at State and National level. The boards study at university level. There are councils for technical and vocational courses of study and specific programmes.

Curriculum Development

Curriculum development is the practical aspect of management of curriculum. The basic assumption of management concept is that no system is perfect. Therefore, there is the need to improve and modify the system empirically. Transaction of curriculum is an aspect of instructional designs. Curriculum development is an approach to 'Curriculum Management. It is also known cyclic process of four steps or activities—objectives, instructional method, evaluation and feedback. It is applied for a specific courses study for specific stage.

The difference between transaction and development of curriculum can be clarified with the help of an example as follows.

Human knowledge is increasing very rapidly. It becomes double within ten years duration in every field of study. In addition to it new fields of knowledge are emerging. The present age is of computer. The new field of computer science (theoretical) and computer application (practical) have evolved during recent years. Thus, it becomes new courses of study. The new courses are managed as transaction of curriculum of computer science in two forms.

Computer-Courses of Study

1. Computer Science	2. Computer Application
B.Sc. Computer	B.C.A.
M.Sc. Computer	M.C.A.
(Theoretical)	(Application)

The content of computer has been managed from school level to university level. The school level computer courses are managed, planned and prepared by CBSE and ICSE boards. The university level computer courses and computer application have been planned and prepared by the board of study of computer discipline at graduate and post graduate level. Every university has its own courses of study. Curriculum development is a technique to improve and modify the courses for future requirements. Education is always for future which is designed by curriculum development technique. It has the empirical basis to assess whether objectives could be realized or not.

NCTE was planned and prepared (Transaction of Curriculum) in 1995. After two years it was realized that it needed modification and improvement. NCTE revised the B.Ed. courses in 1997 which is known as curriculum development. The difference between curriculum transaction and curriculum development has been summarized in tabular form.

Transaction and Development of Curriculum

Curriculum Transaction	*Curriculum Development*
1. It is broad concept and area of curriculum.	1. It is specific or narrow concept of curriculum.
2. Management of curriculum is done at initial stage or introduction of new courses. It is school stages and higher levels.	2. Curriculum development is a cyclic process which is used for improving and modifying the courses at particular state or level.
3. Management of curriculum employs the following steps– (1) Planning (2) Organizing (3) Administering (4) Guiding and (5) Controlling.	3. It is a cyclic process, uses the following four steps– (a) Objectives, (b) Instructional methods, (c) Evaluation, and (d) Feedback.
4. Transaction of curriculum is much more difficult task because it involves planning and preparing the course of discipline at school and university level.	4. It is used for specific course for specific stage. Relatively it is easy and simple task.
5. Curriculum management is done by boards of study and boards of education. There are councils in some discipline which plan and control. At university level there are boards of studies for different subjects.	5. Curriculum development is done by board of studies. The new courses and content are also included in revised curriculum on the basis of try out the new courses.
6. It is based on theoretical aspect and practical.	6. It is a continued process i.e. practical aspect of curriculum.

Research in Curriculum

Ever since Independence, India has been making progress in the different are as of life. In the field of education, different commissions and committees were set up to improve upon the affairs. Research studies have also been conducted to renovate the system of education. But much needs to be done. A sort of revolutionary upheaval is required. Though about five decades have lapsed but still we are not upto the mark as far as school curriculum and text-books are concerned. We have still rigidity dominating the curriculum.

The curriculum development in India is not based on empirical research findings. Undoubtedly in free India, the need for a central agency to undertake research in the area of curriculum was felt. The National Institute of Basic Education did some research work in the curriculum of basic schools. The All India council for Secondary Education tried to develop a new curriculum at the secondary stage. It gave a model syllabus for higher secondary education. The Central Bureau of Text-book Research was established to undertake research in the area of text-books. It developed criteria for evaluation of text books. But no programme of long term research in curriculum is made by any of these institutions. Research in the areas of curriculum and text book was almost absent.

The establishment of National Council of Education Research and Training (NCERT) gave impetus research in curriculum. The Central Bureau of Text-book Research and National Institute of Basic Education were merged with it. Soon in the NCERT, the Department of Curriculum, Methods and Text-boom was established. The recent nation-wide move for implementing the scheme for uniform educational structure (10+2+3) made this need all the more urgent. That is why the Director, NCERT expressed in 'Curriculum for the Ten year School - An Approach Paper (1975): "The necessity of evolving a national consensus on a new curriculum is manifest. It is accepted all round that the curriculum, by way of its objectives, content and methodology, has to serve the current and emerging needs of the Indian Society and the citizen, and these also need to be spelled out so that the ideas may be translated into action." A few studies were carried out about allocation of time to various subjects at school stage, improving the methods of teaching and developing new text-books. The Department of Science in NCERT took up a research project to develop a new curriculum for science at the middle school stage and development of science curriculum at the primary stage with the assistance of UNICEF. The NCERT gave a model approach to curriculum development to all agencies concerned with research in curriculum in the country. During 1960's, State Boards of School Text-books came in existence with the efforts of 1960's, State Boards of School Text-books came in existence with the efforts of Ministry of Education. Each Board accepted curriculum and text-book research as one of its objective.

Research in curriculum and instruction is becoming more and more important day by day. The simple reason being it is that the school curriculum is in a state of continuous change all over the world today. It may be the situation of an advanced country or the advancing one, the school-curriculum is said to be lagging behind in many respects. In our country, this area of working needs special attention of the researchers. The research guides, the authorities responsible for the preparation and provision of curriculum for the schools need be reoriented for doing their jobs in some better ways.

Out of the studies conducted so far in this area, very few of them delved deep into the problems of general curriculum development. Very little has been done on knowledge subjects like Science, History, Geography, Social Studies etc. There is need of developing a scientific curriculum. In the development of such a curriculum, needs, individual differences, growth and development of the child, classroom interaction, social structure etc. need be specially cared for. Some comprehensive research projects which are of long term nature need to be taken up by terms of research workers. Fundamental research should be emphasised and executed to provide empirical foundations to curricular changes. The areas for research may be:

(i) bases of curriculum,
(ii) components of curriculum in different subject areas,
(iii) growth of curriculum,
(iv) barriers to curriculum change,
(v) case studies of specific problems in relation to particular subject field,
(vi) analytical studies on Indian languages,
(vii) teaching of reading and writing skills, and
(viii) teacher involvement in curricular change etc.

In the area of text-books, there may be content analysis of text books at different levels. Text-book writing, editing and publication of text-books require exploration and sustained research. Research in the area of vocabulary will prove all the more beneficial for writer of text-books.

Researches in the Area

A few researches conducted in the area of curriculum are summerized a head in chronological order—

S.R. Gothiverekar worked on the Secondary School Curriculum in the Province of Bombay (A critical Analysis and Examination of its Basis, Present structure and Future Reconstruction) for Ph.D education Bombay University 1947. The main conclusions were :

(1) During to political pressure, there is undue dominance of the English language since the advent of the British rule to the present day.
(2) The undue importance given to the English language and to the matriculation examination have narrowed the purpose of secondary education.
(3) Such subjects as drawing, art, craft, music, physical education, religious-cum-moral instruction are neglected.
(4) Due attention is not paid to practical and vocational education.
(5) Undue emphasis is laid on English medium, consequently the mother tongue and the Indian languages are neglected.

In 1957, *S.L. Chaturvedi* was awarded Ph.D. on the topic 'Craft as an Education Medium in Elementary Schools'. Some of the observations were as follows:

Craft occupies an important place in the education of the child and teaches the dignity of labour. It helps in maintaining continuity between home and school life. Physical activity provides for the healthy growth of mind etc.

E.A. Pires and *K. Katval of C.LE.,* New Delhi worked on 'Building up a Social Studies curriculum for the CIE Basic School' In 1957. The purposes of the study were :

(1) To develop a social studies curriculum suitable for junior basic classes;
(2) To demonstrate how Basic School teachers can and should develop their own curriculum; and

(3) To show how current events can be woven into the social studies curriculum at junior Basic stage.

In 1965, *R.H. Dave* and *R. C. Saxena* (NCERT, New Delhi) worked on 'Curriculum and Teaching of Mathematics in the Higher Secondary Schools'. The objectives of the study were :

(1) To study the existing curricula, text-books and teaching methods in higher secondary schools of various states; and

(2) To develop a new curriculum in Mathematics in the light of the experimental curriculum by adopting suitable techniques of teaching and learning.

In 1967, (NCERT financed) project, 'An Evaluation of the Home Science Curriculum' was taken up by D. Deulkar at Lady Irwin College, New Delhi.

'A Critical study of the Development of the High School Curriculum in the Punjab during the Twentieth Century'. (P.S. Chanana Ph.D., P.U. 1967). In this study, the author inquired into the development of the High school Curriculum in the Punjab during the twentieth Century. By 1869, the high school was a well defined institution in the Punjab. The college, established in Lahore in 1870 was converted into a full fledged University in 1882 and the high school was given a wider and better curriculum. At the close of 19th century, the high school curriculum was undifferentiated. In the beginning of 20th century there was no vocational base. Everybody condemned the narrow and transplanted curriculum. In twenties, there was widening of the curriculum, when provision of extra classroom activities was made. Civics and Hygiene were added to the curriculum in 1927 and house-hold accounts for girls in 1935. In 1940' s, the need for modernising the curriculum of the high school was realised. The Britishers were got in favour of vocationalising secondary education. The high school curriculum was traditional subject centred. The school and the society were widely apart from each other. The high school remained with the university which was primarily concerned with higher education.

Curriculum improvement programme was catching attention of every body. But it was shelved with the publication of the Secondary Education Commission Report which intended to give a national plan of secondary education. The scheme of multipurpose higher secondary schools with its seven streams was launched in public in 1958. But that did not succeed due to the dissipation of resources.

In 1968, *K.S. Pillai* did research for Ph.D. Education at Kerala U. on the topic "An Investigation into the changes in the content and scope of the Primary and Secondary School Curriculum in Kerala during the last thirty years (since 1934) with a view to ascertaining how far these have been helpful to the raising of standards.

In 1972, *M.G. Chaturvedi* and *B.V. Mohale* (NCERT, New Delhi) worked on the project 'A study of the Position of Language in School Curriculum in India.' The main purpose of the study was to assess the position with regard to the study of different languages, at different stages of school education, in the states and Union Territories of India.

In 1972, *S. Rajagopalan* worked on the topic 'A Critical Study of the English Curriculum at the Primary and Secondary Stages of Education in the Madras State (Tamil Nadu)' for Ph.D. in Education from Anna U. The main objectives of the study were: In the light of present position of English in Tamil Nadu to examine and identify inadequacies in respect of objectives of teaching English. Present English syllabus, text-books used, audio visual aids available, methods of instruction followed, organization of English curriculum and the administrative barriers in implementing it, the evaluation procedures utilized, and to suggest remedial measures in all respects.

T. Ghosal for Ph.D. Education (1973) from Cal. U. worked on "An Inquiry into the Curricular Trend in the Secondary Schools of India during the British Rule (A Comparative Study)."

The objectives of the study were :

(i) To test validity of the educational system of the country which had always been, to some extent, the microcosm of the larger social system; and

(ii) To analyse the curricular trends in secondary education in India in context with the developments in English.

P. K. Gupta worked on 'A Critical Analysis of the Elementary School Curriculum in NEFA (Arunachal) with suggestion for improvement' for Ph.D. Education from Gau. U. in 1973. The objectives of the study were :

(i) To analyse the elementary or junior school curriculum in NEFA on the basis of an examination of its socioeconomic and cultural conditions; and

(ii) To offer suggestions for improvement.

In 1975, *J.G. Shah* made 'A Critical Inquiry into the Programme of Home Science Education in the Secondary Schools of India' and got Ph.D. in Education from M.S.U. The main objective of the study was to have a deep look into the programme of Home Science education and to propose an improved four year programme for Secondary Schools.

U.S. Singh took 'Development of a curriculum in Science for Secondary Schools in the State of Maharashtra' and got Ph.D. in Education in 1977 from Bom U. The objectives of the study were:

(1) To evaluate the present science curriculum of standard VIII in vogue from 1972.
(2) To modify the present curriculum with a view to achieving skill oriented objectives of the teaching of science, and
(3) To finalise a practical and progressive science curriculum after a try out.

The study 'Evaluating Commerce Curriculum at the Under Graduate Level in relation to the job Requirement of the bank Employees' was taken up at Raj. U. in 1977 by *K.C.S. Jain* for Ph.D. in Education. The main purposes of the study were :

(1) To analyse and critically examine the prevalent B. Com. (Pass) curriculum for the year 1976 of the University of Rajasthan, with a view to assessing its efficiency in preparing graduates for performing the required bank jobs successfully; and
(2) To study the magnitude of contribution of the independent variables, namely B.Com. degree, job experience, age and intelligence on the job success of bank employees.

In 1977, *S.S. Uppal* got Ph.D. degree in Education from Bombay University on the topic 'Development of Curriculum in Science for Secondary Schools in the State of Maharashtra'. The objective of the study was to develop a curriculum in Science for Standard VIII of the secondary schools in the state of Maharashtra.

In 1978, *R.B. Dewasthalee* was awarded Ph.D. degree from Bombay University for his work "An Investigation into the present Secondary Education Curricula (Std. V to X) in the Maharashtra State with a view to revision in the context of vocationalisation of Education at all levels." The important objectives of this study were :

(1) To investigate the Nature, degree and extent of vocationalisation achieved through the present secondary education curricula,

(2) To locate different areas in which vocationalisation can be achieved, and

(3) To frame syllabi of different vocationalised courses in different areas that can be introduced at all levels of secondary education.

In 1978, *V.Z Sali* of SIE, Poona did research on "The Difficulties in Implementing New Curriculum of the Secondary Schools and Remedies for it : A critical study" The main purpose of this investigation were:

(1) Studying subject-wise difficulties while implementing new curriculum of secondary schools and suggesting remedies for them and

(2) Studying the reasons of poor results at the school leaving examinations.

G.B. Shukla was awarded Ph.D. in Education by Gujarat Vidyapeeth on the topic 'A Critical Study of curriculum development at the stage of elementary education in the state of Gujarat: 1940-1970.' In this study, the investigator highlighted the major defects of primary school curriculum—lack of practical knowledge, inadequate arithmetic in the lower classes, emphasis on information rather than understanding, a heavy load of subject-matter, absence of moral education, devoid of flexibility etc.

D. K. Tharvani worked on 'Critical Study of the Effectiveness of the revised Curriculum for classes VIII, IX and X in Maharashtra State' and got Ph.D. in Education from Bombay University in 1978. The main objectives of the study were:

(1) To examine the various measures taken by the Government of Maharashtra for the effective implementation of the new curriculum in classes VIII, IX and X.

(2) To look at the existing facilities in both the rural and the urban schools in the state for effective implementation of the new curriculum, and

(3) To find out the difficulties experienced by schools in implementing the new curriculum.

In 1979, *A. P. Thakkar* got Ph.D. degree in education from Bom. U. on the topic 'Curriculum in Pre-School Education.' A few objectives of the investigation were:

(1) To seek a rationale for a pre-school curriculum.

(2) To study the existing philosophies, methods and practices in the field.

(3) To carry out an initial explorating survey of the pre-school curriculum in Bombay to elicit the awareness of a cognitive base to the curriculum in the schools.

I. Ghorai made a research study on 'The New Curriculum of Secondary Education in the West Bengal in the light of curricular History in 1980 from Cal. U. The main aim of the study was to know the views and opinions of teachers and the taught on the efficiency of the new Secondary Curriculum.

In 1981, *G. L. Arora* and B. P. *Gupta* of NCERT studied comparison of curriculum, load at the secondary stage in different states (Delhi, Haryana, Maharashtra, Kerala) to analyse the load of curriculum on students of secondary stage viz. class IX and X. The main findings of the study were:

(1) In Delhi, at the Secondary Stage the existing curricula in English, Mathematics and Hindi were considered negligibly heavy while the curricula in Science and Social Studies were considered somewhat heavy by teachers. In the opinion of students, Science was the only subject with a heavy curriculum.

(2) In Maharashtra, the existing curriculum in English and Social Studies were considered negligibly heavy while the curricula in Marathi, Science and Mathematics, were considered to be somewhat heavy. In the opinion of students, science was the only subject with a heavy curriculum.

(3) In Haryana at the secondary stage, the present curricula in the five subjects, namely English, Hindi, Science, Mathematics and Social Studies were negligibly heavy. According to students, mathematics had heavy curriculum.

(4) In Kerala, at the secondary stage, the curricula in English, Malayalam, Mathematics and Social Studies were somewhat heavy while that in Science was considered to be negligibly heavy. Students considered mathematics to be the only subject which had a heavy curriculum.

S.G. Pai was awarded Ph.D. degree in education by M.S.U. in 1981 for his work 'Preparation and try out of curriculum in Environmental Studies leading to Life Long Education for college students.' The main objectives of the study were:

(1) To help students acquire an awareness of the interrelationships, interactions and interdependence existing between biological and physical aspects of the total environment and sensitivity towards the environment and its applied problems,

(2) To help students acquire strong positive attitudes, sound ecological values towards the needs for a better environment and the necessary motivation for actively participating in its protection and improvement, and

(3) To help students develop skills necessary for solving environmental problems and taking preventive measures.

In 1981, *J. Ramdas* got Ph.D. degree from Poona University on the topic 'Curriculum Development in Science relevant to the Indian school system. The objectives of the study were :

(1) To formulate operational objectives to be achieved by science teachers in the classroom,

(2) To implement these objectives and to evaluate their effectiveness in terms of changes in teacher and pupil behaviour, and

(3) To develop and text strategies for curriculum change which could be suitable for Indian conditions.

In 1981, *C.M. Lahi* got Ph.D. in Education from Kerala. U. on the topic 'A Critical Study of the Work Experience Programme in secondary school of Kerala. The main objectives of the study were :

(1) To study the functioning of the work experience programme and the difficulties experienced in its working,

(2) To study the advantages the pupils get from the programme and their difficulties in participating in it,

(3) To find out pupils' attitude towards work experience programme and their interest in it,

(4) To find out parents' attitude towards work experience programme, and

(5) To find out the improvement needed for the proper functioning of the work experiences programme in schools.

In 1987, *Suman Swami* made 'A Critical Study of the Teaching of English in the High Schools of Ambala District, for her M.Ed. degree from Kurukshetra University, Kurukshetra. The objectives of the study were :

(1) To have a deep look into the programme of teaching English in the High Schools of Ambala District.

(2) To identify inadequacies in respect of objectives of teaching English.

(3) To suggest remedial measures for the improvement of teaching of English.

In 1989, *Rashmi Narang* did research on the topic ' A Study of the problems of VII class student in learning English' for her M.Ed. degree from Kurukshetra University, Kurukshetra. The objective of the study were :

(1) To find out the general problems being faced by the student in learning English.

(2) To find out the specific problems of the students in learning English.

(3) To give suggestions for the better learning of English.

Need for Further Research

A probe into the teaching of English as it is being carried out in the schools will bring to light the drawbacks. Naturally something better to overcome the lacunas will be thought of and suggested. The field of research in the teaching of English should be taken up by the researchers very enthusiastically. A few problems of research for the investigators are suggested here below—

1. A study of teaching of Composition in the schools of Haryana.
2. An inquiry into the attainment of objectives of teaching English at the school stage.
3. A study of the methods of teaching English being used in the schools with the view to suggest an appropriate method.
4. A study of the problems related to correction work in teaching 'English being faced by the teachers in the schools.
5. A study of the problems faced by the learners of English at VI class level (Beginners).
6. A critical study of the problems of VII class students of rural areas in learning English.
7. A study of the problems of the students of English medium schools in learning English.

8. A comparative study of the problems of students of VIII class of rural and urban areas in learning English.
9. A Critical, study of the problems of VIII class students of Haryana in learning English.
10. A study of the problems related to text-book being faced by the students of VIII class.

QUESTIONS

1. Explain the term management and enumerate its major components.
2. Enumerate theories of human organization. Describe the modern theory of human organization and indicate its impact on our curriculum.
3. Explain the concept of management of teaching learning Describe I.K. Davies four steps for designing teaching learning.
4. Explain the term 'Transaction of curriculum' and indicate the various activities involved in the management of curriculum.
5. Differentiate between curriculum development and transaction of curriculum. Justify that they are complementary to each other.

11

System Analysis

The third approach of instructional designs which is closely related to both training psychology and cybernetic, is as known 'System Analysis'. It has emerged during World War II. It has greatly influenced management decision making in business, industry, government and military. This new technology is known by several terms, but one term that has gained considerable standardization is, 'System Analysis.'

The Meaning

The word system has been derived from the field of engineering. A system is the sum total of agents working independently and dependently together to achieve the required goals. The term 'system conveys the meaning of analysis and development. The term 'system analysis' actually emerged from the scientific management concept. In general, system analysis involves utilization of scientific mathematical techniques applied to organizational operation as a part of management decision making activities. It has the assumption that no comprehensive system development can take place without prior system analysis. It enables the administrators to use more scientific and quantitative methods for analysing management problems.

The field of educational administration is becoming with the set quantitative-scientific techniques that helps the educational administrators in the decision-making process. System technology brings to educational management a scientific-quantitative approach for solving complex educational administrative problems. It is based essentially on mathematics.

The Procedure

A number of steps are followed to accomplish a System Analysis. The following steps must be utilized for conducting system analysis study-

First Step: Formulation of objectives.

The most important and difficult aspect of the entire system analysis study is to formulate the specific objectives to be achieved. To state objectives in general terms is totally inadequate. An objective may be written in behavioural terms or fiscal functions.

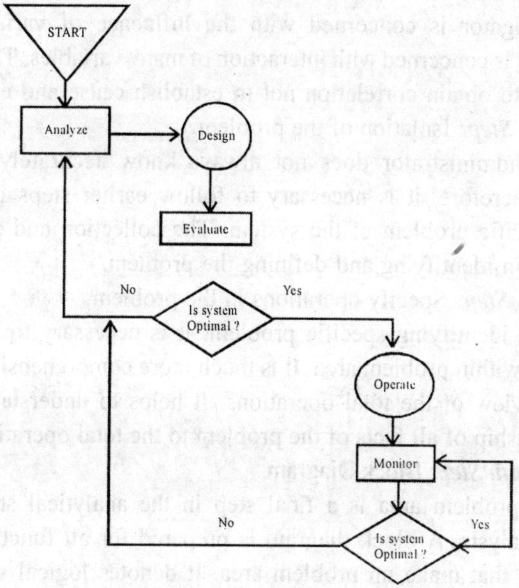

Procedure of System Analysis

Second Step: Review of systems operation.

The second step in system analysis includes a comprehensive review of the systems operation. System analysis is a problem oriented and it is necessary to understand completely the systems operation. The administrators fell in some problems but these do not always turn out to be the main problem.

Under any circumstance a comprehensive review of the whole system is necessary to isolate the main problem to the solved.

Third Step: Collection of data.

The review of system for identifying the main problem yields the data within the problem area. The collection of data involves basically the statistical techniques and procedure. In many situations the aspects as system analysis are the applications of classical statistical procedure.

Fourth Step: Analysis of data.

Analysis of data is done to make it meaningful. The analysis of data is employed to experimental paradigms to study the effect of independent variable upon dependent variable. In system analysis study, an objective analysis is made for determining the influence of variables. The investigator is concerned with the influence of variables. The investigator is concerned with interaction of many variables. The primary concern is to obtain correlation not to establish cause and effect.

Fifth Step: Isolation of the problem.

The administrator does not always know accurately the main problem; therefore, it is necessary to follow earlier steps in order to isolate specific problem of the system. The collection and analysis of data helps in identifying and defining the problem.

Sixth Step: Specify operations in the problem.

After identifying specific problem, it is necessary to review the operations within problem area. It is much more comprehensive than the original review of the total operations. It helps to understand quickly the relationship of all facts of the problem to the total operating system.

Seventh Step: Block Diagram.

The problem area is a final step in the analytical stage of the systems analysis. A block diagram is prepared for all functions of the sub-system that make up problem area. It denotes logical structure of the sub-system operations and similar to the block diagram.

The Design

After system analysis, the investigator attempts to design and tentative solution of the problem. A new solution of the problem is subjected to testing. A tentative solution and retesting the tentative solution continues until analyst reaches to an optimal solution. Once optimal solution is obtained the analyst departs that loop.

The Evaluation

The formal evaluation of the new solution is done for checking out its work ability. It involves implementation of tentative solution in some aspect of the system. The analyst proceeds through the same steps of loop as mentioned earlier. It is advisable to evaluate all new system solutions in small scale of the required operations.

System Operations

The formal evaluation and acceptance for the solution of the problem, the new design has been implemented within the system. It involves two aspects:

(1) It concerns with implementation of new system operation.

(2) It requires the maintenance of the system where a new system is designed. It continues as monitory of the system in order to check the effectiveness of the system.

Criteria for Evaluating a Project

The four general criteria are included in any evaluation system: performance, cost, utility and time. A general criterion is that the total system should operate in an optimal fashion. These criteria have discussed there:

Performance: The effectiveness of a system is evaluated on the basis of performance. The design of the problem solution ascertains how will the new system be effective in achieving the objectives. The performance criterion is the concept of validity of the new system. The system is valid if it does what it is supposed to do. Thus, much of the evaluation of the performance is quantitative.

Cost : Analysis of system is influenced by cost function toa major extent. The amount of resources is being put into the system function in terms of money, staff and facilities comparison are made regarding the investment of resources in the new system and old system of education. This is extremely valuable criterion for evaluation system analysis projects.

Utility: The ultimate criterion for evaluating system project is utility of the system. The return on investment represents the utility of a given function. Many education functions require an assignment of a numerical utility.

Time: Time factors as an evaluative criterion is closely associated with effectiveness. It is particularly relevant criterion in evaluating system projects. There is high correlation between time and cost. Much of the contribution of modern electronic data processing involves time.

The Application

The system analysis has greatly influenced the educational administration and organisation. It provides scientific and quantitative basis for studying the problems of educational system. The educational implication of system analysis have been enumerated in the following areas of education.

(1) It brings to educational management a scientific-quantitative approach for solving complex education administrative problems.

(2) It enables educational administrator to identify the actual problem and abstains a verified solution of the problem.

(3) The training programmes can also be improved with the help of system analysis. The new concept of management may be implemented in training programmes.

(4) The sub-system of education is analysed to understand the actual problem and tentative solutions can be verified or tested on a segment of the system.

(5) Any change in the educational system can be brought objectively, empirically and economically with great utility with the help of System Analysis.

System Approach

The Meaning and Definition : System approach is a rational, problem-solving method of analysing the educational process and making it more effective. System is the process taken as a whole incorporating of all its aspects and parts, namely pupils, teachers, curriculum content, instructional materials, instructional strategies, physical environment and the evaluation of instructional objectives.

The purpose of the system analysis is to get the "Best environment in the best place for the best people at the best time and in the best price."

"The system approach in instruction is an integrated, programmed complex of instructional media, hardware and personal whose components are structured as single unit with a schedule of time and sequential phasing."

The instructional process has become complex these days because of the shift in technological focus for the classroom to curriculum planning. The curriculum should not only specify student behavioural objectives but also suggest the strategies for helping the student to reach the objectives and evaluation instruments to measure the success. It is called the system approach.

Keshaw and Michean (1959) have defined-

"System approach is one of the techniques which aims at finding the most efficient and economically intelligent methods for solving the problems of education scientifically."

The system concept provides a framework for visualizing internal and external environmental factors as an integrated whole. This concept factors are a way of thinking which helps us to recognize the nature of the complex problems and there by provides insight which enables us to operate within the received environment.

System analysis is a systematic way of identifying goals of any system and scientifically working out different steps to more towards these goals.

The approach in general includes the following steps:

1. To analyse the existing situation.
2. To set up the goal for the desired situation.
3. To define the mechanisms to evaluate the achievement of goals.
4. To create alternative situation.
5. To select the most appropriate solution through cost benefit analysis.
6. To work out the layout of the system.
7. To design the monitory mechanisms for the system.
8. To plan for introducing the new solution.

Instructional System

It is a systematic attempt to coordinate all aspects of a problem toward specific objectives in education. This means planned, organized use of all available learning resources, including audiovisual media, to achieve the desirable learning objectives by the most efficient means possible. The system approach focuses first upon learner and the performance required of him. Only then, it makes decisions regarding course content, learning experiences and the most effective media and instructional strategies for realizing the objectives.

The Instructional System employs the following steps:

1. Defining instructional objectives in behaviour terms or measurable terms.
2. Determining functions related to the achievement of the objectives by appropriate multimedia approach.
3. Defining learner's characteristics or entering behaviour.
4. Selecting appropriate instructional strategies for effective learning.
5. Selecting suitable learning experiences for available alternatives.
6. Choosing appropriate instructional aids, resources to facilitate students learning.
7. Defining and assigning appropriate personal roles: teachers of term teaching members and supporting personal students.
8. Implementing the programme: Try out with a small group of pupils in appropriate conditions.
9. Evaluating the pupils learning outcome in terms of learning objectives.
10. Revising if necessary to improve the efficiency of the system to improve student learning.

The system approach applied to educational situations includes: input, process, output and feedback. These are inter linked and interdependent stages and can be described as:

(a) Planned *input* and process involving learning materials and strategies suitable organised to cater the needs of a particular group of students.

(b) Explicitly stated standard of outcome performances, including sequenced behavioural objectives.

(c) Monitoring output which is used to revise, improve and evaluate the instructional system, providing feedback to the learner and teacher, and

(d) A degree of inbuilt flexibility to adjust the individual situation.

The system approach can be effectively used for studying the problems of the following areas of education:

1. Instructional system or procedure.
2. School administration and supervision.
3. Examination and Evaluation system.
4. Non-formal and Adult education.
5. Educational guidance system.

An example demonstrating an application of system approach is discussed in the following paragraph in an instructional system.

Three Phases

Robb (1974) has analysed an instructional system and suggested that an instructional system can be employed into three phases: Planning, Execution and Evaluation. These phases involve eight steps and indicate the development of instructional system.

Phase First: Planning instructional system

Step 1. Defining objective

Step 2. Pre-assessment or determining entering behaviour.

Step 3. Specifying appropriate strategies.

Step.4. Selecting materials, facilities, aids and media.

Phase Second: Execution of instruction Step

Step 5. Defining and assigning personnel roles.

Step 6 Synthesising and implementing the system of instruction.

Phase Third: Evaluation of instruction

Step 7. Evaluation and outcome.

Step 8. Analysing result and modifying the system.

The problem is that the development of an instructional system is for a given target population or class of students. The instructional system can be used by the following eight steps:

Defining Objectives: The objectives for the instruction are identical and written in the behavioural terms which the learners are required to demonstrate.

Determining the Entering Behaviour: The students' entry level is determined by the pre-assessment. The knowledge and skills which the learners are already equipped with, are processed.

Specifying Appropriate Method and Strategies: In this step appropriate method and strategies are specified which can suit to the nature of the students and are helpful to achieve the objectives.

Selecting Materials, Aids and Media: The learning experiences are provided with the help of appropriate material and media. The instructional strategies require the appropriate material and media to generate academic environment. Therefore, appropriate material and media are selected for providing learning experiences.

Defining and Assigning Personnel Roles: In using instructional procedure effectively, the teacher has to play various roles to assist the learner to achieve the objectives.

Synthesizing and Implementing the Instructional System: This is a step of execution phase of instructional system. The system approach, strategies, material, media and roles of teachers are integrated in such way so that specified objectives may be achieved. Under this step learning experiences are provided to the learners.

Evaluation of Learning Outcome: The effectiveness of instruction is examined on the basis of post-test scores of the students. The performance of the students indicate the validity of instruction and fulfilment of the objectives.

Analysing the Result and Modifying the System: The learning outcome is analysed to ascertain the inability of the earlier steps. It provides the feedback to the designer and suggests modification and improvement in the different aspects of instructional system. It ensures the effectiveness of planning and execution phase of the system.

Thus system analysis or approach can be applied for the development of educational administration and organisation, examination system, Instructional system, models of teacher-education, models of curriculum and educational and vocational guidance system. These three approaches can be applied simultaneously for education and training.

A comparative view of these streams of thought has been presented in the following table to make it more understandable:

Instructional Designs

Training Psychology	*Cybernetic*	*System Analysis*
Exponents:		
L. Carter Glaser and Robert Gange	Gulibod Smith and Smith Norbest-Wiener	Frank O. Banghart.
Orign:		
Military training	Principles for Physical Science, Steering boat	Engineering
Goals:		
Task analysis Task Structure	Feedback control Regulation	System analysis. Development
Assumption:		
Task-elements are crucial for developing Skills and competencies	Human being is like a machine. Feedback is important for his development.	Management can be developed by system analysis.
Principles:		
(1) Human task can be analysed its elements. (2) Task-elements functions as mediator for last task	(1) Input (2) Output (3) Process. It is closed loop system. approach.	(1) System analysis for the develop ment. (2) It is a Scientific quantitative
Steps:		
(1) Goals (2) Task Analysis (3) Organization of The elements. knowledge of results. (4) Task efficiency or response functions as reinforcement.	(1) Stimulus in the form of environment (2) Response is the (4) Isolation of problem (5) Confirmation (6) Evaluation	(1) Objectives (2) Data Collection (3) Analysis of data (5) Design
Application in Education:		
(1) Designing instruction (2) Lesson planning (3) Teacher-education models (4) Development teaching skills (5) Branching programme.	(1) Classroom teaching (2) Programmed instruction, system of (3) Teaching models (4) Modification or teacher behaviour by the use of feedback devices.	(1) Educational administrative problems (2) Evolving a new education (3) Reform in the examination (4) Importance in teacher education models, (5) Improvement in instructional system.

Educational Technology can be viewed from the systems approach. A system may be defined as the assemblage of components each having its own purpose. A system is a inter-relation of parts each having a specific function. The parts and their functions are inter-related in specific ways so that they perform adequately to achieve the purpose of the system as a whole. The whole is more than the sum of the parts. It is synergistic., e.g. a bicycle, car, school, college, etc.

The educational system includes students and teachers, and refers to curriculum content, instructional materials, instructional strategy, physical environment, and the evaluation of instructional objectives.

The system is designed on the objectives to the achieved and objectives being defined in terms of obtainable outputs. Inputs are transferred into desirable outputs. For this transformation, interaction takes place with the components.

Each component has its own functions and interactions. These functions and interaction are more important than their description.

The simple system representations (Hary Gray) shows how the inputs' into a system undergo some process of 'transformation' into a product output' and the effects of the output on the environment are monitored so as modify future inputs. Colleges can be thought of as places where the 'process' of education works on the minds and personalities of all the members and the product is the effect of this educational process which will thus be qualitative, as well as quantitative. The 'feedback loop' represents the information on which the educational process is modified to better provide for the needs of learners who are entering the college or leaving it for work situations. The systems approach is a rational problem-solving method of analysing process and making it more effective.

Systems Environment

Input Transformation Process Output

Feedback Loop

The system approach in instruction is an integrated, programmed complex of instructional media, hardware and personnel, whose components are structured as a single unit with a schedule of time and sequential planning.

It is a strategy which utilizes analysis design and management to attain the stated goal effectively and efficiently.

QUESTIONS

1. Enumerate the steps of system analysis.
2. Is system analysis synonyms of instructional designs?
3. Is task analysis the focus to training psychology?
4. Is providing feedback the function of cybernetic psychology?
5. Is system analysis to development process of education and training?

12

Medium of Teaching

The instruction process involves the transfer or communication of information, knowledge and skills from one point (source, the teacher) to another (receiver, the student). For a long period in the history of education, this process depended an printed material and occasionally supported by audio- visual aid. The development of communication technology has made available more sophisticated aids to the teacher to carry out his responsibilities more effectively. The term Educational Technology involves the application of scientific knowledge to education; input, output and process aspects of education; organisation of learning situations for realizing goals of education, development of methods and techniques for effective learning and designing tools for measuring learning outcomes. Therefore, education technology refers to the application of scientific principles to instruction, so that the pertinent technological methods are adopted for communication and effective learning. It involves methods, media and resources.

The two components of educational technology are hardware and software. Hardware aspect refers to instruments or apparatus or equipment useful in the process of teaching such as different types of projectors, recorders, television, closed circuit television, computers, etc. These aids help in transmitting, amplifying, and recording and reproducing stimuli materials for learning purposes.

The software aspect of educational technology indicates the application of psychological principles of learning to the teaching-learning process. In the software approach an attempt is made to manage the teaching-learning process by promoting individual learning towards mastery level through programmed learning and learner-centred instruction methods, instructional modules, teaching modules, instruction methods. Instructional modules, teaching modules, mini courses, and programming material for computer are some of the software aspect of educational technology. Both, hardware and software components of educational technology have far-reaching implications for education. There is no doubt that proper use of educational technology would result in making learning more interesting and rewarding.

Instructional Media

The term media has no specific meaning in the sense that it gives meaning only in relation to terms to which it is related.

The instructional message that stimulates the sense organs (eye, ear and so on) becomes the sensory mode.

The sensory mode in communication (visual, auditory, tactile, Kinesthetic, alfactory, etc) is termed as channels of communication.

The means but not the mechanism of communication, spoken word, printed word, motion pictures are examples of type of stimulus.

The physical means of communication (books, programmed texts, computers, films, video tapes, etc.) are the media.

Some people use the term media to indicate all the above, namely, sensory mode, channels or communication, type of stimulus and physical means of communication. Others use it in association with any one of these. Instructional media are the means by which messages are carried from a source teacher to the receiver learner. The media then interact with the learner through his senses. The learner may make use of more than one sense to receive the information. The media selected by the teacher may range form non-projected aids such as charts and diagrams to projected aids like slides, transparencies and electronic equipment. Aids as such, do not become media. Only when they are used in the process of instruction to convey a massage, do they become media. The process of using the aids for instructional purposes indicates the concept of media usage.

Section of Media

The section of media for classroom instruction is based on certain factors. The teacher should have a clear idea of the objectives of the lesson and the desired outcomes. The learners adopt different patterns of learning. Media should match learning studies. Selection of media depends of the media available, their appropriateness to the lesson under consideration and the physical facilities available in the classroom. Consideration should be given to cost effectiveness, cultural issues related to mass media and the physical and emotional needs and made-up of the learners. Based on the above-mentioned factors, media should be selected by the teacher for effective instruction.

Media and Method

These two terms are very confusing even for teachers. Media and method are used interchangible in education, but they are quite different to one another. These can be differentiated in the following manner—

(1) The universe has two major components: (a) space and (b) time. If we assume instruction as a universe, this way has two components: (i) Instructional space, and (ii) Instructional time.

The 'instructional space' is covered by radio and television. A teacher can reach interior parts of the country and can knock at the door of students. Media is essential for instructional space.

(2) Another way to distinguish between media and method is that method is an abstract entity which is determined by the nature of the content. For example, information through lecture, facts through storytelling or dramatization method, concepts through experiment are taught to students.

Media is a concrete entity which is determined by the mode of communication. The mode of message communication is known as media. For example, information through radio are communicated to the students. The media of communication are: radio, television, video-tape and tape-recorder etc. and mode of communication through various media are: speaking- listening, writing-reading and visualising observing.

Media and method are not contradictory to one another but they are complementary and supplementary to one another. A method can be made effective by using an appropriate media of communication.

Theory of Communication: The basic communication model involves an informational or interpretive process in which messages, information or reaction to information travel from the initiator to receiver through the route called communication channel. The message conveyed by the teacher or the educational media may be verbal or visual and the receiver may listen or see and react in other ways. The communication channel in the classroom should ideally carry both messages and counter-messages; it involves initiation, reception and response which serve as feedback. The communication must be kept open, as only when the teacher and pupils are able to communicate clearly and without interference of understanding and appreciation ensure. But unfortunately many interferences and communication barriers arise which impede the smooth flow of communication between the teacher and his pupils in the classroom, e.g., advertisements and entertainment media. The communication channel employ media of teaching and learning. Type of communication channels have been described here.

Communication Channels

There are three types of communication channel; 1. Speaking-Listening, 2. Writing-Reading and 3. Visualizing-Observing.

Speaking-Listening: In this type of communication, an interaction is face to face as in the case of a teacher. There are situations when the listener can share feelings of the source in the same way as in the case of eye to eye contact. Listening to the radio is an example for this type of communication channel.

Writing-Reading: In this type of communication channel, the 'decoder' is physically separated from the 'encoder' all the time and yet the decoder is able to enjoy and appreciate the feelings of the author. Reading for an instruction material is an example for this type of communication channel.

Visualising-Observing: The observer is physically separated from its producer and yet is able to feel the impact of the ideas conveyed as in motion film or television. The dramatization is an example for this type of communication.

Through these communication channels a sender or teacher conveys his message through some media to a receiver or vice-versa. The function of a sender is to encode the message and receiver- students- has to decode it.

Use of Media

The use of media in the introductory part of the lesson creates readiness in the learner for participating in the learning experience. Media provide clarity, precision and accuracy of the information processed. Media can be used in the development, organisation and summarising phases of the lesson. It brings world events to the classroom and helps in promoting interrelationships and assessing learning outcomes. Media is a very high supporting factor for the teaching and learning process.

Teaching Aids

Media include the various teaching aids that are used in the instructional process. Teaching aids can be classified as projected aids and non-projected aids.

1. The non-projected aids
   (a) Chalkboards
   (b) Graphic material
   (c) Plannelagraph and its modern counterpart, the plastigraph
   (d) Graphic through photo-printing and duplicating
   (e) Pictures
   (f) Models
   (g) Recordings-records, tape and cassettes
   (h) Radio, and
   (i) Teaching machine
2. The projected aids are—
   (a) Diascope, episcope and epidiascope
   (b) Overhead projector
   (c) Filmstrip and slide projectors
   (d) Sound motion film projector
   (e) Micro projector
   (f) Television and
   (g) Computers

Brief explanations are given for some of these aids so that the teachers are aware of their merits and make use of them according to need, purpose, subject-matter and availability.

Chalkboards: Chalkboard is the most indispensable aid for the teacher. If used properly, it becomes the most valuable device for making instruction concrete and comprehensive. Some of the merits of a chalkboard are—

(1) It can capture and hold the attention of students.
(2) It can be used to present learning material symbolically.

(3) Abstract ideas can be presented in visual form.
(4) Chalkboard is invaluable for summarising information.
(5) It affords variety in teaching, and
(6) It is economical, both in terms of time and money.

A college teacher can develop the skill of using a chalkboard. Judicious use of space available on a chalkboard for presenting the material during the course of a lesson is an art. Consideration should be given to the material that can be left on one side of a board, for reference throughout a teaching period. Centre of the chalkboard may, perhaps he used for constant erasing and writing. Diagrams, figure and maps could take up the other end of a board. Use of colour chalks enable the teacher to present important materials in an attractive manner, to catch attention of the students. A chalkboard, though a simple teaching aid has immense potential for presenting instructional material.

Graphic materials consist of charts, graphs, maps, posters, drawings, diagrams, cartoons and sketches, and these aids help in clarifying ideas. Bearing in mind that picture language is the oldest means of written communication', it is not surprising that pictorial or diagrammatic presentation has such a universal appeal. While using some of these aids, points to be considered are size, clarity, accuracy and attractiveness.

Plastigraph is similar to flannelgraph except for the fact that instead of flannelbase, a sheet to PVC is used for the plastic overlays to stick on. The advantage of a plastigraph is that different stages of a process (such as pollination) can be depicted step by step, through figures, diagrams and other representations. The demonstration can be stopped at any stage to give an explanation.

Duplication of material by stencilling or through photoprint is an essential means of communication for educational purposes. This includes the production of copies of written material or typed or printed material, diagrams, figures, drawings and maps for use in the teaching-learning situation.

Aids appealing to the sense of hearing are radio, records, tapes and cassettes. Recorded materials are a source for study material and these have special significance for language learning. If planned properly, educational broadcasts can be used profitably for instruction at various levels.

Slides and Filmstrips

Many of the college teachers are familiar with the use of slides and filmstrips in the regular classes at the tertiary level, especially in science disciplines. Pictures, diagrams and micro-organisms placed on a slide can be magnified when these slides are projected on the a screen by the use of a slide projector. This type of projection enables the teachers to give a detailed view of the material under review and study these in depth for as long a time as needed. Slides can be prepared by several methods. Teachers or students can draw a diagram, graph, or details of a system on glass slide by enclosing a picture in between two glass slides and binding them together. By photo-graphing objects, pictures, landscape and transforming through a special process, slides of photographs can be prepared. The projected photos will be realistic and gaining the attention of the students. Visits to distant places or viewing of rare phenomenon, rare species, etc can be brought to the classroom through photographic slides. Micro-organism can be studied when the fluid in which they live can be smeared on a slide leg. Fresh specimens on slides are invariably studied by reviewing through a microscope. Preserved specimens, in certain cases, are placed between two glass slides by professionals for in-depth viewing.

Projection of slides are very useful in bringing reality to the class. Slide projector has a simple mechanism of projecting the slides on to a screens when the slides are inserted in the slide carrier upside down. After projection the picture is right side upon the screen. Recent models of the slide projectors have circular carrier or a long slide carrier where a number of slides can be loaded at a time and each slide can be projected by remote control without the removal and insertion of each slide at a time. It is also possible to combine a recorded narration in a tape recorder and the showing of slides and thus saving the strain of the teacher's voice.

Filmstrips are similar to slides in their purpose except for the continuous movement of pictures, diagrams, table, etc on the screen. Filmstrips (35mm) have 25-30 frames in a sequential manner on a single theme, topic or story. It can be operated to stop and explain each frame or run through several of them. Frames also carry explanation statements at the bottom. Filmstrips can be hooked to a tape recorder to give the commentary. Remote control system is also available to operate the movement of the frames. As in the case of slide projectors complete darkening of the room is not required in the case of filmstrip projector. Sufficient light can be on the slides and filmstrips can be operated. Teachers can prepare filmstrips especially by the use of camera (loaded with 35 mm film) if the sequence of the theme is planned ahead and the needed material to be presented in each framer is ready so that these forms can be shot in the film of a camera and later process. Since the sequence of the frames cannot be changed when a camera is used, the teacher should be careful to plan and collect the required material, diagrams, sketches, maps, explanations, etc that will go in each frame. Readymade filmstrips can also be purchased.

Overhead Projector

Among the projected aids, the overhead projector is a very helpful aid for college teachers. It has many uses and considerable advantages as a teaching aid. It can be used in full daylight (no need to darken the room) as the projection is by means of transmitted light and not reflected light. The teacher can face the class, operate the projector by writing on the special material provided or use prepared transparencies and the projected material falls behind and above him on the wall or screen for full view of the students. The teacher is in full control of the class as he need not turn his back to the class as different from chalkboard writing. Teacher's production of personal transparencies and commercial transparencies enhances the use of overhead projector. Further it is comparatively a lightweight equipment which is also portable. The teacher can use his ingenuity in the preparation of needed transparencies for his classes. He can so plan that the can present visual materials step by step with the help of overlays or prepare transparencies earlier and use them at the proper time. Transparencies are not difficult to make. Instructional material can be typed, drawn or hand written on a triacetate film supplied in a roll along with the overhead projectors. Felt pens can be used for writing. Individual transparencies can be made and kept permanently and used by placing one at a time on the horizontal stage. As per the dimensions of the horizontal stage where transparencies are placed for viewing, individual sheets can be cut from the role and attached to thick cardboards on four sides to keep it flat and stationary. When a roll of transparency is used it can be continuously used by writing on it and rolling it to move and then get fresh side of the transparency to write again. The written material on the roll can be erased for further use of the same transparency roll.

Method of Use

In the overhead projectors there are two switches other than the one that connects it to the power supply. Of the two switches, one is for the blower and the other for the light. In operating the overhead projector, the blower switch is turned on first and then the lamp. After use, the lamp should be switched off first and then the blower. The power supply should be no to enable the blower to work and thereby the projector is cooled to room-temperature. While the blower is on, the projector should not be moved order to safeguard the lamp. The projector should not be kept in use continuously for a long period. Overhead projectors are subjected to same precautions that would be taken for any other projector. In terms of using voltage stabilizer, keeping dust-free and protecting the lenses and mirror of the projector.

Specific Uses

The beauty of this simple and not so expensive equipment is that the teacher can develop a diagram as he is teaching in a regular class (not dark room) without turning his back and getting the attention of the students by the projected material. By moving the opaque or coloured pointer on the stage, the teacher can focus the students attention on the important aspects. Teacher-made transparencies can be used for step by step development by sliding a opaque cardboard progressively disclosing one part at a time.

Another advantage of an overhead projector is the possibility for using overlays. The information that is to be presented to the class can be split into hierarchical steps. The transparencies are made for each step and starting from the basic one, each additional transparency is placed over the previous one as the explanation is given by the teacher. The development process can be shown step by step, mounting to the final stage. A good example can be from the teaching of Geography, the topic being location of industries. An outline map of India can be the first overlayed and the next, mineral deposits (iron add coal only) followed by iron and steel plants and finally the important centres of this industry. The factors of location can be clearly illustrated by these overlays.

Some of the small living organisms, and aquatic animals, kept in small glass dishes, flower petals and leaves can be projected to study the details.

Overhead projector becomes a very useful aid in the hands of a teacher who has learner to use it properly.

Micro-projector

Micro-projector is a precision scientific instrument and is effective for scientific study and teaching. It is a versatile piece of laboratory equipment and will permit drawing or demonstration at any predetermined degree of magnification. The micro-projector can often assist by projecting the image of a living specimen or slide on to a ground glass screen. Live organisms can be kept in a liquid medium which will reduce heat (e.g. mosquito larvae on watch glass with water). It can also project downward for drawing purposes. With microscopes normally only one student can view a slide at a time and the teacher may not be sure if he has seen the salient features, he pointed out micro-projection technique enlarges the actual microscope slides and tiny objects and projects them on to a screen to be viewed by a small group.

Radio-vision

Radio-vision indicates a 35-mm filmstrip or set of slides and the radio programme which have been created together and the two work in unison. In other words, radiovision is an integrated presentation of. a 35-mm filmstrip and radiovision programme. A relevant broadcast of for a few times, the teacher prepares a filmstrip to, illustrate the points covered in the broadcast as well as additional points for better clarification. The teacher's notes, consisting of a complete script, extra background information on each frame and a list of relevant publications will be the important part of the package. Radiovision should not be mistaken for an improvised television. Radiovision is an independent medium in its own right and is flexible in its use in the classroom.

Audio-Visual Aids

The communication strategy, teaching strategies and tactics are selected for achieving objectives and generating learning structure. The audio-visual teaching aids also play a significant role for this purpose. The learning structure can be effectively generated with the help of audio-visual aids and teaching objectives can be achieved easily. Therefore, the audio-visual aids are termed as educational technology one, i.e., hardware approach to teaching. It is an old view that audio-visual aids can be used to make lesson interesting and involving more than one sense in teaching learning situation. The students can be made active and attentive by the use of teaching aids. The research studies have yielded that a particular audio or visual aids may be used to achieve a specific objective of learning of specific learning condition may be created.

The Characteristics : The following are the main characteristics -

1. It helps in developing perception of learner.
2. It aids in positive transfer of learning and training.
3. It facilitates in understanding and comprehension.
4. It provides reinforcement to the learner.
5. It increases the retention of the learner.

These are the generalized statements about the audio-visual aids, but teacher has to take decision in selecting appropriate audio-visual aids on the basis of students-level and objectives of learning the most crucial feature of teaching aids is aids is to help in creating appropriate learning structure.

Various Types

Initially the origin of teaching aids is from physical sciences and engineering. The use of audio-visual aids has mechanised the education and teaching-learning process. B.F. Skinner comments that our kitchens are more mechanized that education. This statement seems to be true even in our country. The audio-visual aids are classified into three categories—

1. Audio-teaching aids,
2. Visual teaching aids, and
3. Audio-visual aids.

Audio Teaching Aids: This type of teaching aids facilitate audio senses and encourage the listening function. The audio sense is more active by the use of such teaching aids. The audio sense is active in lecture and question-answer strategies. The use of tape-recorder, radio, record player and gramophone make the learner more active and attentive in teaching process. The students take more interest when lesson is displayed with the help of such teaching aids. These aids produce only sounds.

The audio aids are used to realize the cognitive and affective objectives and can not be used in achieving psychomotor objectives.

Visual Teaching Aids: These teaching aids facilitate the visual sense and encourages the seeing function. The visual sense is more active by the use of such aids. Thse sense is more active when teacher uses pictures, maps, graphs, models and line - drawing in his teaching activities. No teaching can be possible without the use of such teaching aids. The visual teaching aids play a significant role in teaching: geography, physics; chemistry, biology and economics, etc. The geography content cannot be taught without the use of maps and globe. The uvsual aids are most useful and economical than audio-aids Generally visual aids are used most frequently in all teaching situations. The audio teaching aids are costly and really used but most useful in language teaching. The language laboratory has been designed for this purpose.

The visual teaching aids are used to achieve the cognitive objectives but affective and psychomotor objectives can also be achieved.

Audio-Visual Teaching Aids: These teaching aids are used to facilitate both audio, and visual senses and encourage listening and observing functions. Thus, these aids involve more than one sense simultaneously and learner is more active. This is most effective and useful than earlier aids. The learning structure can be generated more easily and comprehensively. These aids develop the perception of the learner which is the basis for the understanding of any concept. Television, films, and radio tape are the examples of audio-visual aid. These are costly and rarely used in teaching learning situation.

The audio-visual aids can be used to realize, the cognitive, affective and psychomotor objectives of learning.

The Selection

The audio-visual have significant place in organizing process, but selection of appropriate audio-visual aids is challenging task for a teacher. There are various type of teaching aids, hence selection is the complex problem. The various criteria and principles are used as the basis for selecting appropriate teaching A.V. aids. The studies conducted in this area has revealed that learning objectives and learning structure seem to be important criteria. The effective audio-visual aids may be selected by employing both criteria,

1. Teaching-learning objective, and
2. Learning conditions or structures.

The practical outlines on basis of research findings have been summarized here.

Learning Objectives

The most important criterion in selecting the appropriate audio-visual aids is the learning phase should be considered as criterion for taking decision about the teaching aids. The following are the research conclusions in this regard:

The cognitive and affective objectives may be achieved by the use of radio, still pictures films and educational visits.

The cognitive and psychomotor objectives are realized with the help of tape-recorder, record-players, television and language-laboratories.

The line-drawing is used to achieve the cognitive objectives.

The models are effectively used to realize the affective and psychomotor objectives.

This has also been presented:

Audio-Visual Aids and Learning Objective

Audio-Visual Aids	**Learning objectives**		
	Cognitive	***Affective***	***Psychomotor***
Radio	++++	++++	
Tape-Recorder	++++	++++	++++
Record-player	++++	++++	++++
Line-Drawing	++++		
Still Pictures	++++	++++	++++
Models	++++	++++	
Films	++++	++++	++++
Television	++++	++++	++++
Language Laboratory			
Educational Visits	++++	++++	++++

The above chart indicates the use of the different audio-visual aids in achieving the learning objectives. The plus signs show that a particular objective may be achieved by using a specific teaching aids. The blank place indicates that a particular learning objective can not be achieved by the audio-visual aids of teaching.

This criterion may be supplemented by the learning structure. The audio-visual aids also facilitate certain specific learning conditions or structures.

Learning Structure

For an effective use of audio-visual teaching aids, it is essential that learning structure should also be taken in consideration, because learning objectives can only be achieved by creating appropriate conditions or situations or situations of learning. Thus, appropriate teaching aid facilitates appropriate learning structure. The several studies have been designed and conducted in this direction. The effectiveness of this teaching aids has been evaluated in terms of learning structure. The findings of these studies have been summarized in the following chart—

Audio-Visual Aids and Learning Objective

Audio-Visual Aids Teaching Aids	***Learning objectives***				
	Signal	***Chain***	***Multiple Discrimination***	***Concept***	***Principle***
Radio		+ + +			
Tape-Recorder	+ + +	+ + +	+ + +		
Record-Player	+ + +	+ + +	+ + +		
Line drawings	+ + +		+ + +	+ + +	+ + +
Still Picture	+ + +		+ + +	+ + +	
Model	+ + +	+ + +			
Films		+ + +		+ + +	+ + +
Television		+ + +		+ + +	+ + +
Language Laboratory	+ + +	+ + +	+ + +		
Educational Visits		+ + +		+ + +	+ + +

The plus signs in the chart indicate that a particular aid may facilitate a particular learning structure. The following inferences have been drown:

1. The signal learning structure may be generated and facilitated by the use of tape-recorder, record-player, line drawing, still picture, model and language laboratory.
2. The chain learning structure may be created and encouraged by the use of radio, tape-recorder, record-player, mode, films, television, language laboratory and educational visits.
3. The multiple-discrimination learning structure may be generated and facilitated with the help of tape-recorder, record-player and language laboratory.
4. The concept learning structure is created and facilitated by the use of line drawings, still picture, films, television and educational visits.
5. The principle of learning structure is facilitated and created by the aid of line-drawings, still-picture, films, television and educational visits.

An effective use of audio-visual aids depends upon learning objectives and learning structure this also relates teaching to learning. The successful teaching may be organized by selecting appropriate teaching strategies, tactics, communication strategies and audio-visual aids.

It is evident from the above discussion that different channels of communication serve different purposes. No communication media, is perfect in itself from learning objective point of view. Therefore, more than two media can be used simultaneously for dealing with one learning unit. This approach is known as multi-media approach of teaching and instruction. It has been described here.

Educational Television

Television has come to be part of our way of life. One major use of instructional television is its quality to bring in 'here and now' right into the classroom. The use of closed circuit television system (CCTV) increases the size of the audience by allowing one teacher to address several classroom or colleges at a time. The imaginative use of the T. V. camera can also produce a better presentation, such as the use of close-ups which can focus the audience's attention on particular points or can blow up the details of a demonstration so that all can see clearly.

The CCTV can be used to develop the teaching skills of college teachers. The micro-teaching technique is a training technique in which the selected one or two teaching skills are practised in a simulated condition of teaching a few, five or six; students for a short period of five minutes on a micro- aspect of the content. The emphasis is laid on the development of teaching skills. The feedback to the teacher who adopts micro-teaching is from the observer-teachers and/or video tape. Viewing one's teaching performance on the TV to assess its strong points and drawbacks is more convincing than the observers' comments. After the feedback from the CCTV and observers, the teacher replans his micro-lessons and reteaches and then gets the feedback. This cycle is repeated until the teacher projects the skills and can use these skills in macro-lessons. The feedback from the CCTV is indeed an eye-opener to many a teacher regarding his methods and approaches of teaching as well as his mannerism. Therefore, it is a great asset in improving teaching skills and thereby teaching performance. It should be remembered that micro-teaching is only a training technique and not a teaching technique. Feedback through the video-tape is not a requirement but is extremely helpful and instructive in developing teaching skills.

Portable video-tape and cassette-recorders (VCR\VTR) are now freely available at a reasonable price. These are of great use in the classroom; for programmes can be played at the time decided by the teacher and can be stopped part-way through, restarted and section replayed if required.

In the past few years, computers have come into the classroom in a big way. Teachers and students are now involved in the process of manipulating the computer rather than using it for instructional purposes. In computer-assisted instruction, or computer managed instruction, the learner's response is evaluated immediately and the feedback motivates the student to proceed further, keeping in tune with the rate of reaction of the student and the response from the computer. The instant responsiveness and flexibility of the computer makes it a tool that can revolutionise or at least greatly modify the way teachers teach students.

Satellite Television

The experiments of Satellite Instruction Television have shown that it improves the quality and effectiveness of instruction or as media of communication. Thus, it has the relevance for developing countries.

1. The SITE has the greater significance in domestic use in the developing countries.
2. The SITE is estimated to have cost over Rs. 100 million but the relevance of the Satellite Television. The system for India is also tree like other developing countries.
3. India is ready to design and execute a nation-wide television system and use this medium to educate the masses in rural areas and it is also possible to extend this facility to the whole country.
4. The SITE can carry socio-economic development for the village and it is possible to follow-up the greater awareness and educational knowledge created in the villages.
5. The value of SITE is beyond the monetary investment or even the immediate result.

In short, experiments and research studies of SITE has shown that educational television seems to be effective for instructional purpose. Therefore, it must be an inseparable segment of over-all classroom environment.

QUESTIONS

1. Indicate the need and importance of audio and visual aids of teaching.
2. Describe the role of teaching aids in preparing instructional procedure for teaching.
3. Enumerate the types of teaching aids used for teaching subjects.
4. Differentiate between media and method of instruction Illustrate your answer with examples.
5. Indicate the basis and criteria for selecting appropriate audiovisual aids of teaching.

13

Skills for Teaching

Micro -teaching

Micro-teaching is one of the most important development in the field of teaching practice. It is originated in Standard University in 1963. The workers in the centre for Research and development in teaching have evolved an approach to practical teacher-training. It is more analytical method and completely new approach to provide the feedback. It is considered as a mechanism of feedback device for the modification of teacher trainees.

Historical Background

A doctoral candidate Leith Acheson got information through a newspaper article about portable video-tape-recorder invented by German scientist in 1961. He was working with Robert Bush and Dwight Allen who had received a grant to study those experiences which might be relevant, a grant to study those experiences which might be relevant for teaching in terms of an innovative teacher education programme. Acheson saw the possibility of using the video-tape to provide immediate feedback to the teacher trainees in term of what occurred in the demonstration lesson. Acheson and other Standard graduate students started to explore several different uses of the portable video-tapes-recorder and its potentiality in modifying the behaviour of pupil-teachers towards desired objectives.

Meaning and Definition

Micro-teaching is like a simulated social skill teaching to provide the feedback to teacher-trainee for the modification of teacher-behaviour. It is training concept that can be applied at various pre-service and in-service stages in the professional development of teacher. Micro-teaching provides teachers with a setting or instruction in which the normal complexities of classroom are reduced in which the teacher gets feedback on his performance.

Basically, micro-teaching is a scaled down teaching encounter' in which a teacher teaches in small unit to a group of 5 to 10 students for a small period of 5 to 10 minutes and one teaching skill is practiced during the teaching. Micro-teaching is a new training designed for pupil-teacher which provides an opportunity to practice one teaching skill at a time and with information about their performances immediately after completion of their lesson.

Micro-teaching is a clinical teaching programme which is organized to explore the trainee to an organized curriculum of miniature teaching encounter, moving from the less complex to the more complex.

The basic principles of micro-teaching are simple. A pupil-teacher teaches a short lesson of about five minutes duration to small group of pupils. At the end of the lesson, the pupils are left and student-teachers discuss the lesson with their supervisor. After a short interval, the pupil-teacher re-teaches the lesson with a different group of pupils making use of the feedback from the supervisor and attempts to improve this pervious lesson.

Allen (1966) defines micro-teaching as a 'Scaled down teaching encounter in class size and period.'

Clift and others (1976) have recently defined, "Micro-teaching is as a teacher training procedure which reduces the teaching situation to simpler and more controlled encounter achieved by limiting the practice teaching to a specific skill and reducing teaching time and class size."

Me Aleese and Unwin (1970) suggest that the term micro-teaching is most often applied to the use of closed circuit television (CCTV) to give immediate feedback of a trainee teachers performance in a 'simplified environment', but suggest that micro-teaching is the best viewed as a form of simulated teaching usually incorporating reduced complexity and some feedback placed "along a simulation specture ranging from the purely abstract textbook of teaching practice through the actual classroom teaching."

Micro-teaching is defined as "a teacher education technique which allows teacher to apply well defined teaching skill to a carefully prepared lesson in a planned series of five to ten minutes counters with a small group of real classroom students, often with an opportunity to observe the performance on video-tape."

The Characteristics

The above definitions indicate the following features of micro-teaching:

1. It is a real teaching but focuses on developing teaching skills and competencies.
2. It is a scaled down teaching.
   (a) To reduce the class size 5 to 10 pupils.
   (b) To reduce the duration of period 5;o 10 minutes.
   (c) To reduce the size of the topic.
   (d) To reduce the teaching skill. A single skill is practised.
3. It is a highly individualized training device.
4. It provides the feedback for trainees performance.
5. It is a training device to prepare effective teachers.

The Assumption

Micro-teaching is an idea, at the core of which lie five essential proposition

1. Micro-teaching is a real teaching, but its focus is on the development of certain teaching skills and not the development of pupils-abilities.
2. Micro-teaching lesson reduces the complexities of normal classroom by scaled down class size, content and time.
3. Micro-teaching focus on training for the development of specific teaching skills. One skill is practised during course of teaching and brings it upto the mastery level.
4. Micro-teaching permits for the increased control of practice by providing the feedback to the pupil-teachers. A high degree of control can be imposed on the training programme.
5. Micro-teaching greatly expands the normal knowledge of results or feedback to teaching. It is highly individualized training programme.

The Procedure

Clift and others (1976) have given three phases of micro-teaching procedure:

I. ***Knowledge Acquisition Phase-*** It involves two major activities:
   (a) To observe demonstration skills, and
   (b) To analyse and discuss demonstration.

II. ***Skill Acquisition Phase-***Three activities are performed under this phases in the following sequences—
   (a) To prepare micro-lesson,
   (b) To practice teaching skills, and
   (c) To evaluate the performances.

The evaluation activity provides the basis to re-plan the lesson for re-teaching the same topic to practice the same skill.

III. ***Transfer Phases-***After acquiring skills in the second phases, the trainees are given an opportunity to use the skills in normal classroom teaching situation.

Micro-teaching Procedure

Knowledge Acquisition	*Planning Micro-lesson*	*Teaching Skill Acquisition*	*Re-Planning Micro-Lesson*	*Re-Teaching Skill Acquisition*
To provide awareness of a particular teaching skill.	Prepare a micro lesson no a small unit of content.	Trainee has to teach his micro lesson small class.	The trainee has to replan his same micro lesson in the light of suggestions.	The same trainee has to teach the same micro lesson.
Teaching skill is demonstrated by educator.	One particular skill is to practised.	Small class size teaching practice.	Small class size different student.	Same small size of class, but of different students.
Analysing teaching activities and discuss them.	Small class size to 15 students real class.	Only one particular teaching skill is to be practiced.	Same teaching skill	Same teaching skill is to be practiced in improved way.
	Small duration of teaching 10 to 15 minutes teaching.	The lesson should be complete within 10 to 15 minutes duration.	Small duration of the teaching.	Duration of the lesson is small.

		Stage of Presentation	*Supervision*	*Evaluation*
Assess awareness of the trainee.	Teacher educator has to supervised the learning activities.	Observation or video-taped teaching is followed by discussion, suggestion and demonstration for improvement (feedback).	Supervision of re-planning phase is done.	Observation or video-tape re-teaching followed by discussion and for further improvement (feedback).

The micro-teaching procedure involves the following steps

1. A particular skill is defined to trainees in terms of teaching—behaviour to provide the knowledge the and awareness of teaching skills.
2. These specific skills are demonstrated by an expert or shown through video-tape or film to the teacher-trainees.
3. The student-teacher plans a short lesson in which he can practice a particular skill.
4. The pupil-teachers teach the lesson to a small group of pupils which is observed by supervisor or peers or video-tape or audio-tape.
5. The teaching is followed by discussion to provide the feedback to the trainees. The video-tapes or audio-tape may be displayed to observe his own teaching activities by the trainees. The awareness of own teaching performance provides the reinforcement to the pupil-teacher.
6. In the light of the discussion and suggestions, the student teacher replans the lesson in order to practice the same skill effectively.
7. The revised lesson is re-taught to different groups of same class for the same duration to practice the same skill.
8. The re-teaching is followed by discussion, suggestions and encouraging the teaching performance. In this way, the feedback is again provided to the trainee.
9. The 'teach-reteach' cycle is continued till desired level of skill is achieved.

Various Teaching Skills

Micro-teaching is used for developing certain teaching skills. A teaching skill is defined as a set of teacher behaviours which are especially effective in bringing about desired changes in pupil-teachers. There are various teaching skills which can be developed among pupil-teachers. Allen and Ryans (1969) have suggested the following fourteen teaching skills:

1. Stimulus variation
2. Set induction
3. Closure
4. Silence and non-verbal cues
5. Reinforcement
6. Asking questions
7. Probing questions,
8. Divergent questions,
9. Attending behaviour,
10. Illustrating,
11. Lecturing,
12. Higher order questions,
13. Planned repetition, and
14. Communication completeness.

B. K. Passi (1976) has described the following thirteen skills in his book 'Becoming Better teacher': 'A Micro-teaching Approach'.

1. Writing instructional objectives,
2. Introduction of a lesson,
3. Fluency and questioning,
4. Probing questioning,
5. Explaining,
6. Illustrating with examples,
7. Stimulus variation,
8. Silences and non-verbal cues,
9. Reinforcement to student's-participation ,
10. Increasing pupil-participation,
11. Using BlackBoard,
12. Achieving closure, and.
13. Recognising attending behaviour.

The meaning of importance teaching skills have been discussed here:

Stimulus Variation: This skill involves deliberate changing of various attention producing behaviour by the teacher in order to keep pupils attentive at high level.

Set Induction: It refers to the development of cognitive rapport between pupils and teacher-to obtain immediate involvement in the lesson.

Closure: This skill is complementary to set induction. It is more than a quick summary of the portions taught and the pupils are able to related new knowledge with the previous one.

Silence and Non-verbal Cues: The use of silence and non-verbal cues in powerful device in order to encourage pupil-participation in classroom teaching.

Skill of Reinforcement: It involves teacher encouraging pupils response using verbal praise, accepting their responses or non-verbal causes like a smile.

Fluency in Questioning: This is a skill in asking-questions. By fluency means the use of as many question as possible in a given period of teaching.

Probing Questions: Probing requires that teacher asks questions that need pupils to go beyond superficial first answers of question.

Recognition and Attention Behaviour: The successful teacher is more sensitive to note the interest of boredom of pupils through visual cues.

Recognising and Attention Behaviour: The successful teacher is more sensitive to note the interest of boredom of pupils through visual cues.

Skill of Explaining: An explanation is a set of interrelated statements made by teacher in order to increase the under standing in the pupils about ideas and concepts.

Skill of Increasing Pupil-Participation: This skill involves the four components creating set questioning, encouraging pupil activities and pausing in such a way that pupil participation is maximised.

Skill of Writing Objectives: It involves the following activities-identifying objectives, analysing the task and writing objectives in behavioural terms with regard to adequate learning.

Skill of Using Blackboard: This skill requires legibility, neatness, appropriateness continuity simplicity of blackboard work. It is very essential skill for a successful teacher. The effectiveness of presentation depends upon the proper use of blackboard.

Skill for Class Management: This skill involves a number of activities that a teacher performs for creating and maintaining conducive environment for learning in the classroom.

Skill of Using Audio-Visual Aids: It implies the effective use of appropriate teaching aids to make teaching interesting and desired objectives can be achieved. The effective use of audiovisual aids makes the pupil active and attentive in classroom.

Skill for giving Assignment: This skill consists of the pupils to organize and assimilate the learnt material.

Skill of Pacing Lesson: The pacing of a lesson means the variation in the teaching speed. This skill involves adjustive devices for satisfying the needs of the pupils or student-variation.

Use of Higher Order Questions: This skill involves the questions which can be answered by memory or sensory description. The question consist of rules, principles and generalization.

Divergent Questions: It requires the respondent to organize elements into new pattern, predict, and infer from the situation. This skill involves higher order of thinking creativity.

Lecturing: Requires the effective presentation of content by using appropriate techniques and devices of teaching aids. This is known as communication competency.

Planned Repetition: It is a powerful skill in focusing and highlighting important points of teaching.

Competencies of Communication: It is a skill which is developed by sensitivity training for a clear communication of ideas and concepts in teaching. The teachers are more responsive to possible miscommunication.

Components of Skills

Skill	*Components*
Writing instructional objectives	Clarity, relevance to the content, adequacy with reference to the domains and level of objectives, attainability in terms of pupil outcomes.
Organising the content	Logical organisation according to content and psychological organisation as per need of the pupil
Creating set for introducing the lesson	Greeting, accepting creating, securing attention and giving instructions, establishing rapport, ensuring facilities like chalk, duster, aids, apparatus etc.
Introducing the lesson	Linking with past experiences, link between introduction with main parts, use of appropriate devices/techniques like questioning, examples, exhibits arousal.

Contd.

Skill	***Components***
Structuring class room questions	Structuring questions at different levels which are grammatically correct, precise and relevant to content.
Question delivery and distribution	Questions delivered with appropriate speed, with proper intonation and pitch, allowing pause for thinking, and questions well distributed covering even non-volunteers.
Response management	Management of pupil responses using techniques like prompting, eliciting further information, refocusing and asking critical awareness questions, accepting-rejecting, redirection.
Explaning	Clarity, continuity, relevance to the content, using beginning and concluding statements covering essential points.
Illustrating with explaines	Simple, interesting and relevant to the point being explained.
Using teaching aids	Relevant to content, appropriate to the pupil's level, proper display and appropriate use.
Stimulus Variation	Body movements, gestures, change in intonation and pitch, change in interaction pattern and pausing.
Reinforcement	Use of praise words and statements, accepting and using pupil ideas, repeating and rephrasing pupil ideas. Use of pleasant and approving gestures and expressions, writing pupil answers on blackboard.
Pacing of the lesson	Adjusting the speed of the lesson to the level of the pupils and difficulty level of the content.
Prompting pupil participation	Providing opportunity to pupils to increase participation through asking questions, creating climate of participation, use of silence and nonverbal cues, calling upon pupils' physical participation.
Use of Blackboard	Legible, neat, adequate with reference to the content covered.
Achieving closure of the lesson	Summarization, establishing link between the present learning with earlier as well as future learning, creating a sense of achievement in pupils.

Contd.

Skill	***Components***
Giving assignments	Relevant to the content covered and level of pupils.
Evaluating the pupil's progress	Relevant to the instructional objectives. Use appropriate questions and observations.
Diagnozing pupil learning difficulties and tasking remedial measures	Identifying learning difficulties along with causes, remedial measures suited to the type of the learning difficulties and the level of pupils.
Management of the class	Attention behaviour reinforced and directions given to eliminate non-attending behaviour, clarity of directions, appropriate handling of pupils disruptive behaviour.

Implementing the Programme

After completing the preparation along the lines indicated above implementation of the programme of microteaching in an institution require the following steps.

Orientation about Micro-teaching: Orientation of the faculty was envisaged under step 1 above. Now it is the turn of the student teacher. They need to be given an overview of the concept and procedure of microteaching, analysis of teaching into skills to be practised and the skill learning strategy. This may be done in an atmosphere of free and fair discussion.

Skill Presentation: The teaching skill selected for practice by the student teachers may be presented. The presentation or the modelling exercise includes discussion about its rationale and role in teaching, its meaning, and definition of the allied terms, component teaching behaviours comprising the skill, sample illustrations of the component behaviours, sample microlesson, plans and observation tools. Materials on selected skills has been provided in the second section of this handbook. Material is available in Passi (1976) and "Special Package on Core Teaching Skills" being prepared in the NCERT.

Skill Demonstration: This step is also a part of the modelling. After discussion of the teaching skill, the teacher educator gives a demonstration lesson on the use of the teaching skill. This lesson is observed and the teacher educator is provided feedback on the lesson based on systematic observation and recording as pointed out in Unit IV.

Preparation Micro-lesson Plan: The student teacher selects a concept for the preparation of micro-lesson plan. The concept has to be such that it is reasonably amenable to the practice of the skill. The component behaviours of the skill may be made conspicuous in the micro-lesson through labelling in brackets. Samples are available in section two of the handbook. The lesson is confined to six minutes of teaching.

Creating Microteaching Setting: Seating arrangements for the pupils for practising the skill; the college supervisor and the peer supervisor may be made. Blackboard, chalk, duster and other materials required for the micro-teacher may be arranged.

Practice of the Skill: The students teacher the lesson for six minutes. The lesson is observed using observation schedule.

Providing Feedback: On the basis of the observations, the student teacher is provided feedback on his teaching performance. The feedback is provided in terms of his use of the component behaviours comprising the skill under practice.

Replan-Reteach-Refeedback: The student-teacher replans his lesson in the light of the feedback received. The lesson is retaught and refeedback is provided as in (f) and (g) above.

Repeat the Cycle to Mastery Level: The student teacher repeats the teach-reteach microteaching cycle till he attains mastery over the skill under practice. The mastery level will depend upon the efficiency with which he can use it and the time available for practice.

Integration of Skills: The skills are mastered as outlined under steps: (a) to (i) above. The training in the integration of teaching skills may be provided.

Evaluation Instruments

The teaching skills being developed through micro-teaching lessons are to be evaluated or observed by the peers on supervisor. The rating schedule in used as criterion measure. The most popular evaluative instrument for assessing the effectiveness of micro-teaching is the Stanford Teacher Competence Appraisal Guide (STCAG).

The problem of evaluation of micro teaching effectiveness is much more difficult. The more important question is whether micro-teaching experiences lead to improve the teaching skills in a normal classroom teaching.

Allen and Ryan (1969) have given an evaluation sheet for assessing the skill of reinforcement. It consists of four dimensions of the reinforcement skills.

1. The correct responses of the students are praised or rewarded by saying 'fine', 'good', 'excellent' etc.
2. The teacher uses non-verbal cues (smile) to encourage students.
3. The teacher gives credit to students answering a question partly correct.
4. The teacher refers to positive aspects of a student's previous responses.

These dimensions are recorded by the teacher has used to category number of times. The categories are assessed on scales running from three to seven points. The STCAG consists of a number of scales rating the broad aspects of a teacher's performances.

The Advantages

The following are the main uses of micro-teaching:

1. It is an effective-feedback device for the modification of teacher-behaviour.
2. The knowledge of practice and teaching skill can be given by the use of micro-teaching.
3. It is useful for developing teaching efficiency in pre-service and in-service teacher-education programmes.
4. The specific teaching skills are developed by the micro-teaching experiences e.g. reinforcement skill probing question, etc.
5. It is a training device for improving teaching practice and to prepare effective teachers or better teachers.
6. The mechanism of feedback device can be combined with other devices such as stimulated social skill training and interaction analysis device which provide continuous reinforcement to the trainee-performances.
7. The training of teacher becomes individualized. Each trainee makes progress in developing teaching skills at his own rating depending upon his ability.
8. It permits increased control and regulates teaching practice.

9. Micro-teaching can be done either in real classroom conditions or insimulated conditions.
10. It is an economical device and use of videotape enables the trainee to analyse his own teaching performance.
11. It lessens the complexities of the normal classroom teaching by 'scaled down teaching.'
12. It focuses attention on teaching behaviour to modify and improve in a desired direction.

Reinforcement Skills

While teaching, a teacher encounters a variety of pupil behaviours. Obviously, he would like the pupils' desirable behaviours and criterion responses to be retained and undesirable behaviours to be eliminated. For reinforcing pupils' desirable behaviours and criterion responses, he uses positive verbal and non-verbal reinforcers. These reinforcers not only strengthen the pupils' desirable behaviours, but also develop confidence in them. Besides, they enhance their positive self-concept. Absence of a positive, reinforcer for pupils, desirable behaviours may erode their confidence and lead to poor self image. Positive reinforcement encourages pupils to participate actively in classroom transactions. It stimulates them to achieve more, thereby, creating a sense of achievement.

Skillful management of reinforcers help a teacher to promote pupils' learning. The skill of reinforcement refers to the effective use of reinforcers. It can, therefore, by defined as "the effective use of reinforcers to modify pupils, behaviour in the desired direction."

Skill Components

In order to learn the effective use of the skill of reinforcement, it is desirable to specify its component behaviours which are presented in this section.

Positive verbal reinforcers can be further divided into two broad categories. The first category includes the use of praise words, such as 'good', 'excellent', `fantastic', 'splendid', 'right', 'yes','correct', 'continue', 'go ahead', etc. The second category of positive verbal reinforcers refers to a teacher's verbal behaviour other than the use of praise words. The statements accepting pupil feelings, repeating and rephrasing pupil responses, summarising pupil ideas, etc., fall in this category of positive verbal reinforcers.

Micro-lesson

You have learnt about the specific component teaching behaviours of the skill of reinforcement. Read the lesson given below and identify the component (s) of the skill used in the behaviour. Write the components against the teacher behaviour in the space provided for the purpose.

Concept : Factors of Production

Class: IX

Pupil : What are the factors that contribute to production?

Teacher : Yes (1) any other factor?

Pupil : Teacher nods while the pupil was responding. (2) After pupil's response, he says 'very good' (3) land, water, air and light. So natural resources are important factors of production (4). But can we have production with the help of natural resources only?

Pupil : No, Sir.

Teacher : Yes (5) What are other factors of production then?

Pupil : Labour

Teacher : That is right (6)
Do we need skilled or unskilled labour for production?

Pupil : Production can be more with the help of skilled labour. So, we need skilled labour.

Teacher : (Moves nearer to the responding pupil) (7) says 'very good' after the response (8) and also pats him on his back (9). We therefore, need skilled labour for more production (10)
No doubt that natural resources and the skilled labour manpower are important factors of production. But we cannot have production with the help of these things only. We need something more for production. What is that?

Pupil : Production is not possible without capital.

Teacher : Smiles and nods when the pupil was responding (11) After the response was complete says: "You are correct" (12). Can your think of any other factor or production?

Pupil	:	Another important factor of production is management.
Teacher	:	Excellent (13) Teacher writes on the black-board 'Management, (14) and he says 'qualitative production' (15).
Pupil	:	Can the Government also help in increasing production?
Teacher	:	(Addressing the particular student) you have put a very important question (16). These days the government can help in a number of ways to increase production like enacting and enforcing laws which may be helpful in production.

Observation Tool

Name of the Student Teacher

Class ....

Concept:

Time ....

Session Teach/Reteach

Date ....

Supervisor...........

Instructions

The observation schedule-cum-rating scale for the skill of reinforcement comprises three columns. The first column indicates the tallies against different components of the skill. The second column specifies the components of the skill and the third column contains rating from one to seven against each of the components. The rating scale indicates the adequacy of the occurrence of components. The points on the scale indicate to following.

1. Extremely Weak
2. Very Weak
3. Weak
4. Average
5. Good
6. Very Good
7. Excellent

Tallies	Component	Rating						
(i)	Use of praise words.	1	2	3	4	5	6	7
(ii)	Repeating and rephrasing pupil responses	1	2	3	4	5	6	7
(iii)	Use of Positive non-verbal reinforcers (including extra verbal cues) but excluding writing pupil answers on the blackboard.	1	2	3	4	5	6	7
(iv)	Writting pupils' answers on the blackboard.	1	2	3	4	5	6	7
(v)	Use of discouraging words.	1	2	3	4	5	6	7
(vi)	Use of negative non-verbal reinforcers	1	2	3	4	5	6	7
(vii)	Inappropriate use of Reinforcement.	1	2	3	4	5	6	7

Probing Skills

When a question is put in the classroom, there are a number of possibly pupil response situations such as no response, wrong response, partially correct response, incomplete response or correct response. The skill of probing questioning is going deep into pupil responses through step by step questioning with a view to eliciting the criterion response. Let consider various response situations one by one.

No Response Situation: No response situation refers to the failure on the part of the pupil to frame and express verbally a response to the question that he is required to answer. The opportunity to respond is the essential condition to identify and response situation. Special reference to opportunity for responding has been mentioned because it is observed that teachers tend to think a no response occurrence even without providing opportunity to the pupils to give response. They put questions to the class, pause for a few second and taking the silence in the class as an indication of no response, start explaining, repeating or restructuring the question. This is an unhealthy practice and should be avoided. Only after a designated pupil fails to answer, we may infer a no response situation.'

Micro-lesson Plan Probing Questioning Skill

Concet ....Factors determining the supply of labour in a country.

Class XII

Teacher	:	What are the factors which determine the supply of labour in a country?
Ramesh	:	Birth and death rates, social traditions and wage level determine the supply of labour in a country.
Teacher	:	Any other factor? (1)
Ramesh	:	I do not know.
Teacher	:	If some persons from a village come to your city for seeking employment, what would be its effect on the position of labour supply in your city? (2)
Ramesh	:	It will increase the number of person seeking employment in may city.
Teacher	:	If some persons leave your city and go to another big city for seeking employment, what would be its effect on supply of labour in your city? (3)
Ramesh	:	It will reduce the supply of labour in my city.
Teacher	:	In the light of your answers to these questions, now think of any other factor which affects the supply of labour in a country. (4)
Ramesh	:	Labour supply in a country gets affected if some people go out of the country or come to that country from another country.
Teacher	:	Yes immigration i.e. coming of people in the country, and emigration, going of people out of the country affect the supply of labour in a country. Tell any country where labour supply is on the increase on account of immigration. (5)
Ramesh	:	Labour supply in U.K. is increasing on account of immigration of Asians to that country. Teacher: Why are Asians emigrating to U.K. (6)
Ramesh	:	Because of unemployment and underemployment in their own countries.
Teacher	:	Why has the Government of U.JK. Imposed certain restrictions to check immigration in their country. (7)
Ramesh	:	Because immigrants have affected the supply of labour in U.K. They have affected adversely the employment opportunities of their own people.

Teacher : Does the country from where people go to other countries get benefited by such emigration of men and women? (8)

Ramesh : Yes, it checks the supply of labour in that country.

Teacher : Any other benefit? (9)

Ramesh : These people usually remit money to their dependents in their home country either in dollars or pounds. The remittance in these currencies improve the foreign exchange resources of the home country.

Observation Tool

Name of the Student Teacher ....

Class ....

Concept ....

Duration ....

Supervisor ....

Session .... Teach/Reteach ....

Date....................

Instructions

The observation schedule cum rating scale for the skill of probing pupil responses comprises four columns. The first column indicates tallies against different components of the skill. The second column specifies the components of the skill and the third indicates rating from one of seven against each of the components. The rating scale indicates mastery of the different components of the skill. The fourth column is meant for comments. The observer may give the comments when there is any instance of wrong use of any procedure of probing pupil response or there is any occasion when there is a need to use some component of the skill but the student-teacher failed to use the component. The points on the rating scale are—

1. Extremely Weak
2. Very Weak
3. Weak
4. Average
5. Good
6. Very Good
7. Excellent

Component	*Rating*						
Prompting	1	2	3	4	5	6	7
Seeking further information	1	2	3	4	5	6	7
Refocusing	1	2	3	4	5	6	7
Increasing critical awareness	1	2	3	4	5	6	7

Illustrating with Examples

Many a time, it happens that a teacher explains in the classroom a scientific principle, or a mathematical rule or an abstract idea and observes that his pupils are not comprehending it. In such a situation, the teacher attempts to explain the concept or generalisation more and more but he fails in his attempt. The concept or generalisation requires more than mere explanation for the pupils to understand. This presents a challenge to the teacher. An unskilled teacher may deal with this challenging situation by rebuking the pupils for being inattentive in the classroom and asking them just to memorise the concept or rule. But a skilful teacher handles this situations in a different way. He illustrates the scientific principle, generalisation. This makes them easier to understand for the pupils. Obvious, examples are one of the most effective tools in the hands of the teacher to make to concept or generalisation simple and easier for pupils to understand. Thus, examples can be defined as "the observation or situations of occurrence of a concept or generalisation" and the skill of illustrating with examples can be defined as the selection and presentation of the example, relevant to the concept or generalisation to be taught to the pupils so as to make it easier for them to understand it." The examples, of courses, may be drawn from the pupils' experiences.

Components of the Skill

The next logical question is as to whether all examples make the concept or generalisation easier to understand? If not, what type of examples are helpful and appropriate in realising this objective? Experiences with the use of examples for illustrating concepts and generalisations have shown that effective examples have definite characteristics. A teacher should know these characteristics and keep them in mind while formulating examples for illustrating a particular concept or generalisation. The component behaviours based on these characteristics are presented in this section.

Microlesson Plan

Concept .... Island   Grade VI

Teacher	:	Pupils, open your book of social studies on page 38. You may see that there is a map of India. Locate Andaman on this map. What do you find around Andaman?
Renu	:	There is water on all the four sides of Andaman.
Teacher	:	Yes, there is water on all the four Andaman. Now locate Nicobar in your map. What do you find around Nicobar?
Raju	:	There is water on all the four sides of Nicobar.
Teacher	:	Very good. Like Andaman, there is water on all the four sides of Nicobar. Locate Lakshdweep on the map. What do you find around Lakshdweep?
Ameeta	:	There is water on all the four sides of lakshdweep.
Teacher	:	What is the similarity among Andaman, Nicobar and Lakshdweep?
Manmeet	:	There is water on all the four sides.
Teacher	:	What do we call the places which are surrounded by water? Manjeet: No response.
Teacher	:	These places are called islands. Now define an Island.
Rakesh	:	An island is piece of land which is surrounded by water.
Teacher	:	Can you locate any other island on your map?
Anil	:	Minicoy.

Rating Scale for the Skill of Illustrating with Examples

Name of the student teacher ....

Class .... Concept ....

Session .... Teach/Reteach ....

Supervisor .... Date ....

Instructions

The rating scale given below for the skill of 'Illustrating with Examples' comprises two columns. The first indicates the components of the skill and the second column indicates rating from one to seven against each of the components. The points on the rating scale indicate the following.

1. Extremely Weak
2. Very Weak
3. Weak
4. Average
5. Good
6. Very Good
7. Excellent

An observation should indicate his rating against each component by encircling the numbers which represents his assessment.

Component				***Rating***			
Examples used were simple.	1	2	3	4	5	6	7
Examples used were interesting.	1	2	3	4	5	6	7
Examples used were relevant.	1	2	3	4	5	6	7
Approach used was appropriate.	1	2	3	4	5	6	7
Pupil involvement was adequate.	1	2	3	4	5	6	7

Stimulus Variation

Learning in the classroom depends, to a large extent, on the attention of the pupils on the learning task. It is, therefore, essential for the teacher to secure and sustain pupil attention for making his teaching effective. Continued used of the same stimulus or activity for longer period induces inattention. The inattention is caused in two ways. Firstly, continued focus of the pupils on the same stimulus for a long time restricts his postural mobility. As a result, they feel fatigued. Secondly, the continued use of the same stimulus for longer duration introduces the element of monotony, which brings in dullness. The problem of inattention is further aggravated because of the short span of pupil attention. Their attention tends to shift from one stimulus to another frequently. They find it difficult to attend to one stimulus for more than a few minutes. The problem of inattention is a challenge to the teacher. Unless he is in a position to secure and sustain pupil attention, optimum learning cannot take place. It is, therefore essential for the teacher to secure and sustain pupil attention to what he is discussing in the classroom. How to accomplish this task during classroom teaching, is a problem that confronts every teacher.

Micro-lesson Plan Stimulus Variation Skill

Concet .... Formation of Rainbow

Class VIII

Teacher : Some of you must have seen a rainbow. It is like a bow (Teacher expresses the shape of the bow with the help of his hands and moves to the blackboard). He writes bow and draws it on the blackboard. (1) It appears during .... rainy season before or after rain. (2)

We shall study today .... The phenomenon of rainbow i.e., how is a rainbow formed? (3)

You have already studied the law of dispersion of light. When a ray of light passes through a prism, it gets dispersed into seven colours. What are these colours? (4)

Pupil : The colours are violet, indigo, green, blue, orange, yellow and red.

Teacher : Good, formation of rainbow is based on the law of dispersion of light. Teacher moves to the blackboard and writes dispersion of light. (5) (Teacher comes back to his earlier position).

You know that water vapours are in the air. (Teacher again moves to the blackboard and writes vapours and underlines this word to emphasise it). (6)

How do these vapours remain suspended in air? (7)

Pupil : There are dust particles in the air. Water vapours settle on these dust particles, and thus, remain suspended in the air.

Teacher : Soon after the rain, if the sun rises, these suspended water vapours in the air act as prisms. The rays of the sun pass through these suspended vapours in the air. Teacher stresses the words "these suspended vapours" and through the movement of hand and fingers shows how the rays of the sun pass through these suspended water vapours. (8)

He then moves to the blackboard and writes suspended vapours and draws a diagram showing the rays of the sun passing through the water vapours. (9)

These rays then get disperssed into seven colours forming a rainbow. Do you always see rainbow after rain? (10)

Pupil$_3$: No, sir, it is not seen always after rain?

Teacher : Why? (11)

Pupil$_4$: Its formation depends upon the presence of water vapours in the air. Besides the presence of water vapours in the air, its formation depends upon the angle at which the rays of the sun pass through these water vapours. If they pass through at the critical angle, then only the rainbow is formed. (12)

Teacher : It is a rare phenomenon. Its formation, thus, depends upon two factors i.e. the presence of water vapours in the air and passing of the sun rays at the critical angle through these vapours. Now each of you may draw a diagram in your exercise work showing the formation of a rainbow? (13)

(All start working on the given assignment.)

Observation Tool

Name of the Student Teacher .... Class ....

Concept: .... Time ....

Session Teach/Reteach ....

Date .... Supervisor ....

Instructions

The observation schedule-cum-rating scale for the skill of stimulus variation comprises three columns. The first column indicates the tallies against different components of the skill. The second column specifies the components of the skill. The third one contains rating from one to seven against each of the components. The rating scale indicates the adequacy and appropriateness of the occurrence of the components. The points on the scale indicate the following.

1. Extremely Weak
2. Very Weak
3. Weak
4. Average
5. Good
6. Very Good
7. Excellent

Component	***Rating***						
Movement	1	2	3	4	5	6	7
Gesture	1	2	3	4	5	6	7
Change in Voice	1	2	3	4	5	6.	7
Focussing	1	2	3	4	5	6	7
Change in Interaction Pattern	1	2	3	4	5	6	7
Pausing	1	2	3	4	5	6	7
Pupil Physical Participation	1	2	3	4	5	6	7
Aural Visual Switching	1	2	3	4	5	6	7

Explaining Skills

A pupil is required to learn a number of concepts, phenomena, generalisations, procedures, functions and reasons for certain occurrences. He is to learn about their attributes, constituent elements, relationship and applications. A teacher organises a number of learning experiences in the classroom towards the end. He uses a number of interrelated statements related to the concepts, phenomena, generalisations and functions with a view to developing in pupils an understanding about them. The set of interrelated statement used for this purpose is termed as explanation and the process is termed as explaining. The term explaining can, therefore, be defined as the use of interrelated statements about a concept, phenomenon, generalisation with a view to providing its understanding to someone else.

An explanation to be understood by pupils the explainer has to keep in mind the previous knowledge of the pupils. The previous knowledge refers to the knowledge already possessed by pupils. Since previous knowledge of the pupils of different grades, cultural background and geographical regions is always different, an explanation about a concept which is appropriate for one group of pupils may not be appropriate for another group. The quality of an explanation however, depends on the degree of understanding it generates in the explanation.

Micro-lesson Plan of Explaining Skills

Concept .... Meaning of Consumption

Class XI

Teacher: We have already studied that economics is a study of man related to wealth i.e. economic activities of man. These economic activities may be in terms of consumption, production, exchange and distribution. We shall study today the meaning of consumption (beginning statement).

Man has wants and these can be satisfied by the use of goods. For instance, when an individual is hungry, he satisfies his hunger by taking food. He is said to have consumed the food. Similarly (explaining link), a smoker when uses a cigarette and gets satisfaction, he is said to have consumed a cigarette., Thus (explaining link), the direct use of goods and services for the satisfaction of human wants is known as consumption.

Whenever we consume eatables they lose their utility. Food water, rice, fruit and vegetables get destroyed when these are consumed. Therefore (explaining link) some confuse consumption as the destruction of utilities. But (explaining link) this is not so. Sometimes (explaining link) utility of certain commodities are destroyed of their own. For instance (explaining link) when any fruit decays, it loses its utility. A house may catch fire and get destroyed. The decayed fruit and the burnt house have lost their utilities. But (explaining link) these cannot be said to have been consumed. Because (explaining link) an act of consumption implies satisfaction of human wants. The decayed fruit and the burnt house have not satisfied human want while losing their utilities.

Besides (explaining link) goods, services are also consumed. When a person travels in a bus and pays for the ticket, he consumes the transport services. A teacher's services are consumed by the pupils when they learn from him in the school. In the same way (explaining link) a doctor's, a lawyer's and a tax consultant's services are consumed by the need consumers who pay fees for their services.

Consumption, therefore, (explaining link) stands for the satisfaction of human wants. A commodity which loses its utility without satisfying a human want cannot be said to have been consumed. Besides goods, services are also consumed (concluding statement).

Rating Scale

Name of the Student Teacher .... Class ....
Concept .... Time ....
Session Teach/Reteach ....
Date .... Supervisor ....

Instructions

The rating scale for the skill of explaining comprises three columns. The first column indicates the serial number of the desirable and undesirable component behaviours of the skill of explaining. The second column specifies these component behaviours. The third one contains rating from one to seven against each of the components. The rating scale indicates the adequacy of the acquisition of the components of the skill. The seven points on the rating scale indicate the following. The rating may be indicated by encircling the number which represents the observer's assessment.

1. Extremely Weak.
2. Very Weak
3. Weak
4. Average
5. Good
6. Very Good
7. Excellent

S. No.	*Component*	*Rating*						
Desirable behaviour								
1.	Using appropriate beginning and concluding statement	1	2	3	4	5	6	7
2.	Using explaining linds	1	2	3	4	5	6	7
3.	Covering essential points	1	2	3	4	5	6	7
Undesirable behaviour								
4.	Using irrelevant statement	1	2	3	4	5	6	7
5.	Lacking fluency	1	2	3	4	5	6	7
6.	Lacking continuity is statement	1	2	3	4	5	6	7
7.	Making use of inappropriate vocabulary, vague words and phrases	1	2	3	4	5	6	7

Assessment Battery

You have just taught the lesson. You would like to assess your performance. Below are given 20 items about different aspects of teaching. Read the items one by one. Each item is to be rated on seven point scale. Eccircle the number that represents your assessment.

Topic .... Teacher .... Class .... Date ....

Item	*Rating*						
1. My lesson was effective.	1	2	3	4	5	6	7
2. I was clear about the relevance of the instructional objectives to be realised through my lesson.	1	2	3	4	5	6	7
3. I could organise lesson according to the needs of the subject-matter and level of my pupils.	1	2	3	4	5	6	7
4. Before introducing the lesson, I could secure pupils' attention and ensure availability of the material required.	1	2	3	4	5	6	7
5. I could introduce the lesson effectively.	1	2	3	4	5	6	7
6. I phrased the questions properly.	1	2	3	4	5	6	7
7. I distributed the questions well in the classroom.	1	2	3	4	5	6	7
8. I could lead the pupils to correct and complete answers when they failed to do so.	1	2	3	4	5	6	7
9. I could explain major points of my lesson clearly in a coherent manner.	1	2	3	4	5	6	7
10. I have used simple and interesting examples to clarify difficult points in the explanation.	1	2	3	4	5	6	7
11. I have used appropriate aids for making my explanation easier and interesting.	1	2	3	4	5	6	7
12. I could secure and sustain pupils' attention through variation in my voice, meaningful gestures and movements; and pupil's involvement.	1	2	3	4	5	6	7
13. I appreciated pupils for correct responses and desirable behaviours.	1	2	3	4	5	6	7
14. My blackboard work was neat and it made the lesson easier and interesting for the pupils.	1	2	3	4	5	6	7
15. While-concluding the lesson, I summarised the main point and created a sense of achievement in the pupils.	1	2	3	4	5	6	7
16. Assignments were suited to the content covered in the lesson and needs of the pupils.	1	2	3	4	5	6	7

Contd.

	Item	*Rating*						
17.	I could evaluate pupil learning through appropriate questions and observations.	1	2	3	4	5	6	7
18.	I tried to locate learning difficulties of the pupils and took appropriate steps to remove them.	1	2	3	4	5	6	7
19.	I adjusted the speed of the lesson to the level of my pupils.	1	2	3	4	5	6	7
20.	I could handle discipline problem in the class effectively.	1	2	3	4	5	6	7

QUESTIONS

1. Define the term 'Micro-teaching. Explain its function as feedback device.
2. 'Micro-teaching is real teaching but it is used as training device for developing teaching skills.' Comment on the statement.
3. Micro teaching is known as scaled down teaching; justify the phrase used for micro-teaching.
4. Explain the term 'skill' and differential with competency of teaching. Enumerate important teaching skills.
5. Explain 'Reinforcement skills' and prepare a micro-lesson for developing reinforcement skill.

14

The Evaluation

The Meaning

The evaluation process ascertains the workability of learning experiences and change of behaviour of the students. The term evaluation conveys several meanings in education and psychology. The evaluation is both qualitative as well as quantitative process. The term evaluation has been defined in the following manner.

According to Bradfield and Moredock, "Evaluation is an assignment of symbols to a phenomenon in order to characterise the worth of value of a phenomenon usually with reference the some social, cultural or scientific standard."

According to Hanna, "Evaluation is the process of gathering and interpreting evidence on change in the behaviour of all students as they progress through school."

Writingstone states in the Encyclopedia of Educational Research that "Evaluation is a relatively new technical term introduced to designate a more comprehensive concept of measurement that is implied in conventional test and examination."

It is evident for the above definitions that evaluation in educational context implies broad programme than the examination in which achievements attitudes, interests, personality traits and skills factors are taken in consideration. Thus, cognitive, affective and psychometry learning outcome are measured in the evaluation process. The success and failure of teaching depends upon teaching strategies, tactics and aids Thus, evaluation approach improves the instructional procedure and makes, teaching activities more purposive and objective-centred.

The Functions

The following are the main functions of evaluation process

1. It ascertains that how for could learning objectives be achieved:
2. It diagnoses the weakness of instructional procedures and provides the basis for remediation.
3. It provides the empirical evidences about the effectiveness of teaching strategies, tactics and aids and suggests some modification and improvement.
4. It wives refreshment and feedback to teacher and students.
5. It helps in developing a comprehensive criterion test.

The criterion test plays a significant role in the process of evaluation. All the above functions are accomplished on the basis of criterion test performance.

The Techniques

The evaluation process produces the data for cognitive, affective and psychomotor objectives. The traditional examinations confine to cognitive objectives only. In this way the evaluation is more broad process. The various types of techniques are used in it.

(a) The oral, written, essay type, objective type, practical examination and observation techniques are used for evaluation and observation techniques are used for evaluation of the cognitive objectives.

(b) The interest-inventory, attitude scale, values test and observation techniques are employed for appraising the affective objectives.

(c) The performance test, practical examination and observation techniques are employed for assessing the psychomotor objectives.

The criterion is used rather than achievement test, because criterion test with concerns objectives of teaching and instruction whereas achievement test concerns with content coverage. There are three major characteristics of a criterion test or techniques of evaluation—

Appropriateness: The criterion test must cover the terminal behaviour of teaching or instruction. Each item of the criterion should assess a specific objective. The criterion behaviour should represent the total terminal behaviour.

Effectiveness: The items of the criterion test must have difficult value and discriminative power. The test should be reliable and valid.

Practicability: The test can be administered easily and the scoring procedure should be simple. The obtained data may be interpreted and may be made meaningful. It should be acceptable to teacher and students.

Classifications

All techniques of evaluations can be broadly classified into two categories: (a) Quantitative and (b) Qualitative.

Quantitative Techniques

The quantitative techniques are mainly used in educational evaluation. These are highly reliable and valid. All three characteristics can be classified into three type (i) Oral, (ii) Written and (iii) Practical.

Oral Techniques: The oral techniques of evaluation are used at lower level in organizing and leading teaching activities. The oral questions, debate and drama are used for this purpose.

Written Techniques: In this type, the written questions are asked and students have to write their answers. The written tests are more effective than oral. The written test are usually objectives type tests are now preferred for constructing tests. The objective type tests are now preferred for constructing the criterion test because they are highly objective and reliable.

Practical Techniques: In this type of evaluation, some work is assigned to the student to accomplish it. Such techniques are based to assess the skill or psychomotor objectives. This techniques is used in Science, Geography, Home Science, Agriculture, etc.

Qualitative Techniques

The qualitative techniques are used in schools and colleges for internal assessment. These techniques are subjective and less reliable, but they are used for assessing the affective objectives. These techniques are classified into five categories—

(i) Cumulative Records,
(ii) Anecdotal Records,
(iii) Observation Techniques
(iv) Check-List, and
(v) Rating Scale.

Cumulative Records: Such records are prepared in the schools for each student. The cumulative record of the student includes the educational progress, results of monthly, half yearly tests, attendance, participation in games, sports, co-curricular activities and physical health. The cumulative record of the students provide the awareness about their progress and weakness of the parents, teachers and principal.

Anecdotal Records: This type of record maintains the description of significant event and work or performance of the students. A merit list is prepared in school. The correct information is obtained regarding incident and performance of students in anecdotal records. The interest and learning of the students can be assessed with the help of such records. Such records can also be used to provide guidance to the students.

Observation Techniques: This technique is indispensable in school evaluation. It is used at all the stages of education but most useful for evaluating the small children at primary stage. It is used for evaluating cognitive, affective and psychomotor objectives. The student of higher class can make use of this technique of self-evaluation. The classroom interaction can be evaluated only by the observation technique.

Check-List: The technique is used for evaluating interest, attitudes and values of the students. It includes certain statements of 'yes' and 'no' type. The student has to check either of the two.

Each statement of the check-list evaluates a specific objective of learning. Some examples have been given below

— Are you interested in the steps of teaching'? Yes/No/Not known.

— Do you take interest in lesson-planning? Yes/No/Not known.

— Do you really enjoy in classroom presentation? Yes/No/Not known.

— Are you interested in encouraging the student-activities? Yes/No/Not known.

The above check-list may be used for evaluating teaching interest of pupil-teachers.

Rating Scale: The rating technique is used for assessing the attitude of the students towards teaching and subjects. It consists of some statements which can be rated on three/ five/ seven/ points scale. It is used for higher classes because it requires the power of judgement of the students. A teacher can make use of this technique for evaluating the effectiveness of this instructional procedure, teaching strategy, tactics and aids. The statements of the scale are concerned with the specific objective of learning.

Measuring Learning

Measurement process is also important in the learning system. The measurement has more administrative utility in education than evaluation. An evaluation process is useful in modifying and improving learning system and instructional procedure. The measurement is precise and more objective than evaluation. Hence, it is mostly used in measuring the learning outcome.

Meaning of Measurement: Measurement is a process of quantification. It means precision and quantification of a phenomenon or variable.

According to Bradfield "Measurement is a process of assigning symbols to the dimensions of phenomenon in order to characterise the status of the phenomenon as precisely as possible."

Measurement is always done of a quality, attribute or variable of a thing or a person. We never measure a thing or a person. The psychologists and educationists are mainly concerned with the variables and attributes. The process of measurement converts the variable into variate which is used for drawing the inferences. For example, intelligence is quantified in terms of I.Q. and achievement variable is measured in terms of scores.

Essentials of Measurement: Measurement in any field always involves three essentials—

(1) Identifying and defining the quality, attribute or variable that is to be measured.

(2) Determining the set of operations by which the attribute of variable may be made manifest and perceivable, and

(3) Establishing a set of procedure of definitions for translating observations into quantitative statement of degree, extent or amount.

The Functions

Cronbach (1949) has classified all applications of mental measurement under the following three main functions:

1. Prognosis function,
2. Diagnosis function, and
3. Research Function

Prognosis Function: The first of these functions is that of prognosis function. Any test tells about some differences among people's performance at this movement. All decisions involve prediction when psychological test is mentioned, so called I. Q. test administered to students in school to predict their academic performance come to mind. The measurement provides the extent of a variable which has the specific purpose of predicting future behaviour.

The prognosis has the administrative function such as classification, selection, promotion and gradation of students. The college studies ask a counsellor to help them choosing the best curriculum or job. Thus, the guidance and counselling service are also based upon the prognosis function of measurement. The effectiveness of method instruction and treatment is evaluated on the basis of students achievement.

Diagnosis Function: The second major function of measurement listed by Lee J. Cronbach is that of diagnosis. The prognosis function reveals the level of student with regard to certain characteristics, whereas the diagnosis function identifies the weakness of the student learning. The remedial instruction can be repaired on the basis of diagnosis. It also implies the predicting but there is considerable justification in listing diagnosis for a separate function of measurement. The diagnosis function establishes the cause-effect relationship but prediction implies the simple relationship. The instructional procedure can be improved by this function of psychological measurement.

Research Function: The third major function of measurement listed by Cronbach is that of verification of scientific hypotheses of research. The use of measurement for research purpose, however, is not as great as for prediction and diagnosis. There is a reason for this as measurement is usually considered as completely valid measure of ascertaining human characteristics. An investigator must treat test scores in this experiment as accurate quantification of real and useful variable. Measurement provides a more objective and dependable basis for comparison than does rough impressions. Thus, the valid generalizations are made on the basis of accurate measurement.

In fact, the quantification is generally considered essential for the progress of education particularly at more advanced level. The scales of measurement have also been discussed below.

Scales of Measurement

There are four basic ways for quantifying a variable. They are also called levels of measurement and are commonly referred to as—

1. Nominal Scale,
2. Ordinal or Rank Scale,
3. Equal Interval Scale, and
4. Ratio Scale.

Nominal Scale: The nominal scale is the least precise or crude among the four basic scales of measurement. It simply implies the classification of an item into two or more categories without the classification of an item into two or more categories without any extent or magnitude. There is no particular order assigned to them. The frequency of numbers are used to give a name to something that may be used for determining per cent mode. For example boys and girls; pass and fail; rural and urban, etc.

In the classroom observation, the measurement is done at nominal scale. The teaching and instruction are organized considering the mode of the students, because a teacher cannot pace with each and every student in his teaching and learning process.

Ordinal Scale: The ordinal scale is precise than the nominal scale. It allows the teacher to assign values by placing or arranging the observation in relative rank order. No value is assigned to the distance between positions of ranking. The scale assigns observation to categories by number and arranges them in a logical order. It does not require the relationship of equivalence but also requires one observation to be greater than the other.

This scale is used frequently in the schools for prize distribution and to provide the motivation by the technique of competition. In asking the questions, teacher considers the place of student in the class.

Equal-Interval Scale: The equal-interval scale is more precise and refined scale than nominal and ordinal scale. This scale has all the characteristics and relationship of the ordinal scale, besides this distances between any two numbers on the scale are known. The zero point and the unit of measurement used on the scale are arbitrary or assumed. A linear relationship is established in the equal-interval scale.

The equal-interval scale has the greater use in teaching-learning situation, educational administration, educational guidance and counselling and educational research. The effectiveness to any instructional procedure can be evaluated precisely by collecting the data on this scale. The measurement in education is usually done on equal interval scale. The dependable inferences are drawn in educational research by collecting evidences on equal-interval scale.

Ratio Scale: The ratio scale is the most refined among the four basic scales. It has all the characteristics of equal-interval scale. In addition to that, it has an absolute zero point representing complete absence of the property being measured. It is used in physical sciences and less frequently in behavioural sciences. In school, it is used in maintaining the cumulative records of the students. The cognitive and affective objectives can be assessed by using earlier scales of measurement, the ratio scale may be used for measuring the psychomotor objectives.

The measurement on various scales is done by using different types of measuring instruments. The questionnaire and observation yield ordinal data, educational and psychological tests provide scores or marks and physical measurement yields the data ratio scale. The characteristics of a good measuring instrument have been described here.

The Characteristics

A good measuring instrument or test requires some technical knowledge. It includes the knowledge and understanding of the various kinds of errors which influence the process of measurement. These are known as errors of measurement, and can be classified into four categories: (a) Personal errors, (b) Variable errors, (c) Constant errors, and (d) Interpretive error.

Personal Errors: In the field of measurement, the term objectivity is used to designate that the characteristic is related to personal error. The personal observing exactly the same responses are likely to assign different scores, because they can see the performance only from their own views or biases. The same person examining the same responses on two different occasions is likely to vary. This is known as personal error. It is termed as degree of objectivity.

Variable Errors: This kind of error may occur in psychological and educational measurement. .The variable errors are those arising from accidents and inaccuracies due to many causes. A person making the observation which influences from time to time, test to test and individual to individual, is accountable to variable zero. This is termed as degree of reliability.

Constant Errors: Most of the measurement of education and psychology are indirect. It is neither possible nor desirable to open a person's skull, to look inside. An instrument measures what is claim to measure; which is related to the trait or characteristics.

Testing the problem of constant error is the problem of validity. It is necessary to know whether a test really measures what is claimed to measure.

Interpretive Errors: The test score of an individual has no meaning until it is interpreted in terms of the performance of the other individuals or the performance of the group. Interpretive errors are those which result from understanding as for one or two things.

(1) With what group of the individual is being compared.

(2) The way in which the comparison between the individual and the group performance is expressed.

Interpretive errors may be stated that is the problem of translating the raw scores into the norms. This problem of interpretive errors is taken in care through a process called standardization. This type of error is measured through norms.

The earlier three type of errors are usually considered in constructing the criterion test but the last one is 'interpretive error which is not taken in consideration because the criterion test evaluates the learning objectives in terms of group performance. This error involves when an individual's score is interpreted. Thus, the characteristics of a good measuring instrument may be summarized in the following form:

1. It should be objective.
2. It should be reliable.
3. It should be valid.
4. It should be comprehensive and precise.
5. It should be usable and practicable.

The usability implies the following features:

(a) Ease in administering the tool.

(b) Ease in scoring the answer scripts.

(c) Ease in interpreting scores.

(d) It should be economical from time, energy and money point of view.

Tests for Measuring Learning

According to Glaser, learning outcome can be measured with the help of criterion test. The teaching is organized to provide the learning experiences by generating the appropriate learning structures and situations so that desired objectives may be achieved, these tests are of two types:

(1) Essay type tests or traditional examinations, and

(2) Objective type tests or New type examinations.

Learning and Essay Type Tests: The essay type examinations are most commonly used in our schools, but they are less reliable and less valid and cannot be standardized. The essay type tests can be easily prepared. They can not be abolished from the field of examination though they have certain limitations and disadvantages.

The essay type tests can be used to evaluate lower and higher objectives of learning the objectives type tests can not be used for measuring the higher objectives of learning but essay type tests are effectively employed for higher objectives, hence, both type of tests are supplementary to one another of measuring the learning objectives. The essay type tests are used for evaluating the objectives and affective higher learning objectives.

The oral questions are asked in classroom teaching for measuring the learning objectives. If teacher feels that he would not achieve the desired objectives then he revises and modifies his teaching strategies and tactics. The oral questions also serve the purpose of diagnosis so that teacher who can proceed remedial instruction to his students.

Learning and Objective Type Tests: These are the new type of examinations. They are reliable and valid and can be standardized. A large number of questions or items are included in a test. The construction of such tests is difficult and time consuming, but scoring is easy.

The objective type tests are used to measure lower and middle learning objective, i.e., knowledge, comprehension and application. These are used for both the purpose: prognosis as well as diagnosis.

Managing by Learning Objective: Peter Drocker (1954) has propagated the concept of management by objectives (MBO). Since then it has been used in planning, organizing, leading and controlling the teaching activities. The teaching and testing activities are organized to achieve learning objectives. The concept management by objectives (MBO) is also used in industry, trade and military. It is more useful in the field of education because its principles are applicable in teaching and training activities. The management by objectives is evaluated in terms of learning objectives. In the first step of management for learning objectives are written in behavioural terms and they are evaluated with the help of criterion behaviour included in the criterion test.

The criterion test is a significant aspect of management by learning objectives because its each item measures at least one learning objective. The criterion test may be objective type, or essay type or both. It means that objective type and essay type tests are made objective-centred. The procedure of constructing objective-centred test has been discussed here.

Construction of Objective Test

According to Stanley and Ross, there are four steps of constructing the objective type test: Planning, preparing, trying out and evaluation.

First Step: Planning: This step includes the following activities:

(1) Fixing up the objectives.

(2) Writing objectives in behaviour terms.

(3) Task analysis and content analysis.

(4) Determining the type, forms and items.

(5) Preparation of table of specification.

(6) Taking a decision about mechanical aspects, time, number of items, size of letters and printing, etc.

(7) Evaluating the instructions.

Second Step: Preparing Test Items: In the second step, items are written. The table of specification provides a guide line for this purpose. Generally two types of items are prepared for constructing an objective type test: Recognition and Recall.

Recognition Type Items: The form of items is such that the student has to select the best or correct answers. These may be of the following forms:

(1) True/False or Write/Wrong Type or Alternative responses,

(2) Multiple choice type,

(3) Matching type,

(4) Classification type, and

(5) Analogy type.

Recall Type Items: The recall type items require that student has to supply the correct answer for a question. They are also known as short answer type questions. The recall type items are classified into two categories:

(1) Simple recall type, and

(2) Completion type.

These items may be understood by studying their following aspects (i) Meaning and definition of the type of items. (ii) Example of the form (iii) Formula of guessing (iv) Advantages and limitations and (v) Precautions.

Third Step-Trying out of Test: After writing the items, an initial draft of the test is prepared. The items are improved and modified on the basis of individual and group tryout. The following activities are performed in this step :

(1) Pre-try out is done on small group of students to improve the language ambiguity and difficulty of the items.

(2) Proper try out is done for item-analysis.

(a) Difficult values and discriminative powers are calculated for each item of the test.

(b) Items are selected, rejected and modified.

(c) Final form of the test is prepared. The items are arranged in difficult order. The most easy item is placed first and most difficult at the last.

Fourth Step-Evaluation: The final form of the test is evaluated in terms of various kinds of error measurement. The final form of the test is administered on a large group of target population. The students scores on the test are used for the following purposes:

(1) Estimating reliability coefficient.

(2) Calculating the validity coefficient.

(3) Developing the norms of the test, and

(4) Preparation of test manual.

The objective type tests are reliable and valid. Therefore, they are used in constructing the criterion test for measuring the learning objectives. The form of objective type items has been described in the following paragraph.

Form of Objective Items

As it has been mentioned above that objective type items are recall and recognition type, their meaning, example and advantages are given below:

Recognition Type Items: They are also known as selection type items because item consists of possible answers. The student has to select the best or correct answers. There are various type of recognition items; some important types have been discussed here.

Alternative Response Type or True/False Type Test

Definition :An alternative type test is made of items each of which admits only two possible responses. The usual form is the familiar true-false test. Other similar forms are right-wrong, correct-incorrect. yes - no type, examples.

Learning Objective (L. O.): The learner is able to discriminated between teaching and learning.

Item-There is a difference between teaching and learning.

True/False

L. O.-The learner is able to interpret the meaning of learning.

Item-The change in behaviour through motivation is known as learning.

True/False

Advantages: This of item has the following advantages: (1) Easy to construct, (2) Easy to administer. (3) A wide knowledge is tested. (4) Easy to score.

Disadvantages: The alternative response item has high probability of guessing correct responses. The fifty per cent items are attempted correctly by guessing. The knowledge is tested in bits. There is no freedom for the student to respond.

Suggestions for Modifications: While using this type of item, the following suggestions should be observed

(1) Guessing formula should be used.

(2) There should be three alternatives rather than two, i.e., true, false and not known.

(3) Arrangement of correct alternatives should be random, there should not be a regular arrangement of correct responses.

(4) Item should be written in simple statement form.

(5) The proper instruction should be provided.

Rules and Precautions: In writing such items, the following rules and precautions should be taken into consideration:

(1) Avoid ambiguous statements or long statement,

(2) Exact language or text books should not be used,

(3) Avoid trick statements, and

(4) Avoid specific determiners.

Multiple-Choice-Type Items

Definition: A multiple-choice test is made of items, each of which present more responses and only one of which correct or definitely better than others. E. F. Lindquist asserts that it is definitely superior than other types:

Lee J. Cronbach regards it is being practically free from 'response sets,' and it is one of the corrector best response should be marked is available. Examples

Instructions: The following statements have four possible responses or choices. The correct or best response should be marked by the correct sign (_/)

L. O.: The learner is able to recognise the functions of measurement.

Item: The function of measurement is

(a) Prognosis (b) Diagnosis

(c) Research (d) All the above Ans (d)

L. O.: The learner is able to recall the names of the exponent of 'Behaviour Modification Model' of Teaching.

Item: The exponents of behaviour modification model of teaching is

(a) Robert Glaser (b) J. Bruner

(c) B. F. Skinner (d) D. Ausubel. Ans. (c)

L. O.: The learner is able to classify the activities of organising teaching.

Item: The activity of organizing teaching is,

(a) Identification of communication-strategy.

(b) Selecting appropriate teaching strategies and tactics.

(c) Selecting appropriate teaching aids.

(d) All the above.

Ans. (d)

It is evident from the above examples that each item consists of two parts: statement and choice. The statement is called stern and choice is known as solution.

Advantages: The following are the advantages of multiple choice items:

(1) This is most for measuring cognitive objectives and it is based upon psychological principles.

(2) The scope of guessing is minimum.

(3) It is useful for assessing judgement and discrimination abilities.

(4) The scoring is easy of multiple choice items.

(5) The analysis of such item is also very easy.

Disadvantages: The multiple choice items suffer from the following limitations:

(1) It is difficult to prepare good type of multiple choice items.

(2) There is a scope of guessing the correct response.

(3) An item can be used for assessing one bit of information.

(4) This type of item can not be used for all content.

Rules and Suggestions for writing the Multiple Choice Items

The following rules and suggestions should be taken in consideration for writing the multiple choice items:

(1) Item should be written in simple statement form.

(2) Make all options responses grammatically consistent.

(3) As a rule, use complete statement rather than incomplete statement.

(4) Avoid using any clue for correct response.

(5) Arrange the responses so that correct one should occur in a random order.

(6) Make all responses plausible or homogenious.

(7) At least four six solutions should be provided to one item.

(8) Use the formula for guessing in assigning the of an individual.

(9) Arrange item in groups, group together all items having the same number of choices.

(10) The higher objectives can be measured by increasing the homogenity of the solutions.

Matching Type Item

The matching type item is an improved form of multiple choice items.

Definition: A matching type test consists of two columns, each item in the first column is to be paired with a word or phrase in the second column on some basis is suggested. In the simplest form of matching test item, the number of responses is exactly the same as the number of statements.

L. O.: The Students are able to recall the exponents of model of teaching.

Item: There are two columns A and B. In the column A several statement are given and their answers arc provided 10 column B but they are arranged randomly. Write the correct word of second column in the respective statement of first column in the blank space.

Column A ***Teaching Models***	***Column B*** ***Exponents of Teaching Model***
1. Developmental Model	A. I. K. Davies
2. Basic Model of Teaching	B. David P. Ausubel
3. Operant Conditioning	C. Ned A. Flanders
4. Advance Organizer	D. Hilda Taba
5. Managing Teaching learning	E. William Gardon
6. Interaction Model	F. B. F. Skinner
	G. Jean Piaget

Advantage: "The matching exercise is particularly well adapted to test in who, what, and where types of situations or for naming and identifying abilities" -E. E Lindquist

(1) It is an economical item from time and construction point of view.

(2) It is easy to construct and score.

(3) It is easy and convenient form of exercise for measuring events and dates, events and person, events and place, terms and definitions.

(4) It is very useful for measuring knowledge objectives.

Limitations: These items have the following limitations:

(1) There is a scope of guessing.

(2) The analysis of such items is difficult.

(3) It is not well adopted by the measurement of under-standing as distinguished from memory.

(4) When the equal numbers of items are in both columns that last item can be attempted correctly without knowing it.

Rules and Suggestions: The following rules and suggestions should he considered using and preparing matching type of items:

(1) The homogeneous type of material should be included in each matching exercise.

(2) The each exercise should be checked carefully for unwarranted clues by indicate matching pairs.

(3) The items in the response column should be arranged in a systematic order.

(4) The basis of matching should be clearly indicated.

(5) There should be more words or phrases in the paired columns.

Classification Type Items

A classification type item consists of several words. Out of these words, one word does not belong to that group. The learner has. to identify the word on the basis of his understanding.

L. O.: The learner is able to discriminate between the functions of measurement and characteristics of measuring instrument.

Instruction: There are five words but one word does not belong to the group. It should be underlined.

Item: (1) Prognosis, Reliability, Diagnosis, Prediction and Research.

2. Validity, Objectivity, Prediction, Reliability and Norms.

Advantages: (1) The classification type items are easy to construct, easy to score and easy to interpret.

(2) This type of item is useful for measuring comprehension and discriminative abilities.

Limitations: It has the following limitations:

(1) There is a scope for attempting item correctly by guessing.

(2) These types of items can not be used for all type of content and for all school subjects. It has very limited scope.

The Analogy Type Items

This type of item includes both, selection and supply type of situations. This type of item consists of two situations. The first situations is complete and another is incomplete. The second situation is completed by the student on the basis of first situation.

L. O.: The learner is able to state the purpose of different steps of managing teaching learning.

Instructions: There are two situations. The first situation is complete and second is incomplete. It should be completed on the basis of first situation.

Item: 1. Planning : Objective : Leading: ....

2. Controlling : Evaluation : Organizing ....

Ans.: 1. Motivation 2. Teaching Strategies.

Advantages: (1) The analogy type items are easy to prepare and easy to score.

(2) This type of items are used to measure the verbal reasoning ability of the students.

(3) The analysis objectives are best measured by this type of items.

(4) These items are included in both recall and recognition type items.

Item: Tryout : Items Analysis : Variable error..............................

Ans.: Reliability

Recall Type Items

These are also known as supply type of items, because student has to supply the response on the basis of his memory. There are two categories (1) simple recall and (2) Completion type items. The brief description of these items has been given here.

Simple Recall Items

Definition: The simple-recall test is defined as one in which each item appears a direct question, a stimulus word or phrase or specific direction. The response must be recalled or supplied by the pupil from his experience rather than identification.

The simple-recall test is different from eassy type, primarily the basis of length of response is required. It is sometimes called a short answer test.

L. O.: The student is able to recall the exponents of taxonomy of objectives or learning conditions or managing teaching-learning.

Instruction: Give the answer of the following questions in the space given in front of each question.

Item: 1. Who is the exponent of the concept of learning conditions? (..........)

2. Who has propounded the idea of managing teaching-learning?

3. Who has contributed the concept of taxonomy objectives?

Answers: (1) Robert Gagne (2) I K. Davies (3) B.S. Bloom.

Advantages: The following are the major advantages of recall type of items:

1. There is no scope for attempting question correctly by guessing.
2. It is easy to prepare and score.
3. These are valuable for measuring factual knowledge.
4. These items are useful for evaluating the knowledge objectives.

Limitations: The following are the limitations of recall type of items:

(1) The recall type items tend to measure highly factual information.

(2) The response of item mainly depends upon memory aspect.

(3) One item measures our bit of information.

Suggestions: The following suggestions should be followed while using recall type of items:

(1) The item should be a direct question in the statement form.

(2) The response should be brief and well worded or single-worded.

(3) The question should be so written that it requires a specific response.

The Completion Type Items

Definition: The completion type test may be defined as a series of sentences in which certain important word or phrase has been omitted and blank submitted to the pupils to fill it. A sentence may contain one or more blanks Each blank counts one point.

L. O.: The learner is able to recall the name of exponent has who given an approach for writing objectives in behavioural terms.

Instruction: The following statement are written in incomplete form. The blank should be completed by providing an appropriate word

Item: An approach for writing objectives in behavioural term is given by Robert Mager.

L. O.: The learner is able to recall the name of exponent of basic model of teaching.

Item: The basic model of teaching is developed by Robert Glaser.

Advantages: The completion type test has the following advantages:

1. There is no scope for guessing the correct response.
2. This type of item is easy to construct and easy to score.
3. It has a wide applicability as far its subject matter is concerned.
4. It depends upon understanding while recall type depends upon rote memory.
5. It measuring linguistic aptitude and language comprehension also.

Suggestions: The following suggestions should be followed while using the completion type items.

(1) The indefinite statement should not be used.

(2) The key words and phrases should be omitted.

(3) The grammatically clues should be avoided.

(4) The statement of item should be so written that it requires a single response.

Evaluating Learning Objectives

The process of management by objectives can be successfully applied in the organization of teaching. The classroom teaching objectives can be evaluated easily. The learning objectives of various school-subjects may be tested by preparing objective-centred items.

Items for Teaching Technology

Knowledge Objective: (1) The learner is able to recognize the level of teaching.

Instruction: In the following item, a statement has been given and four responses are given. The right response should be marked by correct sign.

Item: Teaching levels are,

(a) Memory level (b) Reflective level

(c) Understanding level (d) All the above. Ans (d)

(2) The learner is able to recall the steps of managing teaching learning.

Instruction: In the following statement a blank is provided. It should be completed by giving a suitable word.

Item: In managing teaching learning process .... steps are to be followed.

Ans. Four

Comprehension Objectives: (3) The learner is able to identify the characteristics of a measuring instrument.

Instruction: The following item consists of five words. One word out of these does not belong to that group. It should be underlined.

Item: Reliability, Objectively, Validity, Diagnosis, Norms and Prediction.

Ans. Diagnosis

Items for General Science

Knowledge Objectives: (1) The learner is able to recognize the functions of a leaf.

Item: The functions of a leaf are

(a) Respiration (b) Transpiration

(c) Carbon Assimilation (d) All the above Ans. (d)

Comprehension Objectives: (2) The learner is able to classify animal kingdom.

Item: Cow, Horse, Frog, Elephant and Camel. Ans. (Frog)

Item of Geography

Knowledge Objectives: (1) The learner able to recognize the capital of India.

Item: The capital of India is

(a) Bombay (b) Madras

(c) New Delhi (d) Lucknow. Ans. (c)

Comprehension Objectives: (3) The learner is able to generalize the causes of lunar eclipse.

Item: The lunar eclipse is due to

(a) The earth rotates on its axis.

(b) The earth rotates round the sun and moon revolves round the earth.

(c) The earth is larger than moon.

(d) The sun is greater than the earth.

Ans. (b)

Item of History

Knowledge Objectives: (1) The learner is able to recognize the date of India's Independence.

Item: 1. The date of India's Independence is

(a) 26th January 1950 (b) 2nd October 1947

(c) 30th January 1948 (d) 15th August 1947 Ans. (d)

2. The learner is able to recall the date of republic day.

Item: The republic day of India is ....

3. The learner is able to recall the name of first Prime Minister of India.

Item: The first Prime Minister of India was ....

Ans. (2) 26th January (3) P Nehru.

Essay Type Test

The essay type test is not reliable and their validity is also poor. Even that the essay type test can not be eliminated from the field of educational measurement. The essay type test is used objectively from measuring the higher-learning objectives. The effective type test can not be successfully used for evaluating the higher objectives to teaching and learning. Therefore, the essay type examination needs improvement. Three types of improvement can be made for their effective use.

(1) The improvement should be made in the form of questions.

(2) The improvement should be done in question-paper, and

(3) The improvement should be made in marking the answer-books.

Improvement in Questions: The following types of improvement should be made in the essay type questions:

Each question should measure a specific learning objective. The emphasis should be given on the coverage of learning objectives rather than content coverage. The content of a question should be correct and real. The language should be simple and clear. The formation of question should be written in such a way that it should require a definite answer. The words of a question should have a single meaning. The difficulty level of a question should be according to the level of the students. The vague statement should not be used, e.g., what do your understand by 'Teaching technology '? The answer of this question is not definite.

Improvement in Question-papers: The form of question-paper should be such so that all learning objectives can be measured. There should not be many choice in the paper but there should be choice within the question. The instructions should be simple and clear. The marks should be distributed for each question. There should be a distribution of marks even for the parts of the question. The model answers should be supplied to each question for evaluating the answers.

Improvement in Evaluating the Answer-books: The essay type tests are easy to construct but difficult to evaluatee. There should be an improvement in evaluating the answer-books. The experienced and eminent persons should be appointed for evaluating the answer-books. The instruction for evaluation should be given in simple and clear language. The model answers should be sent to the examiners. The marks should be assigned for each part of a question separately. The rank or grades may be used in evaluating the answer books. The central evaluation system should be introduced and the examiners should be assigned the question rather than answer-books. It means, that answer of some questions of all the candidates should be examined by the examiner only. While assigning the marks, the examiner should justify why has he deducted the marks'? What else should be there so that full marks would be given?

The essay type tests can be successfully used for measuring the higher-learning objectives.

Essay Type Questions

In the process of management of teaching-learning, the essay type tests can also be used successfully for measuring learning objectives. The essay type questions can be made objective-centred rather than content-centred.

Essay Type Question in Teaching Technology

Creative objective: (1) The learner is bale to evaluate the meaning and definition of Teaching Technology.

Question: "The scientific knowledge applied to classroom teaching is known as Teaching Technology." Discuss the statement.

(2) The learner is able to examine the merits and demerits of essay type and objective type tests.

Question: "The essay type test should not be abolished but should be mended." Comment on this statement.

Question: "The objective type tests are not contradictory to essay type tests but these are complementary to one another." Give your views on this statement.

(3) The learner is able to analyse the elements of teaching process.

Question: "Teaching is not only an art but also a science." Explain the scientific aspects of teaching.

Essay Type Questions in History

The following questions can be used for measuring the creative higher learning objectives.

1. The learner is able to analyse the influence of geographical factors on Indian history.

Question: 'The northern boundary of India and influenced the ancient Indian history.' Describe the statement in detailed.

2. The learner is able to fine out the contribution of Ashok for human-welfare.

Question: 'Ashok was not only ruler but also he was a great social reformer.' Discuss the statement.

or

Describe the contribution of Ashok for human-welfare in detailed.

Essay Type Items in Geography

The essay type question can be contributed in geography for measuring higher learning objectives or creative objectives.

1. The learner is bale to analyse the relationship between Geography and History.

Question: "Geography provides the statue to man's (History) activities." Comment on this statement.

Question: "Geography is a study of earth and man." Discuss this statement.

Question: 'Geography and History are not contradictory but supplementary.' Comment on this statement.

The essay type questions and objective type items should be used for measuring the learning objectives. The criterion test for the management of objectives for both types of items should be included for the coverage of learning objectives.

In the following table, the comparison of objective type and essay type tests has been provided.

Comparison between Essay and Objective Tests

Point	*Objective Type Test*	*Essay Types Test*
Purpose	Measuring Achievement prognosis, diagnosis, research, Counselling and guidance.	Measuring Achievement prognosis, classification and promotion.
Construction	The construction is difficult, time consuming, costly and needs knowledge and training.	The construction is easy and economical, need no training.
Scoring	The Scoring is simple and easy. The answer key is used. The mastery over subject for the evaluator is not essential.	The scoring is difficult. The evaluator should have the mastery over subject-matter.
Reliability	They are highly reliable and various methods are used for estimating the reliability index.	They are less reliable and also difficult to estimate the reliability.
Objectivity	They are objective in scoring the answers of the students. The personal factors do not influence scoring procedure.	They are subjective. The scoring procedure is highly influenced by the personal factor, of the evaluator.
Validity	They are valid and validity co-efficient is estimated by employing various methods.	They are not valid and the validity co-efficient is difficult to obtain.
Norms	The objective type tests are standardized by developing norms.	The essay type tests can not be standardized and it is difficult to develop norms.
Guessing factor	The items can be attempted correctly by guessing. The guessing formula is used for the correction.	There is no scope for guessing but the students can cheat and bluff the examiner.

Contd.

Point	***Objective Type Test***	***Essay Types Test***
Hand writing	The language and hand-writing do not have in fluence on scores. The expression and language can not measured.	The hand-writing and language have great influence on socres. The expression, organization of content and language can be measured.
Learning Objective	The objective type tests are useful for measuring congnitive lower objectives. They can not be used effectively for affective and psychomotor learning objectives.	The essay type tests are applicable for measuring cognitive and affective higher learning objectives.
Administration	The administration of objective type test is difficult. The specific instruction are given. It needs training for administering test effectively.	The administration of essay test is easy. The specific instructions are not essential and no training is required for this purpose.
Fatigue	The student feels fatigue because in a short period a large number of questions are to be answered. One hundred items are to be answered in an hour approximately.	The student relatively feel less fatigue, because five questions are to be answered within three hours.
Content	It has high content coverage, because large number of items are included in this test.	It has poor content coverage; the sampling is done. The five questions cannot cover the content.
Number of Question	It has usually large number of items in one test ranging 50 to 100 or more.	It has usually eight or ten questions but five questions are usually attempted in three hours of duration.
Preparation of students	In this type of test, students have to study thoroughly the minute concepts are prepared.	In this type of test, students have to prepare broad and important concepts.

Criterion-referenced Tests

In the 1960 a new term entered, in the vocabularies of measurement specialists, criterion-referenced test. It referred to a particular kind of test and unconventional approach to the measurement of educational achievement. Test of this kind were also referred to objective- referenced or domain referenced and were contrasted with the more conventional standardized or teacher-made tests, which are referred to norm- referenced tests.

Strong advocates of the new test, who were usually rather critical of conventional tests claimed that criterion-referenced tests constituted a significant and generally applicable improvement in the conception and methodology of achievement testing. They suggested that norm-referenced tests should be abandoned as quickly as possible in favour of the new type. An alternative view, which we support, is that neither type is superior the others for all measurement purposes. Each has special characteristics that make it uniquely well suited to particular situation and uses.

On way of becoming familiar with the characteristics of criterion-referenced tests is to consider some of the ways in which they differ from or are similar to, norm- referenced tests. Comparison of this kind is bound to involve some over simplifications and in accuracies, since there are many different forms of each type to test. Nevertheless, the forms have enough features in common to make the comparison useful, even if not always completely accurate.

Difference Between Criterion and Norms Referenced Tests : One difference is as the kind information they are intended to provide. Criterion-referenced tests are used to determine which of certain specified objectives of Instruction a particular pupil has attained. Norm-referenced tests are used to determine how much overall knowledge of some subject a particular pupil has achieved. The basic report for a norm-referenced test is a count of the number of test questions that are answered correctly.

A second difference is as the basic interpreting the information provide. The criterion is a criterion-referenced test for the attainment of all instructional objectives. The excellence or deficiency of a particular student's achievement in earning is judged by the propagation of the prescribed objectives, the student has attained. The 'norm' in a norm-referenced test is the achievement of some specifical group of students on the test. An excellence or deficiency of a particular student's achievement in learning is judged by that student's standing among those in the specified group.

A third difference is as the distribution of items over the domain of achievement sampled by the test. The items in a criterion-referenced test cluster around a limited number of specific objectives. For example a criterion referenced test might focus on 20 distinct objectives, using five items for each objective in order to determine whether or net the student had attained it. The result would be a 100 items criterion-referenced test. The items in a norm-referenced test would be diffused more widely across the domain of learning. Each of the 100 items would involve a separate aspect of achievement.

A fourth difference is as the use made of the test information. The purpose of a norm-referenced test score is simply to indicate a student's degree of success in learning of criterion-referenced test, on the other hand, is after used with instructional procedure intended to ensure that certain things will be learned.

Despite these major differences, there are substantial similarities between criterion-referenced and norm-referenced tests. Both have essentially the same job to do that is to measure achievement in learning. Elements of quality are essentially the same for both. An individual test question used in the two are indistinguishable.

In general, criterion-referenced tests are best to assist in categorical pass-fail decision with respect to separate specific terms or competencies.

The norm referenced form is useful in measuring a person's general level of knowledge or understanding of a subject. While categorical decisions are sometimes made on the basis of scores on norm-referenced test, as in the case of certification examination.

Proponents of criterion-referenced test have performed a valuable service in emphasizing the importance of clearly defining test goods.

Proponents of criterion-referenced test sometimes criticize standardized test (norm-referenced) for their level of specific relevance to what is being taught in a particular unit of study in a given local school system.

The norm-referenced for is useful measuring a person's general level of knowledge or understanding of a subject.

Summative and Formative Test

Summative Test: Summate test is given to the student after he has passed successfully all the formative tests given separately in the last of each unit of the content. Form summative test, the general level of student is judged and on the basis of students performance, the effectiveness of teaching and instruction is evaluated. Thus it provides reinforcement to teacher and instruction and help in planning and organising of further teaching. On the basis of student's performance, it can be judged, to what extent objectives could be realized. These two test, formative and summative are complimentary to each other in teaching-learning. In formative test, the difficulties of student's learning are important while in summative test, the effectiveness of teaching is measured.

Formative Test: In teaching and instruction, the whole content is presented in small units. Therefore, in the end of each unit, students should be given test and weaknesses should be diagnosed. After diagnosis, remedial teaching should be done and then formative test is given. Formative tests are used to make teaching-learning more effective and to give opportunity to students to get mastery in the content here more emphasis is on the achievement of objectives.

QUESTIONS

1. How can the process of 'Management by learning objectives be implemented in the classroom teaching? Discuss this statement with examples.
2. Indicate the functions of Measurement? Differentiate between Evaluation and Measurement.
3. Describe the ferns of objective type items and illustrate their forms with suitable examples.
4. The essay type tests are detective even then we can not ignore them. Comment on this statement.
5. Distinguish between criterion-referenced test and norm-referenced test. Which should be preferred in educational measurement and why?

15

Learner's Control

When teaching-learning situations are controlled by the learner, it is known as 'Learner-Controlled Instruction'. Teacher has the secondary role, he is an observer, helper and provides assistance to the learners. It assumes that learners have the capacity of decision-making and problem-solving. The curriculum transaction is based on modern theory of human organization which is task and relationship centred.

John Brubecher has defined the term teaching according of learner-controlled instruction methods:

"Teaching is an arrangement and manipulation of learning situations in which there are gaps and obstructions which a learner will seek to overcome and from which he will learn in the course of doing so."

It is evident from the definition of teaching that student is more active than the teacher. Teacher's job is to assist the learner for creating the learning situations. The instructional procedure and sequence of content is determined by learner, which in teacher-controlled instruction the sequence of content is determined by the teacher logically, which may not be workable psychologically. In LCI the sequence of content is psychologically workable which has been decided by learning.

In programmed instruction, the sequence of the content elements is determined empirically which is psychologically workable as controlled by the learner. The term LCI is very popular in programmed instruction. The following are the main methods which are known as Learning-Controlled Instruction Methods.

1. Kellar Plan.
2. Programme Instruction.
3. Computer Assisted Instruction.
4. Mestery Learning.

Individualised Learning

Individualised learning is something of a blanket term covering a wide range of activities. The promise that all students are individuals and that there are many permutations and combinations of individual difference leads one to conclude that a totally teacher-centred approach to teaching is likely to be inadequate.

Every students is an individual and a class of students is heterogeneous regarding background and prior knowledge of a subject. Self pacing helps to smoothing the initial inequities in a group. Students can be diverted to complementary study packages, remedial material, materials constructed for specific needs or study in small groups of two or three or individually under the tutelage of tutors. Fellow students, senior class students or teachers can help in the organisation of the courses for individual learning or in the testing programme.

During the sixties, independent learning was encouraged through programmed instruction which required the students to work through small steps of subject material that were sequenced very carefully. Students were frequently rewarded by confirmation of the correctness of their responses. Norman Corwder's branching programmes helped students who selected an incorrect response by directing them to remedial branching frames. Further research work of Mager, Pask and Scott (1961, 1972) indicated the need to match the learning style of the student and the way in which learning material was structured, giving importance to the student rather than the teacher to have control over the sequences of topic in a learning programme. The most recent approaches to independent learning are, Keller plan and audio-tutorial approach. These approaches allow the students to work through the learning material in their own way. However, they have to master a block of work of mini-course before proceeding to the next. Postlethwaite's (1972) audio-tutorial approach seeks to overcome what are not predetermined. Audio tape presentations which other appropriate resources are presented using study carrole in a learning centre or in a library.

Independent Learning

Independent learning or independent study that includes a variety of practices enables a student, on his own, to formulate problems, find answers through systematic procedures of reference work, hypothesising, experimenting, field work, etc, and evaluate one's own progress and achievement. It is of value to a student of high ability as well as to a student who needs time to go at his own pace and perhaps with the help of a remedial programme. The teacher or the tutor has to be conscientious and capable of providing initial enthusiasm, guidance at regular intervals and encouragement for further progress. As there is no pressure for competing with other group, the students work at their own pace to complete a courses or a programme.

Independent learning would generally take up some of the following forms-assignment work, laboratory work, reference reading, programmed learning, mastery learning, learning by Keller plan, learning through audiovisual aids such as films, filmstrips, slides, cassettes, tapes, television, etc. Centres of educational technology, self-learning centres or cells and libraries in colleges and University Departments of Education could cater to the needs of those students who would like to enrich the teaching-learning process by independent study. In this chapter, the following four approaches of independent learning are discussed in detail: Tutorials, Mastery Learning and Keller Plan, Programmed Learning and Computer assisted instruction.

Keller Plan

Similar to Mastery Learning is Keller Plan which has been developed mainly from Skinnerrian principles of operant conditioning. This approach has been adopted widely at the college level, especially in the United States. Keller Plan combines mastery learning approach with the programmed instruction concepts, of learner control, self-pacing and contingency contracting. At the beginning of a course, students have a contract-agreement with the teacher regarding what work will be done and then they proceed at their own pace and initiation. The teacher is available for tutorial assistance or small group discussions. Thus giving general feedback and guidance. Since this approach depends on the learners to manage their own learning, the students should be mature and have self-discipline to manage their own learning.

Keller Plan advocates the use of a sequential set of self-study units pursued by each student at his own pace. A student must demonstrate mastery of a unit by means of a written test before going on to the next unit. Failure to pass an unit is not held against the pupil.

The Course

The course is divided into 30 units. Each unit approximates a week's work. The students are assigned reading, which may include programmed texts, material only available from the library and handouts. It always includes questions and exercises. As with other courses, students may go to particular rooms at specific times, and if they do so, they will find other students working at the reading materials, and not a formal period of teaching. In scientific subjects, the rooms may be laboratories, and the tasks and exercises may include the conduct of experiments, or other kinds of observations. 'Proctors' who are undergraduates and have been chosen for their mastery of the course, their maturity of judgement, their understanding of learning problems, and their willingness to help, are students from more senior years, and are available to help with any difficulties that may arise. Laboratory work is normally under the direct supervision of a laboratory assistant.

When a student thinks he has completed one of 30 units of work he may report for a test, which consists of about 10 short questions to be answered. If he does not reach a satisfactory standard, he will have to re-study the course material. If his score is on the borderline, he may make another attempt on the same day. If his score is satisfactory, he is given the next assignment.

Lectures and demonstrations are provided as an added bonus to the course for those students who have completed a requisite number of units successfully. Thus attendance at lectures and demonstrations is not compulsory, but a privilege earned by successful study.

In Keller's original course, 25 percent of the course grade marks is obtained from the final examination which partly consists of questions the students had already received as part of the assignments or in the follow-up tests. Keller calls a follow-up test, 'readiness' test, because it indicates the readiness to receive the next assignment. As the course is criterion referenced, the number of readiness tests passed counts to their credit, but the number they fail is not held against them. Nevertheless each students' progress can be monitored throughout the course to permit counselling where necessary. This counselling is initially given by the proctor, but the teacher may help as required.

The system gives students the feeling that they are receiving a great deal of personal attention although in reality they are receiving less than in a typical course with lectures and discussions. The teacher's role is to select reading materials, to organise their presentations, to design test and to make the final evaluation of students' progress. He will also provide lectures and demonstrations and act as a clearing house for complaints and disagreements.

Use of the Keller Plan

The Keller Plan can be adopted as a possible means of solving several problems of teaching. The most severe problems are:

(a) The high failure rate of first year students due to inadequate preparation in high school.
(b) The wide spectrum of interest and motivation of students at this level.
(c) The needs of the highly gifted student who may not be challenged by the materials presented in a conventional course.
(d) Students in the course, who have very different background and ability, say in physics, include those who will study physics as a major subject, students requiring physics as an ancillary subject (e.g. biologists, engineers) and a few who will not continue in physics at all.

Problems Encountered

1. There is a tendency towards non-coordination of theory with laboratory experiments. In general, the theory in the units is more advanced than is required for the laboratory and the theory required for most laboratory experiments is not very demanding. However, even the simplest theories may be confounding if encountered in the laboratory write-up before the study guide for the associate unit is available and read by the student.
2. Organisational difficulties arise, such as that of providing help and testing facilities for students when they want it.
3. Accommodation is strained and staff resources can be inadequate.

4. There is danger of testing becoming an automatic production line process instead of being a relaxed discussion between students and tutor.
5. The Keller Plan facilitates assessment of skills both verbally and by written tests. But, in subjects like mathematics, use of mathematical language, in a clear and precise way is a vital skill; but students are passing Keller Plan tests without practising this skill. A possible solution to this problem is to include at least one question in each test for which a clearly written answer is required, verbal addition being unacceptable.

Modified Plan : The Keller Plan can be modified to suit the needs of students and teachers. It is not necessary to always have the student proctors, specially to administer the tests. Responsibility can be left to the students or teachers to complete the test. Further, units can be grouped and test administered.

Programmed Instruction

The programmed instruction is a new strategy of teaching. It is highly individualized instructional strategy for the modification of behaviour. It is used for instructional purpose but it can also be employed as a mechanism of feedback device for improving teaching efficiency. The theoretical knowledge of programmed instruction is essential to use it as feedback device for the modification of teacher behaviour.

Origin: The origin of modern programmed instruction is from the psychology of learning and not from technology. It is an application of 'operant conditioning' learning theory to teaching-learning situations. It has got a historical momentum only after the publication of "the science of learning and art of teaching" articles by *B.F. Skinner* in 1954.

Meaning and Definition : Programmed instruction has been defined as a method of given individualized instructions in which the student is active and proceeds at his own pace and is provided with immediate knowledge of result. The physical presence of teacher is not essential in this strategy.

Susan Markle has tried to give a wider definition of programmed instruction: "It is a method of designing, a reproducible sequence of instructional events to produce a measurable and consistent effect on behaviour of each and every acceptable student."

Programmed learning is a designed strategy in which various kinds of intellectual economical and motor experiences are provided to the learner in a controlled situation through a variety etc.

The Principles

A good programmed instruction is based upon the principles of learning. The principles on which programmed instruction is based, are discovered in psychological laboratories. There are five fundamental principles of programmed instruction:

1. Principle of Small step,
2. Principle of Active responding,
3. Principle of immediate confirmation,
4. Principle of Self-pacing, and
5. Principle of student testing.

These principles are functional in nature and explain the procedure of programmed instruction strategy. The brief description of these principles has been given here.

1. *Principle of Small Step:* The subject matter is broken down into a sequence of small step. A student can take a step at a time. He has to read a small step by being active.
2. *Principle of Active Responding:* The student learns that he should actively respond as he learns. The learner has to construct the response. It is an integral part of learning.
3. *Principle of Immediate Confirmation:* The student learns the best if he confirms his response immediately. The confirmation provides the reinforcement to the learner.
4. *Principle of Self-Pacing:* In programming, each student can work each step as slowly, or as quickly as he can. This is known as principle of self-pacing.
5. *Principle of Student-Testing:* A student leaves the record of his study because he has to write a responses for each step on a response-sheet. This reminds the principle of student-testing.

The Assumptions

The programmed instruction has the following basic assumptions:

(1) A student learns better by being active.

(2) A student learns better if he is motivated to learn by confirming his responses.

(3) A student learns better if the content matter is presented in small steps.

(4) A student learns better if he commits minimum errors in his learning.

(5) A student learns better if the sequence of content is psychological workable.

(6) The learning may be effective if the pre-requisites are specified on the part of the learner.

The Objectives

The objectives of this strategy have been summarized as follows:-

(a) To help the student to learn by doing.

(b) To provide the situation to learn at his own pace.

(c) To help student to learn without the presence of a teacher.

(d) To present the content in a controlled manner and in logically related steps.

(e) To study by himself and assess his own performance by comparing with it the given answer.

The Characteristics

The following are the main features of programmed instruction strategy:

1. It is not audio-visual device. It is a part of education technology, *i.e.*, instructional technology.
2. It is not a test. It is a new strategy of teaching and learning.
3. It is not the solution of educational problems. It is a new instructional strategy for the modification of behaviour of the learner.
4. It can not replace the teacher from the field of teaching because the effective teacher can prepare a good programme.
5. It requires more creativity and imaginative efforts to develop highly individualized instruction.

Steps for Development

The development of programmed instruction is a very challenging job for a teacher. The mastery over the topic; knowledge and practice or programmed instruction are essential for it. The following steps are important in preparing programmed instruction material.

1. Selection of the topic to be programmed.
2. Identifying the objectives.
3. Content analysis for developing the instructional procedure.
4. Writing objectives (Entering and Terminal) in a behavioural terms.
5. Confusing of criterion test.
6. Deciding appropriate paradigm and strategy of a programme.
7. Writing programme frames and individual try out.
8. Group try out and editing the programme and preparing final draft.
9. Master validation or evolution of programmed instruction in terms of internal and external criteria.
10. Preparation of a manual of the programme.

These steps are followed in preparing an effective programme or instructional material. The procedure is very time consuming and laborious. The programmed text is different from conventional text, because the workability of the material is determined on the basis of student's responses.

Feedback Device : The procedure of development of programmed instruction provides the deep insight and understanding about the elements, structure, and their sequence.

During teaching practice, the pupil-teachers are asked to teach a lesson by following the traditional approach of lesson planning. The classroom teaching is recorded or evaluated. After that, they are asked to develop the programme instruction frames on the same topic and asked to re-teach the same topic to another class of same level. The same criterion measure should be used to record and evaluate the classroom teaching. The experimental studies of this type has yielded significant improvement in teaching. The preparation of programmed frames provides the awareness about content structure and functions as feedback to the trainees.

The following skills are developed by giving the training of programmed instruction:

(1) The skills of content analysis and arranging content in learning sequence and developed.

(2) The pupil-teachers are able to present the content in small step.

(3) They are able to provide the reinforcement to learners by confirming their responses.
(4) The pupil-teachers are able to develop the situation for achieving the desired learning objectives.
(5) The trainees are able to consider the individual variation and generate the learning situation so that they can learn according to their own pace.
(6) The pupil-teachers are able to identify the objectives and are able to write them in behavioural terms.

Computer Assisted Instruction

The most striking innovation in the field of educational technology is the use of computers. The main objective of computer assisted instruction is to provide the needed flexibility for individualising the educational process. It meets the specific needs of the student in a way in which it is almost impossible to do so in a face-to face student-teacher relationship.

Computer : A computer has the facilities to store information as well as retrieve it. The stored information is in a particular computer language so that the computer understands and reacts. When the necessary procedures to process the information are given to it, it interacts and manipulates the information and the answer is typed on a teletypewriter. The different parts of the computer that are involved in this process are input equipment, memory store, processing unit, control unit and output equipment. The input equipment translates the information given to the computer. The input equipment translates the information, in terms of several operations such as adding, subtracting, multiplying, etc., and also selects particular information that is needed, which in turn is translated back to an understandable form by the learner. This is the working of a computer in its most simple form.

The Characteristics : There are two basic characteristics of computer assisted instruction (CAI). The first is that the computer can evaluate a student's (Learner's) responses instantly and indicates whether the response is correct or incorrect on the basis of predetermined Key words indentified within it. Where the student's answers (responses) correspond to the anticipated incorrect answers, then the computer gives corrective hints or offers general hints where the answer does not relate to any of the anticipated in correct answers. It would also call for a modified or new answer. In this way, every student is involved in the learning process as different from a conventional classroom where only a small percentage of the students respond to the teacher's questions. Each student responding and receiving necessary feedback through CAI is led towards the goal of effective learning. Secondly, the computer can individualise instruction in a number of specified ways. Instruction can be individualised according to differential aptitude, achievement and interest. The computer makes note of the learner's performance and progress in learner a unit and on the basis of the evaluation of his ongoing achievement and as per his needs, it can modify his programme for further learning. The great asset of the computer is its instant response and its flexibility to suit the learner's needs and requirements through tutorial interaction and dialogue.

CAI and PL : Computer assisted instruction is one example where programme instruction has been combined with powerful media and technology to produce expensive and impressive learning systems. In this case, the monitoring and feedback functions of a teacher are handled by the computer. Computer assisted instruction is based on the same principles as the ordinary programmed instruction but students work from computer terminals. They observe displays shown on monitors or typed on a computer output, instead of programmed textbooks or workbooks. Students type information into the computer or respond to it by pressing the related (buttons) keys. In addition to manipulating an interesting, sophisticated and responding equipment, the students find that they cannot cheat, as answers are given (or appear on the screen) only to the student's responses. It also permits the students to proceed according to their abilities and pace of learning.

Various Types : There are a number of ways by which computers can be used for instruction. Computer assisted instruction (CAI) or Computer aided learning (CAL) refers to situations in which a computer system is utilised in the learning process.

The *first* application involves utilisation of the computer as a record keeper and retriever. Teachers and administrators programme the computer for processing data of the students for instruction purposes such as printing report cards, storing and retrieving rest and examination results, pertinent details about students (age, sex, community, family background, etc.) and scheduling students for classes in the case of streaming of students ability-wise or due to large strength of the college or shift system. For the purpose of guidance and counselling, cumulative records, counsellor's records, file and details about vocational interest, aptitude, and information and psychological test results can be stored in the computer and retrieved as and when needed.

The *second* is to use the computer as a laboratory computing device, which is one of the most frequently used educational application. A single terminal, teletype or electric typewriter is installed in the classroom with a direct access to an externally placed computer. Students are encouraged to develop their own computer programmes relating to their regular classroom assignments. Talented and over-achieving students can be encouraged to develop their own software or help the peer group in preparing software to suit the different abilities of the learners. At the tertiary level, this will be a very stimulating experience.

The *third* from of CAI uses the computer as a tutor. One form of tutoring is to provide drill and practice to the student at a computer terminal. In this form, a complete lesson/course is also presented in the computer to the student and the computer keeps track of his performance and can give a summary of his performance to the teacher whenever asked for. In drill and practice branching type of remedial programme is also provided for those learners who are in need of such remedial teaching.

The *fourth* application is simulation which is effective when presented in CAI. Through specific input, computers develop models of processes or structure. Simulated conditions are shown on the computer screen such as working of the circulatory system of the human body or the effect of interactions on the operation of a system or other models from company management, biology, mathematics or ecosystem. Such simulations have tremendous potentials for instructional purpose. Simulations are also planned as competitive games to motivate and increase the interest of the learners.

Computer Managed Learning : Computer-managed learning (CML) as different from computer-assisted instruction or computer assisted learning, involves decision-making. On the basis of the initial interaction with the student, the computer suggests the type of models of instruction for him. The computer notes down the attainment as well as the drawbacks of the learner in order to construct his profile. This profile is used to plan the learning unit for the student, whether it should be modified, enriched or a remedial module should be added. This decision is taken on the basis of the measurement and assessment it makes on the learner's performance. Students' achievement is measured in relation to criterion attainment with reference to the syllabus of the module and assessed in relation to the course requirement. Following the computer's decision, there could be discussions with the student and teacher (tutor) and the instruction of the student is so managed that efficient personalised learning takes place.

The Advantages : In describing undergraduate computer-assisted learning in biology, chemistry and physics, McKensie (1977) cites eight advantages and four criticisms of the method. The advantages of CAI are:

1. The immediate feedback provided by interactive terminals keeps students interacting and eager to keep trying.
2. Wesker students are obliged to participate actively. They often remain passive in lectures.
3. The computer will wait patiently for an answer and will not express annoyance with wrong response.
4. The graphics facility is a powerful aid in enhancing intuition, especially in giving insight into mathematical formulae.
5. Interactive graphics make it possible to sample many more illustrations than could easily be shown in a textbook.
6. Mathematical calculations can be done as readily for realistic examples as for artificially simple case that can be solved analytically.
7. Large volume of data can be handled with accuracy and without druggery.
8. The novel technique provide enrichment of a course through added variety.

The Limitations

1. A programmer cannot cater for every possible response and may give unexpected and unhelpful responses to unusual input.
2. A few students are intimidated by the strangeness of a computer terminal (less likely for physics and chemistry students).
3. Packages can become boring if a student is alone at a terminal for too long. Most packages should run for an hour or so.

4. A package will not be appreciated unless it has a perceived goal and will not be considered important unless it is integrated into a course to the extent of being assessed by a teacher.

Computer assisted instruction provides for individualised instruction, motivates students to go through a unit or course through its varied presentation modes and by instant feedback, encourages learners to proceed with the lesson. There is a tremendous saving of students' and teacher's time. Computers are adaptive to students changing performances and relate the learning to suit their cognitive potentials. However, computers can never replace teacher as the 'human aspect' is vital for learning and behaviours of the effective domain can only be developed by a teacher.

Mastery Learning

The Mastery Learning approach proposed by Bloom (1968) and Block (1861) takes into account individual differences among learners in learning rates, the principle of over-learning (learning beyond immediate recall) and the concept of learning objectives (objectives for each unit of the syllabus specified in terms of students' behaviour). The underlying assumption in this approach is that most students can master a major portion of the syllabi if enough time is given to them to do so. Further, attainment level is fixed high to have a mastery of learning in the subjects. Evaluation followed in the mastery learning approach is criterion-reference based and not norm-based. Certain standards are set against which the concerned individual's performance is evaluated. There is no common norm for all the students. However, there will be great individual differences in mastery rates among the students. But this approach would avoid the majority of the students in a class moving from course to course without mastering the concepts involved. As an individualised learning process, it puts a premium on the mastery of what is learnt and perhaps, students with higher mental abilities profit more. The others may take a longer time to reach that level but what they learn is more meaningful and comprehended thoroughly.

B. S. Bloom has developed mastery learning strategy. It is a new instructional strategy which is used for developing mastery learning and objectives of curriculum can be realized. It includes classroom teaching, reinforcement techniques remedial instruction and individual learning device. The poor students are allowed extra time. Thus, story learning is the group-based instruction. It is followed by remedial techniques. The following steps are used in Bloom's mastery learning approach.

1. Teaching content is divided into learning units.

2. In the second step instructional objectives are identified. The objectives are formulated for every unit separately. The learning outcomes are understood in detail.

3. Mastery level of each unit is determined in view of the objectives of the unit. It is counted in terms of the percentage of questions which are included in the test. For mastery level 80 to 85 per cent questions should be attempted correctly for each unit.

4. General teaching activities for learning are performed for each unit separately. It is done in group. This step is same as conventional teaching.

5. After teaching criterion test is administered to evaluate the mastery level of each unit. The performances of student provides reinforcement.

6. The students are diagnosed who have not attained the level of mastery and their causes of difficulties of students provides reinforcement.

7. Remedial instructions are prepared on the basis of the causes of learning difficulties of the students. Extra time is given for going through remedial instruction. For this purpose some other books are also suggested to study the content. The branching remedial programme can also be used. Tutorial classes are also organized for the learning difficulties for the weak students. After these programme criterion test is again administered to examine their mastery level.

8. The remedial instructions or teaching is organized for each unit separately so that students who have the learning difficulties on every unit will get an opportunity to remove their difficulties and attain mastery level. Thus, the students are classified on the basis of their learning difficulties. In this way every student is able to attain mastery level.

9. The purpose of unit test or formative test is to provide remedial teaching or instruction for weak students. The purpose of criterion test or summative test is to classify the Students Tests are used for evaluation and remediation.

10. The criterion test also provides the feedback to students as well as teacher, for organizing mastery learning strategy or revising and improving instructions and teaching for attaining mastery level.

Group Controlled Instruction

Teaching is a group activity. There are students and teachers who work together in classroom or teaching learning situations. When teachers dominates in teaching, it is known as Teacher Controlled Instruction. When learners dominate in teaching-learning situation it is called learner controlled instruction methods. There are teaching-learning situations in which interaction or participation of both is essential, is called interactive process of teaching.

The fourth type of teaching-learning situations where group participation is encouraged which is known as action-oriented method. Some educational objectives can only be achieved by Group Controlled Instruction such as feeling of cooperation, feeling of team work. Psychomotor skills. Verbal skills and habit formation etc. Action-oriented method provides the opportunities to do some thing or social productive work.

The role of teacher is like a friend and guide. He provides the awareness and guideline for organizing group activity. Every learning has work. The learning by doing principle is followed in group-controlled instruction methods. Each and every learner remains active while doing something. It is also based on the modern theory of human organization *i.e.,* task and relationship methods. The following are the Group Controlled Instruction (GCL) methods.

1. Small Group Instruction.
2. Role Playing or (SSST)
3. Educational Excursion of Field trips,
4. Tutorials.
5. Project Works.

The details of there methods (GCI) have been provided in the following paragraphs.

Small Group Instruction

Teaching in large groups invariable results in the traditional one-way communication in which the teacher assumes a dominating role. The teacher's tendency to lecture has encouraged educators to find ways and means of designing techniques in gropes that would avoid domination of one person and encourage student participation. Teachers and educators have considered the small groups as uniquely structured to achieve educational goals. In small groups, the teacher is able to give individual attention to all the members of the group according to their needs. The students get an opportunity to get more actively involved in their own learning, as well as participate in discussions. Further, small group are conducive for the development of leadership qualities as there is two-way communication between students and students and teacher and students. Small group instruction involves groups, ranging in size from 5 to 15 or 20 students depending on the topic, the technique of instruction adopted and the teacher's experience. There is no minimum or maximum number of persons to be included in a group, for group discussion. When the number decreases to five or four there is a likelihood that they pair off rather than interaction with all members. At the same time, when the number increases to fifteen or so all the members may not participate. However, size of the group depends on the type of group discussion that is carried on.

Group Discussions

In small group instruction, group discussions form the core of all the strategies used. A discussion indicates an exchange of ideas accompanied by active learning with all the members of the group participating in it. Effective small-group discussions do not take place accidentally. The planned learning activities that emerge from carefully structured student behaviours. Therefore, the teacher has to learn to plan, organise and conduct effective group discussions.

The following are some of the principles related to small group discussions:

1. Every small group discussions should have educational purposes and, therefore, need to be goal-oriented and moving towards that goal.
2. The topic for discussion is related to the common needs and interests of the participants. Students are motivated to discuss, if the topic for discussion is of vital importance to them.
3. Student should have sufficient information and knowledge about the discussion topic in order to effectively participate in the group discussions.
4. Through group discussions, students are enabled to vocalise their thoughts and ideas in the right form and in correct language. Group discussions are helpful means to develop such skills through the cooperation of the teacher and the peer group.

5. For effective group work individual student should be assigned responsibilities.
6. Teacher should stimulate students to ask thought-provoking questions but at the same time each student is encouraged to do his own thinking.
7. Teachers should encourage students to evaluate the progress of group work.
8. An ineffective discussion session should not be permitted to be prolonged. Change of activity, topic, or seating arrangement are some ways of discontinuing the ineffective discussions.
9. Group discussions can be combined with role playing or panel discussions.
10. Conclusions arrived at in small group discussion can find further application in the classroom.

Research done by Human Resources Research Organisation indicated five instances where it is most feasible to use small group methods (Olmstead, 1970):

1. To increase depth of understanding and grasp of course content.
2. To enhance motivation and generate greater involvement of students in the course.
3. To develop positive attitudes towards better use of material presented in the course.
4. To develop problem-solving skills specific to content of the course.
5. To provide practice in the application of concepts and information to practical problems.

In small group discussions, students are expected to use skills such as critical thinking, inferring, evaluating, problem solving and human relations responsibilities and skills like understanding others' point of view, taking turns to discuss instead of dominating the discussions, initiating and supporting shy, quiet members, patience in dealing with opposing and negative remarks, etc. Students can get a feedback about their techniques by the use of in-group and out-group strategy. The group members are divided into two groups, each member having a partner who sits in the in-group circle. When discussions are going on, the out-group partner in the out-group circle evaluates his or her in-group partner. The out-group partner does not participate in the discussions and only evaluates his or her own partner and nobody else. After a specified time, the partners switch places and the discussions continue. This process enables the partners to get an insight into the techniques and skills adopted by them and their effectiveness. The partners are provided with checklist for evaluation.

The teacher plays an important role in small group discussion as its leader. The concept of leadership in group discussions is viewed as a functional leadership in that the leadership is shared among the group members. A group member who enables the group to fulfil the task assigned to it in reality has assumed the leadership role, if only for a short duration. The teacher as the group's status leader ensures that members fulfil some leadership functions during group discussion sessions. The teacher's responsibility is to provide an opportunity for each student of the group to become a leader. It is evident that conducting group discussions involve considerable amount of planning, organisation and effort to make it effective and worthwhile.

Major strategies of group discussions are brain storming, buzz sessions, simulation approach (role play and gaming), case study, group tutorial and assignments.

Role Playing

A number of techniques are being used currently in India as well as in other countries for the modification of teacher-behaviour. The simulated social skill training is one of them. Cruick Shank (1968) has developed a teacher training system. This system of training is being denoted by several terms such as: Role playing, Artificial teaching, Pilot training, Laboratory method, Clinical method and Inductive scientific method.

The current teaching practices of our teacher education programmes have the following limitations:

(a) The pupil-teacher are sent to actual classroom teaching during teaching practices programme without inducing the role of teacher. Some training institutions have the provision for demonstration lesson.

(b) There is no provision for providing reinforcement for the pupil-teacher behaviour. The supervisors give remarks for their teaching task in general, may be as criticism of lesson. There is no scope to follow the suggestions given by the supervisors.

(c) The teaching practices involve risk and humiliation for pupil-teacher because they do not known even the classroom manners.

The simulated social skill training (SSST) has the direct improvement over these limitations of traditional teaching practices.

Meaning and Definition : The simulation technique is to induce certain behaviour in an artificial situation. A pupil-teacher has to play several roles as a teacher, as a student and as a supervisor.

Simulation gives greater control over the teaching variables. It is based upon socio-drama. The socio-drama is very much related to the practice. The most important aspect of simulation is the introduction of the student to teaching is non-stressful conditions.

The simulated social skill training can be defined as mechanism of feedback devices to induce certain desirable behaviour among pupil-teachers by playing the role of teacher in their own group as an artificial situation of classroom teaching.

The Assumptions : The SSST is based upon the following assumptions:

1. The teacher behaviour is modifiable by the use of feedback devices.
2. The basic assumption is that there are certain patterns of teacher-behaviour which are essential for effective-teaching. These behaviour can be described and practice like any other skill. The observer identifies those behaviour and teacher practice, those pattern of teaching-behaviour.
3. The teacher-behaviour has its taxonomy. Carl Openshaw has developed the taxonomy of teacher-behaviour by the use of simulated techniques.
4. Another assumption is that social skills are developed by practice and imitation in a group. All members of the group have an opportunity to practice in controlling and improving their own behaviour for teaching purposes.

Procedure of SSST

The technique is used for developing the social skill of teaching in classroom situation. This is generally employed for the pupil-teacher before sending them in real classroom in their teaching practices. Certain steps have been outlined merely as suggestions. The teacher educators can develop their own procedure of SSST. Generally the following six steps are used in SSST technique:

Step 1- The pupil-teachers are assigned the roles which they have to play in SSST. Each individual has a chance to be as teacher, student, and an observer.

Step 2- After assigning the role, certain social skills are discussed which are to be practised. The skills are discussed for a topic. Each candidate has to select a topic of his interest.

Step 3- A schedule of organizing SSST is prepared who will start? Who will stop? When should it be stopped? And who will intervenes the conversation?

Step 4- The procedure and technique of observation is also decided. What kind of data of observation are to be recorded? How can the data be best interpreted?

Step 5- The schedule is followed for the first practice session. The teaching is organized and observations are taken for evaluating the teaching task of an actor. The teaching is followed by discussion and demonstration to provide the feedback to the pupil-teacher by giving the awareness of his social skill of teaching and suggestions for the improvement.

Step 6- The procedure is now changed by changing topic, teacher, pupils, observer and social skills. Every pupil-teacher should have which is assigned to him. The topic and social skills should not be too easy or too difficult.

Elements of Simulated Training

The procedure consists of three roles: teacher, pupil and observer. Cruick Shank considers that this teaching paradigm also includes three elements: 1. Diagnosis 2. Prescription, and 3. Evaluation. These elements can be observed with the help of the following diagram:

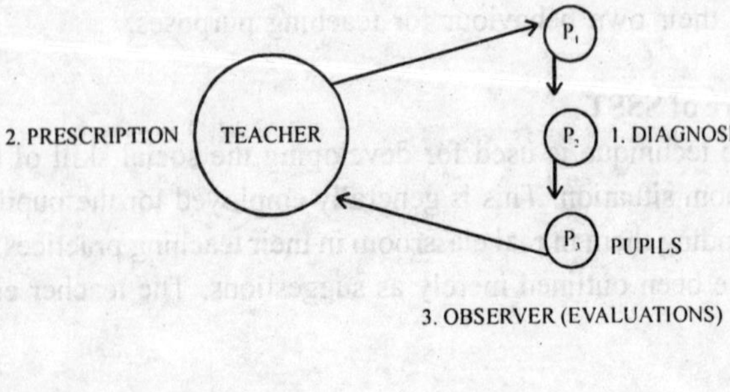

Taxonomy of Teacher Behaviour

Under this teaching the student-teachers simulate a particular activity or role and they try to develop an identity with the actual classroom situation. The whole simulated teaching programme becomes a training in *role perception* and *role playing.* The handling of behavioural problems of classroom are better mastered through simulated teaching sessions :

1. A Source Dimension,
2. A Direction Dimension,
3. A Function Dimension, and
4. A Sign dimension.

Each of these dimensions of teaching, according to Carl Openshaw, is observable and quantifiable, the analysis of which provides empirical evidence about what a teacher does. how he behave, while teaching:

(1) The source dimension of teaching provides interaction between the relationship of students and teacher at a basic level. Teaching is an interaction between projector entity called teacher and receptor entities within a classroom situation.

(2) The identification and classification of the nature of receptor entities provides the direction dimension to teaching in the study conducted by K. Openshaw and others.

(3) The teacher has to perform certain tasks. These tasks (presentation of subject-matter) should be dealt with beliefs, attitudes, skill and process of instruction. The second task in to establish and to maintain interpersonal relationship among students in classroom. The third task is to facilitate the learner process. These three tasks constitute the function dimension of teaching.

(4) In order to observe a behaviour it should be communicated in some way. The communication may require more than one mode of expression in fulfilling a given function. The mode of behaviour makes the sign dimension. The following diagram illustrates the taxonomy of teacher behaviour—

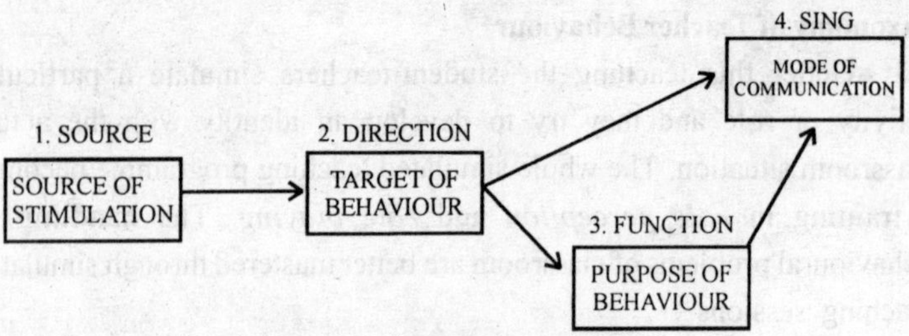

Taxonomy of Teacher-Behaviour

Source	*Direction*	*Function*	*Sign*
This indicates the origin of an encounter.	Indicates the target to which the behaviour is directed.	Indicates the purpose of the behaviour within an encounter.	Indicates the mode of Co-mmunication.
(a) Orginate (b) Respond (c) Class (d) Object	(a) Individual (b) Group	(a) Structure Intiate order assign (b) Develop Infrom Explain Check, Elicit Test Reinforce Summarize (c) Administer Manipulate and Manage (d) Regulate Set Standard (e) Evaluate	(a) Speak (b) Read (c) Gesture (d) Perform (e) Write (f) Laugh (g) Silence

This diagram indicates that the source of behaviour controls other dimensions of teacher-behaviour but it may be determined through the observer's recognition of the target of focus, the direction dimension. The mode of interaction together with the purpose of behaviour gives meaning to all behaviour. Some modes limit the range of possibility of purpose while other purposes may limit the modes behaviour available to the teacher given behaviour may be classified in more than one category of the function direction. Each encounter may have a number of shifts within sign dimension. Any change in the source and direction dimension indicates new encounter.

Advantages of Simulated Training : Cruick Shank has suggested a number of advantages of Simulated Technique as feedback device:

1. The major advantage is that in using the technique, we are forging close links between theory and practice.
2. The student-teachers are given an opportunity to study and analyse critical teaching problems.
3. The students can acquire classroom manners thought the technique of simulation.
4. The student can understand behavioural problems of classroom and develop insight to encounter them.
5. The technique provides reinforcement to students to develop teaching skill and avoid the risk of actual classroom encounter.

Use of Simulated Social Skill Training : This technique may be used in the following problems of teaching:

1. The appropriateness of open or closed question skills are ascertained in teaching situations.
2. The ability to ask questions is developed in which the concepts and logical sequence have been expressed previously by pupils.
3. The confidence in teaching is developed to encounter the face to face situation in pupil-teachers.
4. The SSST techniques provides a situations to expose the pupil-teacher to play the role of teacher and observer prior going to actual classroom teaching. It helps in developing social skill of teaching.
5. It is a best replacement of demonstration lesson because every teacher-educator is not an effective teacher. It eliminates an opportunity of imitation of certain skills of teaching.
6. The ability to demonstrate and explain the rules of logic in classroom teaching helps in maintaining consistency in the meaning of words.
7. The micro-teaching can be best used for developing certain teaching skills but it is difficult to use in our teacher-education programme during teaching practices. It can combined with SSST to be employed in our situations to develop teaching skills.
8. It provides the feedback to each pupil-teacher and also helps them to act as teacher, pupil and observer to perceive the role

in each situation. This may provide insight to take a decision about his own teaching activities. It helps in predicting consequences of teaching and may change the flow of activities of teaching.

Education Excursion

The purpose of education process is to generate learning conditions for realizing objectives. The learning experiences are the means for bringing desirable change in behaviour. The learning experiences are provided in classroom and out side the classroom. Thus learning experiences are the means for implementing curriculum. In the classroom teaching real experiences are not provided, verbal and non-verbal languages are used in teaching. The students do not get first hand information.

Rein had introduced the technique "short excursion" in 19th century to make history and geography more interesting and realistic. These are also termed as 'Field Trips'. If a teacher has to teach Tajmahal' Waterfall, Mountain, sea etc. he can make use of this technique of organizing educational excursion. It makes social studies content interesting and realistic. This technique can be effectively used in history, geography teaching.

Meaning and Definition : The term school excursion has been defined by Henary Johnson comprehensively.

"The school excursion as developed by Rain was prized for the reality which is imparted to geography, nature study, history, and other social and physical subjects. It was also prized for the open air exercise which is brought for the initiative and freedom it made possible, the opportunity it created for school training."

This technique is very effective for school programmes. It can also be employed for developing teaching competency for in-service teacher training. They get an opportunity for visiting other professional institutions and observing the functioning of technical institutions.

The Characteristics : The following are the main characteristics of this technique of teaching—

1. It provides the real experiences and perception of learning content.
2. It is a psychological technique which involves more senses in learning situations.

3. It makes history geography and other subjects for interesting and realistic.
4. It provides freedom in learning or self-learning out side the classroom.
5. It provides the first hand information or knowledge about the teaching content and objects.
6. It provides the real experiences which are easily comprehend and retained for a longer time.
7. It reduces the scope of rote memory and memorize the social studies content.

Theoretical Basis : This technique is based on the following principles—

(1) It is based on psychological principles i.e. observation and perception by involving more senses.

(2) It is also based on social principles and feeling of group work, cooperation. It is group centred instructional technique.

(3) It is based on real learning experiences out side the classroom by observations imagination and inventions.

(4) It provides the opportunity to develop the ability of appreciation and praising natural places or spots.

(5) It provides direct contact with real content of teaching school subjects.

Apart from these principles, it is a fact that real experiences are very costly and time consuming. Today multimedia approach and distance learning are being used for this purpose which are economical devices.

Planning and Organizing Field Trips : The following steps are used in organizing educational excursion—

1. Formulating specific objectives for the field trip.
2. Planning and organizing the activities so that the objectives can achieved effectively.
3. Permission should be taken from school or college authority for organizing field Trip.
4. A schedule is to be prepared for the field trip (a) Date (b) Time (c) No. of students (d) Incharge of the field trip (e) Specific programme for the trip and (g) Financial assistance.
5. Incharge of the field trip has to contact the places or institutions for the permission as per schedule.

6. A guideline and schedule paper is prepared for each and every student.
7. Incharge of the trip has to prepare schedule for boarding and lodging at different places during the field Trip.
8. A list of the required items is prepared for the journey.
9. The specific instructions are given for the starting place and time.
10. Incharge has to prepare code and conduct which every student has to follow during field trips.

A guide sheet is prepared and it should be checked that every student should be well aware about the guide sheet. Every student has to fillup the guide sheet. The format of guide sheet should be very comprehensive and specific. Proper instructions are given for completing the guide sheet by the students.

Use of Field Trips : The field trips should be organized in such a way so that objectives of teaching learning can be achieved. It should function as an effective technique for providing learning experiences or real experiences out side the classroom. These should be planned and organized for achieving specific learning objectives. The following five steps should be employed for organizing effective field trip:

(1) To prepare and motivate students for field trip.
(2) To organized field trip systematically.
(3) Follow-up programme should be used.
(4) To test the students for which field trip will be organized.
(5) To review the learning out comes of the students.

Preparing Students for the Field Trip: It is the job of the incharge and subject teacher to create curiosity for seeing the place which will provide real experience and perception. The students should be well informed with help of maps, charts, pictures, films etc. They should be provided guide sheet for the educational excursion.

Conduct of Field Trip: The incharge has to prepare a guide sheet for the organization of field trip. It shows the schedule for visiting places, objects etc. It should be related to their study subject.

Follow-up of Field Trip: After conducting a field trip, a follow-up programme should be organized to make use of guide sheets as completed by the students which will enable them to provide full awareness about the visited places. The guide sheet should be completed by each and every students as a report of field trip. The incharge should organise group discussion and highlight the points which may be given in the examination.

Testing Students: This step is most important to make field trip much more useful for the students learning. Generally students consider the field trip a means for recreation. It should have specific objectives. There should be evaluated by administering test. They should be informed that these will be a test after the field trip, then they will be attentive and serious about their observations and they will note down simultaneously. It will provide feedback to the subject-teacher and the students. Technical terms should be explained by the incharge and subject teacher.

Review of Learning Experiences: It is group controlled instruction technique of teaching. It can also be termed as self learning or open training. The students assessment provides the basis for the effectiveness of this technique. The students are provided opportunities to work upto their satisfaction. It is highly individualized technique of teaching learning.

The Examples : Educational excursions are organized for various school and college subjects: geography, history, natural studies, botany, zoology, commerce, civics, agriculture etc. The following are the example of field trip of these subjects.

Geography: It has the great importance in teaching geography e.g.

(1) Hilly area and mountains (2) Sea shore (3) Water falls (4) Dams (5) Aboriginals and (6) Mines etc.

History: It can be effectively used in teaching history e.g.

(1) Historical building (2) Tajmahal, Lalkila, Sarnath chittavgarh (3) Kurkshetra (4) Amirtsar jaliyana wala bagh. etc.

Commerce and Economics: To visit village industries, Traspartation, food grain storage, factories, mills etc.

Civics and Social Studies: To visit parliament house, assembly, Rashtrapati Bhawan, Governor house. Tinmurti, etc.

Education: To visit other type of educational institutions e.g. Blind school, deaf-dumb school, Technical training institute, vocational institutions etc.

The Importance : The field trip technique has the following importance—

1. It makes teaching interesting specially history and geography.
2. It provides the real experiences through perception.
3. It develops faith in natural scenes and human works as dams.
4. It develops the insight and imagination by perceiving historical buildings.
5. It develops cognitive, affective aspects of the students.
6. It develops the ability of observation and imagination and feeling of appreciation.
7. It develops the feeling of cooperation and group work.
8. It helps in self teaching:

The Limitations : It has the following limitations.

1. It is a costly technique of teaching learning from time, money and energy points of view.
2. Mostly students think it as source of recreation.
3. It can not be used for all the topics geography and history.
4. The poor students can not participate in these field trips.

Tutorials

According to Hale Commission (1961), tutorial is a discussion period at which not more than four students are present and which is one of a series of such periods, extending for at least a term in which each period is conducted by the same teacher (tutor). The tutorial system has its origin in Britain and the British model has three types of tutors— (1) The moral tutor or general counsellor who is responsible more for the personal aspect of the student than his academic, (2) The discussion group leader type of tutor, and (3) The academic tutor who gives regular instruction to a small group of students or to a single student for a specified period of time. It may be noted that in the Indian context all the three types are needed in large institutions at the tertiary level, flexibility being permitted to the roles and responsibilities of a tutor so that individualised learning could take place to the maximum.

Each student is expected to spend at least an hour a week with his tutor if it is the British model. In other patterns, the students meet the tutors as and when required for academic guidance. The tutors should have qualities such as personal appeal and integrity to arouse confidence and devotion in students capacity to create enthusiasm and motivation, good organisational ability and ready sympathy and consideration. The tutorial system gives opportunity for discussion in small groups, personal contact with the tutor\teacher and tutorial group members and satisfies the social and psychological needs of an individual in a group situation. The atmosphere of a tutorial system is as informal and free as possible but the tutor is clear on the objectives of the tutorials which in turn are made clear to the students as well. Planning and organisation are as important as in a regular class teaching. Tutorials, in small groups can also follow lectures, after students have consolidated their learning. Tutorials should help in the academic progress, personal intellectual development original contribution and student's ability to critically appraise and discuss.

Some of the colleges in India follow a tutorial system, the tutorial group consisting of 15-20 students with a college teacher as the 'tutor'. The main purpose is to give individual and personal attention to the students and help them solve problems. The role of the tutor is that of a counsellor and not that of an academician involved in promoting individualised learning.

Various Types

Tutorial covers a wide range of teaching activities. These may be classified under three heads:

Supervision Tutorials: In this type of tutorial students and teacher meeting are arranged regularly. A student reads an essay and defends it with arguments. This strategy can provide an opportunity to deepen his understanding of subject for able student. It stresses on the mastery over the basic skills of scholarship.

Group Tutorials: These tutorials are useful for an average student. These can satisfy the needs of less exceptional students. The teacher should have the background of social psychology and group dynamics so that he can deal with group tutorials effectively in solving their problems.

Practical Tutorials: These tutorials are commonly used for both group and individual basis to achieve psychomotor skills in laboratory, workshop and rehearsal. These tutorials are basically employed to achieve the psychomotor objectives.

Project Work

It is a new teaching strategy and it has been evolved as a result of social tendency of education. The advocates of this opinionate that the education should be related to life situations. It is experience-centred teaching strategy. The exponent of project method is W.H. Kilpatrick. The main focus of this strategy into socialize a child.

Objectives: It is used to achieve cognitive and affective objectives. The main focus is to socialized a child and to develop the ability of problem-solving.

Structure: The teacher places the real problems related to life situations, and the learner realizes its utility in his life. The learner prepares a plan for solving the problem. The students collect several information for solving the problem. The teacher's job is to provide guidance. The students themselves make an effort to seek solution of the problem by studying the materials.

Principles: It involves the following principles

(1) Principle of utility: The problem of study is related with life situation of the learners.

(2) Principle of readiness: The problem of study is related with life situation of the learners.

(3) Principle of learning by doing: Learner has to perform certain tasks in project strategy.

(4) Learner gels freedom to work: The learning situations are realistic.

(5) Principle of socialization: It develops the feeling of co-operation and group work.

Various Types : Kilpatrick has classified the project strategies under four types:

(1) Constructive - In this type learner has to complete certain task.

(2) Artistic - This type of project develops the aesthetic tests of the learner.

(3) Problem-centred -A problem is presented before the learner and he has to seek the solution of the problem.

(4) Group Practice - A task is assigned in which group work is required to complete it.

Procedure of Project: Usually six steps are followed in each type of project strategy.

Step 1 : To identify a problem related to life situation of the learner.

Step 2 : To select and define the problem.

Step 3 : To prepare a plan for finding out the solution of the problem.

Step 4 : To implement the plan.

Step 5 : To evaluate the workability of the project plan.

Step 6 : To prepare a record of the project.

Advantages: It has the following advantages:

(1) Project strategy is based upon psychological and sociological principles.

(2) The new knowledge is imparted by linking it with their life situations.

(3) It develops insight toward life problem.

(4) All school subjects can be taught by an integrated approach.

(5) Project Strategy provides an opportunity for work experience, divergent thinking and social efficiency.

Limitations: It has the following disadvantages:

(1) The subject-content can not be taught systematically or in a sequence.

(2) The plan projects cannot be designed for all school subjects and on the whole subject-matter of school subjects.

(3) It is very costly and time consuming strategy of teaching.

(4) It can not be used in teaching for higher classes.

(5) MI social qualities cannot be developed by this strategy.

Suggestions: The following precautions should be taken in using this strategy:

(1) It should be used in agriculture and technical institutions.

(2) The problem of the project should be economical and useful.

(3) It should be employed as a supplementary teaching technique.

(4) It should be used at primary and secondary levels.

QUESTIONS

1. Explain teaching according to learner-controlled instruction and enumerate the important instruction methods used in LCI.

2. Describe the main characteristics of programmed instruction and justify it is self-study method.
3. Describe and justify that Kellar Plan is as mastery learning. Indicate the procedure for giving personal attention in this plan.
4. Explain the phrase Group-Controlled Instruction and justify that it is an activities-method.
5. Describe the project-method as group-controlled instruction method.

16

Textbook Programme

The process of education which every school-going child wades through is midst of prescribed text books with which the child's satchel lies packed up. The prescribed books are everything for the learner. They are his main source of attention of studies both in the school and at home. They serve the purpose of a tool in the hands of the teachers. Thus they are able to carry on their routine of teaching in the classroom situations. The school text books need to be excellent through and through. Only then the teachers in the schools will be able to discharge their duty more efficiently.

The Meaning

A text-book is a prescribed book for the student of a particular age group. It covers items as given in the syllabus. Such a book forms the basis of teaching learning in the class. Later on the students can revise their syllabus by studying that book whenever they feel like doing so.

Text-books are standard works or manuals of instruction in a subject of study. They are the never failing friends of the students as well as of the teachers. A text-book has been defined as an instrument of instruction that facilitates teaching learning process. It is written on the basis of a prescribed syllabus in which the major ideals of the subject-matter are selected and summarised judiciously. They are organised logically according to the mental make-up and psychological requirements of the students so as to facilitate teaching, sometimes a text book is called "The teacher in print." Nevertheless, it can by no means, replace the teacher. Rather it is to be used to aid and supplement his work."

The Definitions

According to Webster's Dictionary, "A text-book is any manual of instruction, a book containing a presentation of the principles of the subject used as a basis of instruction." The Shorter Oxford English Dictionary says, "A book used as a standard work for the study of a particular subject, a manual of instructions in a subject of study."

According to the Encyclopaedia America "In the strict sense of the term, a text-book is a book that presents a body of knowledge in an organised, and usually simplified manner for purposes of learning. Text book is frequently the most important teaching tool because it can determine not only what will be taught but also how it will be taught. Although television and other new media are rivalling printed materials of communication, text books remain major resources in schools and colleges."

Education Commission Report (1964-66) puts forth the view, ' A good text-book written by a qualified and competent specialist in the subject, and produced with due regard to quality of printing, able illustrations and general get up, stimulates the pupils' interest and helps the teacher considerably in his work. The provision of quality text-books, and other teaching and learning materials can thus be an affective programme for raising standards."

Among various instructional aids such as text-books, supplementary books, reference books, maps, charts, film strips, films, Misra says, "The text-book is presumably the most important because it is used in formal as well as in informal situations of instruction and also in situations of self-study. This is the cheapest of all the aids enumerated above and this is the only aid available to a large majority of the pupils and also the teachers."

According to the writer's Handbook for the development of education materials, "Text-book is the term for a book used in a course as the base around which the course is built."

L.J. Lewis says that text-book is a tool both for the pupil and the teacher.

According to Mukerjee, "Text-book may be looked upon as the symbol of National Culture. They are not national symbols in the same sense as Ashoka Chakra, but they are perhaps more revealing of national ideas, ideals and values than the figures on our coins and flags."

The term text-book is broader than the term school book. To Hall-Quest it is "a record of racial thinking organised for instructional purpose."

To Lagne, "It is a standard book for any particular branch of study."

Bacon means by text book "a book designed for classroom use, carefully prepared by experts in the field and equipped with the usual teaching devices.

According to Encylopaedia of Educational Research (Third Edition), in the modern sense and as commonly understood, "the text-book is a learning instrument usually employed in schools and colleges to support a programme of instruction. In ordinary usage the text-books is printed, it is non-consumable, it is hard bound, it serves as an avowed instructional purpose, and it is placed in the hands of the learner."

About the text-book Dictionary of Education says, "It is any manual of instruction, a book dealing with a definite subject of study, systematically arranged, intended for use at a specified level of instruction, and used as a principal source of study material for a given course."

The Characteristics

Analysis of the definitions of a text-book give us a few characteristics which are given below:

(1) It is a standard book in the subject.
(2) It is meant both for the teachers and the students.
(3) It is a manual of instruction.
(4) It is both content and technique.
(5) It is used for formal as well as informal education.
(6) It is the foundation on which the course is built up.
(7) It is a tool for realising the instructional objectives of the subject.
(8) It contains selected material.
(9) It presents material in graded form.
(10) It is a principal source of study material for a given course.
(11) It is a learning instrument used by the students.

The Importance

Text-Books occupy a very important place in the field of education. In Indian situations, their importance is all the more as we have shortage of instructional materials like films, TX, teaching machines etc.

According to the Encyclopaedia of Education; "Text-books have been associated with schools for as long as schools have been known .... Undoubtedly text-book is the core around which subjects are taught. In a very real sense, the text book is the curriculum."

1. They determine not only the subject-matter to be taught but also the methods of teaching.
2. They are the only tools in the hands of teaches in Indian situations with which they are able to run their teaching programme smoothly.
3. They are good learning instruments for the students as they can revise their lessons whenever they want to do so.
4. They are the chief vehicles for attaining the goals of curriculum.
5. They indicate clearly what the teacher is required to know and what the pupils are supposed to learn.
6. They always focus the attention of the teacher as well as the learners. Thus chances of deviations are reduced to the minimum.
7. Text-Books give concrete form to the curriculum. Scope of any topic can be better known with the help of text-books.
8. Text-Books usually have graded material which is arranged according to the needs and requirements of the learners. They help the teacher in right planning of the yearly work.
9. They lead to economy in effort and save much time and emerge. Thus the teacher need not dictate notes in details.
10. Text-Books encourage the students for self-education.
11. They give uniformity to teaching in different classroom situations where text-books are used.

Thus the use of text-books, undoubtedly, have good many advantages. A few draw backs are also there which are explained here below.

The Drawbacks

1. Too much dependence on text-books gives temporary bookish knowledge.
2. There is lack of direct experiences. The students acquire second hand knowledge.
3. Teaching and learning become very rigid. The teacher has to teach whatever is given in the book. The learner too has to learn the things given in the book exactly.

4. The text-books oppose the dynamic methodology of teaching learning. They are, in fact, not suitable for teaching according to new progressive methods.
5. The text-books are sometimes exploited for inculcating wrong ideology like narrow nationalism, racial prejudices etc.
6. Sometimes the text-books replace the teacher. When the students find material better explained in the text-book, they do not shown due regard to the teacher.

It is, undoubtedly, right to say that there are some drawbacks in the text-books used in the schools. At the same time advantages cannot be set aside especially Indian classroom situations. Here in this country we need well graded, organised printed material in the form of text-book and this we shall ever need in times to come. Without text-books our system of education may lag behind. The best way out is to have good books written by distinguished writers.

By means of books, knowledge is accumulated into a permanently available store or fund and of all books, text-books are the most important for such funding. There is need of new books for new purposes and revision of existing books to meet special needs. It goes without saying that text books shape the little thing and, increase the power of expression. They form the backbone of school structure.

With the advent of independence and acceptance of free and compulsory education, new trends in the field of education have made fresh demands. Our educational system is to be reoriented. For bringing about the necessary changes, the importance in text-books ranks high in order of priority. There is a great need of standard text-books high in order of priority. ranking

On Different Subjects

There is need of different types of text-books for students belonging to different levels of learning. A good text book remains according to the mental level of the learners. For subjects like science, Social studies, etc. we need text-books where knowledge is important to the learners. For languages we need the type of books which help the student to have better command over the language. In such books there is repetition of vocabulary items, structure patterns of sentences so as to enable the learners have full command over the language. In the same way text-book of Mathematics are expected to give sufficient practice to the learners.

Good Books

A text-book is called good one if it contains some specific and general qualities. General qualities are found in all type of similar books. The specific qualities refer to some books which are written with specific purpose. Usually in a book, the general qualities include binding, get up,, printing, quality of paper etc. The specific qualities are seen differently in different in different type of books. Thus the language text-books, Science text-books, Mathematics text books, History text book etc. will differ from one another in many respects. Only merits of the book will win applause for it.

The general qualities are seen externally in a book whereas internal qualities are specific and they are known if we make efforts to find them out.

Physical aspect of the text book can be seen externally. We may see to it under the following heads: (1) Physical aspect and (2) Academic aspect of the text-book.

Physical Aspects

Size of the book

(i) It is suitable for the learners.
(ii) It is convenient in handling and carrying.
(iii) It is neither too big nor too small for the students for whom it is meant.

Printing of the Books

(i) The printing is neat and clean.
(ii) It is free from any type of errors.'
(iii) The inking in the printing is balanced throughout.
(iv) The blocks are clearly printed in the book.
(v) There are sufficient margins on all sides of the page.
(vi) The spacing between the words is even.
(vii) The spacing between the different lines contained on a page is suitable.
(viii) The spacing between the different paragraphs is satisfactory.
(ix) Design of the pages is open rather than crowded.
(x) Each chapter begins on a fresh page.
(xi) Length of a line is within the eye span of the child.

Type Size of the Books

(i) Different type size are used for the cover page, title, text and captions.

(ii) The type size used in the book is suitable for the age group.
(iii) A balance in the use of different type size is maintained.
(iv) It does not strain the eye sight of the pupils.

Paper Used in Books

(i) Paper used in the book is of white colour.
(ii) It is adequately thick.
(iii) It is smooth.
(iv) It is durable.
(v) It is reasonable of good quality.

Binding of Books

(i) The binding of the book is sufficiently strong..
(ii) It opens flat easily,
(iii) The sides of the book are properly trimmed.
(iv) The folding of the paper is proper.
(v) The cover page of the book is durable.

Price of Books

(i) The price of the book is reasonable. It suits the pockets of majority of the parents.

Over all get up of Books

(i) The get up of the book is fine.
(ii) Its title page is attractive.
(iii) The material is presented according to some accepted norms.

Academic Aspects

From academic point of view, a good text-book has the following characteristics:

Thematic Content

1. The subject-matter is according to the mental level of the learners.
2. It is capable of sustaining interest of the student.
3. It is related to the physical and social environment of the learners.
4. There is a variety of themes.
5. The facts given are correct and up-to-date.
6. It provides new information to the learners.
7. It is free from such incidents and references as may hurt the feelings of the children.
8. It inculcates the qualities of good citizenship.
9. It contains enough humorous material.

Organisation of the Contents

1. The subject matter is divided into convenient units.
2. Length of each lesson suits the learners.
3. The reading material is graded in order of difficulty.
4. The presentation suits the nature of the contents.
5. The different themes are presented through variety of forms such as essays, stories, poems, dialogues and plays.
6. The style of presentation is simple and clear.
7. The title of each lesson is brief, meaningful and suitable.

Textual Language

1. The textual language is according to the mental level of the learners.
2. The language used is correct.
3. It is appropriate to the situation or context.

Illustrations (Visual Aids)

1. Abstract concepts of the book are clarified with the help of pictures and diagrams. It makes easy to comprehend.
2. The pictures used in the book are drawn well.
3. They are realistic.
4. They are relevant to the text.
5. They motivation the learners.
6. They are properly distributed throughout the book.

Textual Exercises

1. Every lesson is followed by exercises.
2. Instructions to do the exercises are clear.
3. There is a variety of exercises are on each lesson.
4. They help the teachers in diagnosing the areas of difficulty.
5. The exercises for each lesson are purposeful and adequate.
6. They help the teacher to evaluate the achievements of the students.

Science Books

Apart from the usual characteristics of academic and physical aspects, the text-book of science should possess the following:

(1) It should aim at teaching science successfully keeping in view the aims and objectives of teaching science fixed up for different levels.

The different topic should centre round everyday life situations and thus make the learner really interested in the subject. This is rather of immense value especially in this fat growing and developing age which is heading towards an era of science and technology.

(2) It should compensate the drawbacks occurring there due to the shortage of material facilities. Sometimes costly equipment and apparatus are not available due to the paucity of funds. It should encourage the teacher as well as the learners by drawing their attention to certain low cost aids. Some sort of suggestions for improvised apparatus should be there.

(3) The terminology used in the book should be standard one. It is very essential in the case of text-books written or being written in regional languages. The terminology evolved by the Central Ministry of Education and State Governments should be used.

(4) A Science text-book should be accompanied by a laboratory manual. That will help the science teacher to be of more practical type. It may inspire all concerned for more practical and hence and inclination towards research.

(5) For a few questions given in the exercises, hints or guidelines should be there. For numerical questions, answers should be given in the book. It is all the more important and useful if teacher's guide book is made available for each text-book.

(6) The subject-matter of science should be given in the book in such a way that it is not dull and boring material for the young learners. Its correlation with other subjects, with child's life and the community be maintained as far as possible.

(7) In the subject of science, illustrations and diagrams hold unique position. So special emphasis be laid on these. Labelling the diagrams should be done accurately. If they are coloured, registration of colours should be done correctly.

And above all, the text-book should be written by some experienced teacher who is highly qualified and is well read.

Mathematics Books

The text book of Mathematics should process the external and internal qualities of a book explained fully in the preceding pages. Besides, the following qualities are there is a good text book of Mathematics:

(1) Every question of the book motivates the students fully. The problems are taken from day to day life situations. Seemingly they are real problems. Thus no question will read that a coloured T.V. set costs Rs. 10/- or 200 and a pencil costing 5 paise each.

(2) It contains guiding exercises, testing exercises, practice exercises. All the questions are not solved in it. There may be some questions in which a few hints or guidelines are given.

(3) The book satisfies all type of learners. The average students, the below average and brilliant students remain contented by the study of the book. It does contain a few different exercises which pose challenging situations for the extra ordinary students. In their case, real learning starts from this point onwards.

(4) In case some new terms are used in the book, they are fully explained. Then any user of that book remains fully satisfied. The symbols used in the book are popular ones. It is free from any type of controversial facts. The subject-matter of the book is up-to-date and is up-to-the-mark in every way.

(5) The author of the text book is a Mathematician in the real sense of the word. He writes the book in a natural way taking material from environment of the learners. He presents things in such a way that the book becomes interesting. It also motivates the learners.

Social Studies Books

The text book of social studies concerns the social aspect of life in its wider sense of the word. In academic as well as physical aspects, the books should possess the qualities discussed in the preceding pages of this chapter. Besides, it should possess a few more qualities which are explained there below.

(1) As far as subject-matter of Social studies book is concerned, it is expected to deal with the environment of the learners very thoroughly. The subject-matter has to be up-to-the-mark and up-to-date in every way.

(2) Since the main purpose of social studies is to reveal to the children where they are in time, space and society-contents

dealing with all these things have to be there in the book in a very systematic way.

(3) Usually the subject of Social studies is taken up as dull and boring. The text-book for this subject has to be really a good one which should arouse interest in the learners.

(4) The text book writer of this subject is expected to be fully aware of things all around the learners. He should be busy in modifications and revision of the book every now and then in this age when we are seeing a large number of changes almost in everything.

(5) The book should be free from any type of bias. It should not contain undesirable element.

(6) Facts supported by evidences should be given in the book. Truths and facts-should not be concealed by any type of efforts.

(7) The style of the book should be such that it stimulates a spirit of further enquiry in the learners. They become fully well awakened students ever ready to add to their knowledge.

Various Types

There are four different categories of books which are given below:

1. Students' Text-Books,
2. Teachers' Text-Books,
3. Work Books,
4. Supplementary Readers.

Students' Books

Students' Text-Book is a well known type of text-book. Almost everyone concerned with the sphere of teaching-learning is well aware of it. Text-books of this type are used by the students community. They form the foundations mainly on which stand almost the whole of their knowledge. In school stages, text-book is considered to be the be all and end all of life for the students. They are called intensive readers in the case of languages. The students do intensive study of these books. The main objective of such readers is to acquaint the students with books. The main objective of such readers is to acquaint the students with proper linguistic material. It is generally called the course book of the students. The course book need be taught to the students in such a way that they come out with all-round development of personality. Sometimes the teachers use the student's text-book in such a way that the students known only that much what is given in the book. The text book should not be used as the be-all and end- all of life. It need be used as an aid for teaching-learning. It helps to revise and reinforce the material taught to the students.

Importance of text-book varies from subject to subject. In some subjects, studies are not possible without the text-book. For example, study of a language is not possible without the text-book. In subjects like History, Geography, Social Studies - the students may do without books for sometime though at some later stage they may feel the necessity of the book. In Mathematics, the students may do without the text-book.

Place in School Curriculum

A text-book is the central string round with the whole teaching-learning process is woven. It also fixes up the target for the teacher and the taught. It is useful in the following ways—

1. The text-book is a guide for the teacher. He is able to proceed along with the lines indicated in the book.
2. The book prescribed for the class is a memory aid for the pupils.
3. It is a permanent record or measure of what has been learnt.
4. It serves the purpose of a uniting factor in the language learning of a wide area.
5. It is a means of extending linguistic experience beyond the local scene and the limited experience of the pupils.
6. It is an exercise ground for reading.
7. The examples given in the book serve a very useful purpose. The learners are able to learn a good deal from them.
8. It brings a system in the teaching work.
9. The text books check unnecessary repetition and omission.

Teachers' Books

Along with the students text-books some books are available which are meant for the teachers. Books of that category are called teacher's text-books. They provide a sort of guideline to the teachers for using the student's text-books in a better way. Solutions to some problems which the teachers are likely to face are given in them. A few hints, guidelines, meanings of some specific words, answers to some typical type of questions etc., are given in that book. Naturally the teacher will then be able to teach better without facing any sort of problem. There has been shortage of such books, but now they are being made available along with the students' text-books.

Teacher' text-books are not popular as yet. In some subjects, teachers, text-books have not been prepared even. The controlling authorities should get such books written along with the students' text-books. That will help in the improvement of teaching being conducted by the teachers.

Work Books

These are practical type of books which help the learners to have a lot of practice in some selected items of learning. In books of this type, there are a large number of exercises. A few exercises may be reading exercises, learning exercises, writing exercises, testing exercises etc.

Teaching of languages provide more scope for work books. In languages, different language items may be, practised by the students in different situations. In one chapter, vocabulary items may be the main teaching point. All exercises of practical nature may centre round vocabulary. In the next chapter, emphasis may be on the structures. Multiple type of learning exercises are provided there.

Work books are combination of book material and the note book. The students read the questions and they write the answers on the blank space provided in front of the question or in the next line following the question. Exercises like full in the blank, correction of sentences, changes the narration, change the voice etc., are given in such a way that the students attempt their answers on the space provided in the book itself. Naturally a work book once completed by a student cannot be used again. Of course, for revision purpose or for just consultation, the students may use it when he or she feels like doing so.

But there is dearth of books of this type. There is a lot of scope in this area of producing books. Actually the diluting standards of languages teaching can be improved by providing the learners with more and more work books. Work books can also be produced in subjects other than languages. It is high time that the writers tend to produce books of this type.

Supplementary Readers

Supplementary reader is a variety of books used to supplement the material learnt in the text-book. Student text-book provides basic knowledge to the students. They study their text-book provides basic knowledge to the students. They study their text-book very intensively. The supplementary reader helps them to have a better grasp over the subject-matter. The supplementary readers have their immense value in the case of languages. In the supplementary reader, the vocabulary and the structures are almost the same as are in the text-books. They are certainly according to the mental level of the students. The situations are different and the story element also is new one. When the learner goes over them rapidly, his interest in the language is aroused. The language items like vocabulary and structures do not create any problem for him. Rather he is able to have a revision of the language item.

According to Menon and Patel: "Supplementary Reader should be of a standard of language at least as simple as that of the book used for detailed study in the next lower class. It must be written within the vocabulary and structures of the next lower class." In supplementary reading, the learner is his own guide. He needs less guidance from the teacher than is needed in intensive reading. Further about supplementary reading programme Menon and Patel have suggested: "One period a week should be set aside for supplementary reading. The teacher should not teach the supplementary reader as though it were a detailed text. It is his function to create in the pupil the capacity for and the habit of silently reading books for the thought and ideas they contain."

The Importance

1. The supplementary readers help the learners to grasp the subject-matter of prescribed text books in a better way.
2. They make the students interested in extra-reading.
3. The students are able to compare things. Through comparison, things are better clarified and they are more retained in the minds.
4. Through supplementary reading, the students become habitual of doing fast reading.
5. Self-study habits are formed in the students.

Present Position

Supplementary readers are available but we need more in quantity as well as of good quality. Supplementary readers strictly related to the text books prescribed for the different classes is the need of the day. That is bound to improve the situation with regard to teaching-learning of English language in our country. It is high time that the authors try their hand on bringing out relevant supplementary readers really useful for the school-going children.

Various Types

(i) Progressive Readers: This type of supplementary reader gradually brings in new vocabulary. The main purpose of readers of this variety is to extend the readers' command of the language at recognition level.

(ii) Plateau Type: Supplementary readers of this type are written throughout at a fixed level. The purpose is to consolidate the vocabulary which the reader has already acquired. .

Out of the above two type, we need both the types for the learners of the language.

The Characteristics

1. The language items like vocabulary and structure should occur in the book in accordance with the mental make-up of the learners. There should be different lessons for the revision of language items which the learner has already come across in the text-book. New language items may occur if the supplementary reader is designed to be of progressive type but that should be presented in a scientific way keeping in view the principle of selection and gradation so that learners don't face problems.
2. The story element and the situations in the supplementary readers have to be different. Some pictures/illustrations should be there to simplify the problems that the learners are likely to come across. The pictures should be colourful for the lower classes and for the senior students, they maybe in black and white.

3. The supplementary readers are meant for rapid reading, So they should contain good stories, incidents, or dialogues which might captivate the attention of the learners.
4. A good supplementary reader always inspires and encourages the learners to read more and more.. It should, therefore, serve the purpose of a means and not an end in itself.
5. At the end of each chapter, there may be elementary exercises which should judge that overall grasp of the learners. These exercises should not be detailed once because that will make the book an intensive reader.
6. From technical considerations point view, the book should be attractive in appearance, get up etc. In this connection, the following points are important—
   (a) The paper used in the book should be of good quality.
   (b) The printing should be free from any error.
   (c) The size of the print should be neither too big nor too small.
   (d) The binding of the book should be strong.
   (c) The size of the book should be neither too big nor too small. It should be in accordance with the age group of the learners for whom it is meant.

Need to Improve Quality

The Education Commission (1952-53) found that there was great deterioration in the standard of text-books prescribed for the students. It recommended that

1. With a view to improving the quality of textbooks prescribed, a high power Text-Book Committee should be constituted with should consist of a high dignitary of the judiciary of the State, preferably a Judge of the High Court, a Member of the Public Service Commission of the region concerned, a Vice-Chancellor of the region, a headmaster or headmistress in the State, two distinguished educationists and the Director of Education; this Committee should function as an independent body.
2. A fund should be maintained from the amount raised from the sale of publications which may be utilised for awarding scholarships, and providing books and certain other amenities for school children.

3. The text-book committee should lay down clear criteria for the type of paper, illustration, printing and format of the book.
4. The central Government should set up a new institution, or help some existing Art schools to develop training in technique of book illustration.
5. The Central and State Government should maintain libraries of blocks of good illustrations which could be loaned to text-book committee and publishers in order to improve the standard of book illustration.
6. Single text-book should not be prescribed for every subject of study, but a reasonable number of books which satisfy the standards laid down should be recommended leaving the choice to the school concerned.
7. In the case of languages, however, definite text-book should be prescribed for each class to ensure proper gradation.
8. No book prescribed as a text-book or as a book for general study should contain any passage or statement which might offend the religious or social susceptibilities of any section of the community or might indoctrinate the minds of the young student with particular political or religious ideologies.
9. Frequent changes in text-book and books prescribed for study should be discouraged.

State Efforts

At the state level, the state Governments set up some organisation for improving the quality of text-book either through state production or by improving the machinery for approving text-book produced in private sectors. At the national level, the Government of India tried to develop a programme for helping the state Government to improve text books first under the Central Bureaus of School Text-Books and later on under the NCERT.

Education Commission (1964-65) observed that text-book writing and production did not receive the attention they deserved and therefore there was a proliferation of low quality, sub-standard and badly produced books, particularly in regional languages. It recommended: A comprehensive programme of text-book production at the national level should be implemented by mobilising the best talent in the country. The Ministry of Education should take steps to establish in the public sector an autonomous organisation, functioning on commercial lines for the production of text-book at the national level, at the state level, the production of text books should preferably be contrasted to an autonomous agency functioning in close liaison with the State Education Department, the entire organisation of State production of text-books should be run on a no-profit no-loss basis.

National Policy of Education

The resolution issued by the Government of India on National Policy of Education (1968) and as approved by the parliament iterated that the quality of books should be improved by attaching the best writing talent through a liberal policy of incentives and remuneration. It suggested: The possibility of establishing autonomous book corporation on commercial lines should be examined and efforts should be made to have a few basic text books throughout the country.

National Board of Education

In 1969, the Government of India established the National Board of School Text-Books with the object of providing a forum to discuss all the matters relating to qualitative improvement, production, distribution and sale of text-books; adopting criteria for text-books; advising the Central and State Governments or, all matters concerning text-books; and recommending measures which would promote national integration through text books.

First Meeting : The Report of the first meeting held in April, 1969 recommended: The state education department should assume direct responsibility of producing quality text-books. Appropriate agencies such as text-book corporation or bureau should be established for the purpose with the required autonomy and official support of work effectively on a no-profit-no-loss basis. Special measures should be adopted to improve the quality of text-books attracting best available talent to write text-books, conducting pre-production field tryouts, applying new technological innovations, etc. There should be a continuous evaluation of text-books particularly those required for History, Social Studies, Languages and Sciences; co-ordination should be effected through exchange of materials, production of certain materials at the national level, maintenance of a national centre for textual materials and the creation of a Department of Text-Books in the NCERT to undertake national programmes of research development, training and extension for all States.

Second Meeting : The second meeting of the National Board made the following four recommendations:

1. A crash programme of evaluating school text-books, as proposed by Ministry of Education and Youth Services, may be launched.
2. Modern management techniques in the production of text-books should be introduced.
3. A status study may be made by investigating relevant issues, such as the number and nature of minority language groups in each State, and how text-books are provided in the minority languages.
4. Up-to-date estimates of the need for paper for nationalised textbook and that for note-books, etc., may be obtained from the states. They may be requested to work out projections of their paper requirements for the next five years.

Teacher's Guides

A good text-book, written by a qualified and competent specialist in the subject, and produced with due regard to quality of printing, illustrations and general get-up, stimulates the pupils' interest and helps the teacher considerably in his work. The provision of quality text-books, and other teaching learning materials, can thus be an effective programme for raising standards. The need to emphasize it is all the greater because it requires only a relatively small investment of resources.

The Quality

Unfortunately, text-book writing and production have not received the attention they deserve. Most of the books at school level including the ones in original languages are of sub-standard. Reasons are:

(i) Lack of interest shown by the top ranking scholars.
(ii) Malpractices in the selection and prescription of text-books.
(iii) Carelessness and cheating done by the publishers.
(iv) Lack of research in the preparation and production of text-books

State Production

With the spread of education, the text-book industry became a more profitable field for investment and the above mentioned evils became more and more conspicuous. To improve things it was decided that the state Governments should take over the production of text-books. The result is that many states have taken over production, distribution and sale of books under their control. The quality of books has improved and private profiteering has also disappeared. In some states, education Departments have taken over the responsibility of text-book production but they have not organized themselves fully for it. In their cases, short-comings are seen such as failure to revise books for long periods, misprints, poor production, failure to supply books in time etc. State production of text-books is only step in the direction of improving the quality of text-books. The books need be checked.

National Level Programme

The best talent available in the country should be brought together to produce the text-books at school and University levels. It can be done at the national level by agencies set up by the Government of India.

1. For the University Stage, the Ministry of Education is bringing out a series of low priced and subsidised books in collaboration with USA, USSR & U.K. It should also be made use of for books at undergraduate stage.
2. N.C.E.R.T has produced books with the help of scholars available in the country. The State Governments can use these books with some changes or without any change.
3. The Ministry of Education should take steps to establish in the public sector, an autonomous organisation functioning on commercial lines for the production of text-books at the national level, especially scientific and technical books. A small Committee may be set up to work out the details of the project.
4. The effort at the national level should be supported and augmented by each state setting up an expert section for the production of text-books.

5. The preparation, tryout and evaluation of text-books should be the responsibility of the State Education Departments. The production aspect of text-books may preferable be done by the State Education Departments. The sale and distribution of textbooks are better left to the student co-operatives.
6. The production of text-books and teaching aids at the state level should preferable be entrusted to an autonomous agency functioning in close liaison with the Education Department.
7. The machinery set up should be such that the text-books are subjected to continuous revision and improvement.
8. At least 3 or 4 books should be provided in each subject to provide a multiple choice of books for the schools.
9. Liberal policies should be adopted for remunerating authors.
10. The entire organization of state production of text-books should be run on a no-profit-no-loss basis.
11. Manuscripts should be invited from a variety of sources including teachers, and a high level committee of professional persons should select and approve manuscripts.
12. Teacher's guides and other instructional material should supplement text-books.
13. Lists of minimum teaching aids and equipment needed by each category of schools should be prepared and steps taken to provide the equipment to every school on a high priority basis.
14. Education Departments should work with the All India Radio for the use of radio lesson, supplemented by printed guide materials for teachers and pupils. Broadcasting of special radio talks specially designed for teacher in the mornings and evenings will help teachers in lesson preparation. Sophisticated forms of newer techniques would not be suitable at present in the general run of schools but may be tried out experimentally in training institutions.
15. Teachers should be helped and trained to rely on inexpensive and locally available or improvised teaching aids. Costly equipment should be shared by schools in a neighbourhood.

Need for Research

As curriculum and methods of teaching are in the process of development, so change in text-books is needed. Text-Books are selected or revised in accordance with the instructional objectives and requirement. Again selection or revision of text-books cannot be a sporadic or a haphazard process. This has to be done on the basis of systematic evaluation and research. UNESCO observed, "In an era of revolutionary changes in education and far-reaching programmes for expanded school enrolment, planning is required to ensure an adequate text-book component for the development of education systems. The quality and content of educational books need constant improvement in all countries of the world." According to the Report of Education Commission (1964-66): "It should be an objective of policy to see that a text-book is continuously revised and kept up-to-date and that a through revision takes place at least once in five years if not of tener. The need for frequent revisions of text-books is obvious, even if the curricula were to remain unchanged."

A book declared a good book once may become bad and outdated with the passage of time. There is need of continuous revisions and updating it from time to time. No doubt, the text-book plays certain unique roles in the system of instructions and instructional materials. But it is not possible for any written record to be completely current and up-to-date. It is not the function of a text-book to compete with the daily newspaper, and further even the newspaper is at a disadvantage in reporting the news in competition with radio and television. To view the text-book as a compendium of current information is to see it as for ever out-of-date. It goes without saying that production of good text-books requires a number of experts with good knowledge of their subjects as well as the ability to write text-book in accordance with the known principles of learning.

Improvement of school text-books has been an endeavour of continued interest in the hands of controlling authorities and the research workers. Several committees and commissions have also been appointed for this purpose by the Central and the State Governments. The Central

Bureau of Text-book Research (CBTR), National Board of School Text-books (NBST) and National Council of Educational Research and Training (NCERT) have done commendable work in this field. Ministry of education has Book Promotion Division and even UNESCO has exclusive regional institutes for the Book Development. As a result, therefore, a good deal has been done so far but a lot still needs to be done.

Evaluation is, undoubtedly, a valuable process. It is a necessary factor in human progress. The doctor who prescribes needs to ascertain the results of his treatment. The effectiveness of the lawyer's plea is evaluated by the jury. The quality of carpenter's work is judged by the owner of the house. The farmer must measure his crops to know the effect of fertilising and cultivating. The parent is constantly observing the effects of his controls in the behaviour of his offspring, so it is with the teacher. He needs to ascertain the effectiveness of the text-books, methods, etc. Evaluation of text-books pinpoints the good and bad points and thus suggests ways for improvement.

In the field of English text-books, Central Institute of English and foreign languages Hyderabad and NCERT have done a lot of improvement by bringing out a set of school books which have been adapted by the different states through the Directorate office and the State School Education Boards. According to Indian Express, New Delhi, Jan. 29. "The Central Board of Secondary Education (CBSE) and live states and Union territories have completed the work of evaluation and revision of text-books to remove passages prejudicial to national integration. These states and union territories are Gujarat, Punjab, Himachal Pradesh, Mizoram and Delhi according to studies carried out by the National Council of Education Research and Training NCERT, which has been guiding the programme of evaluation of school text-books from the standpoint of national integration, has completed evaluating its own text-books. The first effort to evaluate school text-books from the national integration point of view was undertaken by NCERT in 1969 and this was followed by another programme in which text-books published by private publishers and used in English medium schools of the country were evaluated."

QUESTIONS

1. Describe the relationship between curriculum and text-books.
2. Justify that text-books and curriculum are most significant components of learning experiences and instruction.
3. Indicate the importance of text-books and enumerate drawbacks in using text-books.
4. Enumerate the characteristics of good text-book and indicate its physical aspects and academic aspect.
5. Indicate the types of books and describe the role of text-books in educational process.